CHIEF JUSTICE OF THE UNITED STATES

WILLIAM HOWARD
TAFT

HERBERT S. DUFFY

"A good man, and a just."
—LUKE xxxiii, 50

New York
MINTON, BALCH & COMPANY
1930

TO

MY GRANDMOTHER

MAGDALEN FOX SMITH

FOREWORD

In the preparation of this biography, access was had to the private papers of William Howard Taft located in the Manuscript Division of the Library of Congress, Washington, D. C. This book, however, is not in any way to be considered or construed as an official life of Mr. Taft.

I wish here to record my gratitude to those who in the years I have been preparing the work have counseled and assisted me in its preparation. Their names are omitted for the reason that many who rendered valuable aid have declined to permit me to express my appreciation publicly.

H. S. D.

CONTENTS

ix

CONTENTS

ILLUSTRATIONS

". . . whatever fate betide the Federal judiciary, I hope that it may always be said of them, as a whole, by the impartial observer of their conduct, that they have not lacked in the two essentials of judicial moral character, *a sincere desire to reach right conclusions and firmness to enforce them.*"

*from Taft's speech before the
American Bar Association, in
Detroit, 1895.*

WILLIAM HOWARD TAFT

WILLIAM HOWARD TAFT

CHAPTER I

BEGINNINGS AND BACKGROUND

THE life of William Howard Taft displays a beautiful consistency and coherence, the sort which few lives have, because it was infused with one animating principle —his constant and incorruptible devotion to justice. This special gift of his, and his genius for the law, flowered out of a rich family heritage. Behind him was a long line of fine, staunch men of pioneering intelligence, most of them devoted to the legal profession and all rooted deep in the best American tradition: Robert Taft, who came from England to Massachusetts in the seventeenth century; Aaron Taft, who fought in the Revolutionary War and made a clearing in the backwoods of Vermont to establish his homestead; Peter Rawson Taft, Judge of the Court of Common Pleas and the Probate Court of Wyndham County, Vermont, who also served as State Legislator and County Commissioner.

Alphonso Taft, the father of William Howard Taft, traveled by stage coach from Wyndham County, Vermont, to New Haven, in order to study at Yale, during that transition period when industry was superseding agriculture and New England villages were fast becoming manufacturing centers. After five years spent in Ellington, Connecticut, where he taught in the high school, and in New Haven, where he tutored University students in order to earn for himself a legal education, he resolved to make the West his home. He had heard much of the rapid growth of Ohio and had read, among other magnified legends about it, the *Toledo Blade's* prediction that Cincinnati "within one hundred years . . . will be the greatest city in America, and by the year two thousand, the greatest city in the world." This was the type of place he sought, a growing community, abounding in opportunities, seething with activity, a pleasing city, set in the midst of hills, with the Ohio River sweeping westward.

Alphonso Taft came west and saw Cincinnati. Walking along Pearl, Fourth, Walnut and Main Streets, he surveyed the large, compactly built store-rooms, facing upon poorly paved and worse kept streets. He visited the river landing, where live stock and farm products from Ohio, Kentucky and Indiana poured into the Cincinnati markets, and observed with bewildered interest the landing and shipping of goods, at the docks, from floating wharves adapted to the rise and fall of the river—a procedure accompanied by riotous chaos and confusion. He found Cincinnati prosperous, its industries increasing and expanding with incredible rapidity, its trade and commerce, stimulated by the railroads and constant growth of the population in the West and South, assuming fabulous proportions. He was much impressed. Of course everything was so new that the city seemed to possess something of the bizarre, unlike the staid, conservative dignity of the New England cities that he knew. And he determined to make Cincinnati his home.

Alphonso Taft married twice. His first wife, Fanny

Phelps, the mother of Charles P. Taft and Peter R. Taft, died in 1852. Two years later he married Louise M. Torrey, and while they were living on their estate in Mt. Auburn, on the hills just outside of Cincinnati, William Howard Taft was born, the fifteenth of September, 1857.

His was the usual, happily uneventful childhood of a small boy born into a well-bred family of easy circumstances and good background. He was only four on that April day when Cincinnati hummed with news of Fort Sumter's surrender, and, after the mass meeting presided over by Rutherford B. Hayes, two impromptu regiments paraded the streets amid high excitement—the Turners in white linen roundabouts, led by Colonel Robert L. McCook, with a sword buckled to his civilian suit and the effect topped with a stovepipe hat, and the Guthrie Grays in their red flannel shirts. And since his home was not in the path of the storm, the Civil War made little impression upon his childhood. He went to school and played games and grew up and of course went to Yale, as had his father and his two older brothers, matriculating in 1874 and graduating four years later.

Taft was an excellent student, of course, a big young man, quiet, good-natured, humorous, with an enormous interest in college politics. He loved to direct college activities, promoting and helping to elect a personal slate, a group ticket for class offices. One of his classmates said later,

"He was in every bit of politics that he could be, right through the college course. If there was a 'Lit' Board to be elected, or the Manager of the baseball team, or junior prom

5

officers, there was Taft doing the electing. It was his gift of organization that led him on. His close personal friend, Judge Hollister, was quite often on the opposite side in these class fights. Taft had a way of slapping his opponents on the back and saying. 'Well, I got you that time,' or else if his man got beaten, he would say, 'I'll get you the next time.' "

With John Addison Porter, who later became secretary to President McKinley, he revived the ancient and distinguished Linonian Society which, founded in 1753, had died as a result of student indifference. Taft and Porter managed to enroll some two hundred new students, and the society took on a fresh lease of life.

During Taft's four years at Yale, inter-collegiate athletics were by no means the important part of University life that they have since become. Yale played its first football game (defeating Columbia) two years before Taft entered college, and played the first game with Harvard during his junior year. Because Yale owned no oval Rugby football, Harvard loaned the Yale players a round, non-regulation rubber ball to practice with. The *Harvard Advocate,* reporting the game, said the players wore knitted caps as head-guards and "presented a very pretty appearance in their bright new uniforms . . . pieces of clothesline supplied the crossbars, and there was only a faint streak of lime to mark the touch-lines. Disputes among the players began immediately and were kept up during the game."

Taft's father had forbidden him to play football, a stricture which fortunately did not mean the sacrifice it must have meant in these days, when to keep a young

6

Photograph, Underwood and Underwood, N. Y.

THE YALE JUNIOR

man of Taft's massive build and determination off the gridiron would bring real grief to any coach and fellow-students!

It was pre-ordained, of course, that William Howard Taft should study law when he graduated from Yale, and carry on his family heritage of legal accomplishment, entering the Cincinnati law school in 1878 and graduating two years later. The one spectacular event of which his law school career has left us a record, is the incident related in this half-column from the *Cincinnati Commercial*.

"A sensation sheet edited by Lester A. Rose contained in its weekly issue yesterday a lot of trash of vile nature, hardly worth mentioning because of its absurdity, that was apparently construed by the Editor to refer to Alphonso Taft. It would not have attracted much attention had not the boys hawking the paper kept up the cry, 'All 'bout the Judge Taft scandal.' Early yesterday morning, Mr. Will Taft, a tall athletic young man about twenty-two years of age met his brother Charles at the *Times* office and stated quietly that if he could find Rose he would whip him.

"Rose was described to Will Taft as a tall, rawboned man with a broken nose who was known to be a bruiser of considerable physical courage and great endurance. It was related to him that Rose had been slungshotted and clubbed by Ed Hudson and others, and that his head had been found to be like a block of granite. Mr. Taft listened attentively to the information and appeared to appreciate it. He did not make much talk about the task that he set out for himself, but seemed to be in a hurry to get at it with as few words as possible. His brother, Charles, accompanied him, not with the intention of assisting, but merely to be on hand in case of interference that might be improper or unfortunate. They walked up to the corner of

7

Fifth and Elm Streets and quickly found Rose, who was accompanied by a lady and another friend.

"Will Taft is only a year or so out of Yale where he developed his muscle at the manly exercises of the college, and he seems to have retained it. He approached and asked the person if he was Rose. A prompt 'that's my name,' and a blow in the face revealed to Mr. Rose the object of the call. The first blow was a left-hander, not so effective as intended, but he made up the deficiency with repeated blows until Rose went down. The rules of the ring were not observed. When Rose went down, Mr. Taft pounced upon him and was getting in heavily with some blows when a bystander, more powerful than Mr. Charles Taft, interfered and prevented any further punishment. The bystander objected because the head of Mr. Rose was being used as a hammer on the pavement, but since he learned the nature of the difficulty, he has not ceased to regret his interference. As the case stands, the Messrs. Taft were questioned by a policeman as to the nature of the difficulty and quietly walked away without further interference."

Like his two older brothers, Taft began his law practice in Cincinnati, but he had been at the bar only a few months when Miller Outcalt, newly elected Prosecuting Attorney of Hamilton County, tendered the post of assistant to Taft. Taft accepted, assumed his duties January first, 1881, and labored under the pressure of a heavily congested docket, framing indictments, taking depositions, consulting witnesses and trying cases.

Then, in March, 1882, a vacancy occurred in the post of Collector of Internal Revenue for the Cincinnati District, and Representative Ben Butterworth recommended Taft's appointment to President Arthur. The President, who had shortly before appointed Alphonso Taft the United States Minister to Austria, readily accepted Butterworth's suggestion. Taft, however, after serving a few months, became dissatisfied because, although his position enhanced his prestige in Republican political circles, it interrupted his legal career. Consequently when his father's former law partner, Major H. P. Lloyd, approached him with an offer of partnership, he gladly accepted and for the next two years practiced with Major Lloyd.

But Taft, who loved nothing so much as the private practice of law, seemed doomed to public life and to politics, from the earliest years of his career. And he dated his public life from the events growing out of the Berner case, which resulted in the Campbell disbarment proceedings.

There was at that time a definite conflict between two factions in Cincinnati's political life—the decent and the corrupt. And the decent element, much as it deplored the outrageous tactics of the corrupt, under the leadership of the notorious Tom Campbell, had remained somewhat inactive, chiefly for lack of strong direction. Taft understood the situation thoroughly. He had learned from his father plenty of facts concerning the murky activities of the machine during elections, and those tactics included everything shady—bribery, repeating, false counting, and the stuffing of ballot boxes. While Taft was still studying law, these offenses became so flagrant that the United States District Court appointed Joseph Benson Foraker, later Governor of Ohio, to superintend the election. And as reporter for the *Cincinnati Commercial,* familiar with all

9

legal proceedings from those which took place in the smoke-hazed chambers of the Justice of the Peace to those in the District Court, Taft had seen that the Campbell organization had its talons deep in the judiciary. The whole situation came to an unsavory climax, in 1884, with the Berner murder case.

A man named Berner killed his employer in the act of robbing him, and retained Tom Campbell as counsel. The peculiar atrociousness of the murder had aroused public sentiment to the point of demanding that Berner hang. It was a sensational case—the trial opened with the courtroom crowded to capacity; five hundred and four people were called and examined before the jury was chosen. Days were consumed in the examination and cross-examination of witnesses . . . then the jury brought in a verdict of manslaughter.

The *Cincinnati Legal Bulletin* published this comment:

> "The result of the Berner murder trial last week has caused the deepest feeling among all classes. Six times the prisoner had confessed to his participation in the most brutal and cold-blooded butchery, giving all the details of the horrid affair, and only a few days before his trial had offered to plead guilty to murder in the second degree, the Prosecutor refusing on behalf of the public, as the evidence was absolute and unquestioned. Yet the jury brought in a verdict of manslaughter only. The finding is condemned in the severest terms everywhere by the people and by the papers."

A meeting, in protest against the verdict and the Campbell organization, was held at the Music Hall on the Friday following the verdict. It ended in a riot, during which some forty people were killed and over a hundred wounded, before order was restored by the calling out of the state militia.

On the following Tuesday, the Bar met to discuss plans whereby such disasters as this riot and the troubles rising out of it, might be remedied by legislation. William Howard Taft moved that a committee of five be appointed,

> "who shall consider the code of criminal precedure and recommend, to a future meeting of the Bar, legislation that shall so reform that code as to quicken the trial of cases and hasten the bringing of criminals to justice."

The motion was carried and Taft appointed a member of the committee.

Shortly afterward, Campbell was indicted, charged with bribery; he had approached one of the Berner jurors and offered the release of a debt in exchange for a satisfactory verdict. A committee of ten, with the object of making charges preliminary to disbarring Campbell, was appointed by the Cincinnati Bar Association. Taft was a member of this committee. After a thorough and painstaking investigation, the committee recommended that charges be preferred against Campbell. E. W. Kitteredge and William M. Ramsay, two leaders of the local Bar, were selected to direct the prosecution, while William Howard Taft and John R. Holmes were chosen as junior counsel to assist them. Laboring through a hot summer and fall, Taft traveled over the state interviewing witnesses and taking depositions, collecting evidence in his own mercilessly thorough and painstaking way. On the first day of the hearing, in November, William M. Ramsay, senior counsel, wearied by overwork and harassed by covert threats from the Campbell faction, became too ill to appear before the court to make the opening argument. In his absence, Taft assumed the burden, and, for four and a half hours, he outlined the case of the prosecution against Campbell.

His leadership in the disbarment proceedings against Campbell established him definitely as a power in the civil and legal life of Cincinnati, to be counted on thereafter as a solid and valuable man, able and just. He had displayed initiative, thoroughness and a gift for lucid and persuasive argument. More than that, he had, in the minds of every one, aligned himself unmistakably on the side of justice and of decency.

CHAPTER II

THE CINCINNATI BAR

IT was interesting, as well as remunerative, to practice law in Cincinnati. With the abundance of litigation which had accompanied mercantile progress and development, the city became a Mecca for distinguished lawyers of the Middle West. The Bar of Cincinnati contained on its roster the names of seven hundred men, many of whom had achieved national prominence. Many of them formed partnerships which became especially illustrious. Probably the most outstanding of these was Hoadley, Johnson and Colston, its members being ex-Governor Hoadley, Edgar Johnson and George Colston, engaged in general, as well as corporate and probate, practice. Eventually, Edward Louterbach, a prominent practitioner of the Manhattan Bar, invited Hoadley and Johnson to join him in a partnership. Unwilling to practice alone and determined to retain the established prestige of the firm, Colonel Colston invited Judson Harmon, then a judge of the Superior Court, to become his partner.

When Harmon went to Columbus to notify Governor Foraker of his resignation, the two fell to discussing the qualifications of various men, among them William Howard Taft, who might succeed Harmon. Harmon urged the Governor to appoint Taft, and Foraker replied that he had known Taft "ever since he came out of Yale University, when he appeared in my courtroom one morning as a local court reporter for the *Commercial*. His bright face and agreeable manner at once attracted to him my favorable attention and excited for him a friendly regard." The Governor went on to relate how favorably he had been impressed by Taft's work in the Campbell disbarment proceedings, saying that he felt he knew Taft "well enough to know that he had a strong intellectual endowment, a keen, logical, analytical mind, and that all the essential foundations for a good judge had been well and securely laid." [1]

Foraker, however, was above all a politician, and Taft's appointment had no special political expediency. Taft did not even know he was being considered. There were no letters on file urging his cause, and no ward and precinct leaders were calling upon Foraker to appoint him. And the Governor, feeling that an older and more experienced man—Taft was only twenty-nine—should be given the first offer, tendered the post to John Williamson Herron, and only after Herron's refusal did he appoint Taft.

The *Weekly Law Bulletin* thus noted Taft's acceptance:

"W. H. Taft, third son of the Honorable Alphonso Taft, has been appointed by Governor Foraker to fill the place of Judson Harmon in the Superior Court of Cincinnati . . . he is twenty-nine years old . . . and only admitted to the Bar seven years ago, is a very bright young man, who already enjoys great popularity and personal respect. He will no doubt soon work himself into his new position, which came to him unsolicited. The appointment seems to be generally well received."

[1] *Notes on Busy Years*, by J. B. Foraker. D. Appleton & Co., New York, 1916.

Delighted with his appointment, Taft wrote to Foraker,

"You have told me a number of times that you are in favor of young men. I little expected to have so strong and to myself so gratifying a proof of your conviction on that head. Considering the opportunity so honorable a position offers to a young man of my age and circumstances, my debt to you is very great. The responsibility you assume for me in making this appointment will always be an incentive to an industrious and conscientious discharge of my duties."

It is interesting to know that, in acknowledging Taft's letter, Governor Foraker advised him to resign after one term. Foraker explained that he did not depreciate the service rendered by the judiciary, but believed that with the serving of one term, Taft would have established himself sufficiently well so that he could resume the active practice of law with absolute certainty of success. Taft replied:

"I wish to thank you for the very kind words of your letter in regard to my appointment. When I showed the letter to my father he said, 'That is good advice. Be sure and follow it.' I shall hope to express to you my thanks and obligations for your great kindness in person this week."

This appointment of course increased Taft's professional prestige. Six months before, in June, 1886, he had married Helen Herron, the charming and popular daughter of John Williamson Herron and Harriett Collins Herron. This marriage brought to Taft a particularly busy and interesting social life. And Taft loved people—loved to surround himself with friends in his own home, to chat with them, learn about them and recount anecdotes, which he did extremely well, with such infectious relish of a joke that his enjoyment was bound to be shared. He had the reserved manner of the Tafts, to be sure, a little aloof, as people usually have to whom things of the mind come first. But that it was the aloofness of dignity, not coldness, no one who knew him at all well could doubt.

The Superior Court of Cincinnati to which Taft had been appointed was notable in the state judiciary of Ohio. It had been first created by an act passed by the Ohio Legislature on the fifteenth of March, 1838, which designated a single judge to pass upon all matters that came within the jurisdiction of the court. In the early fifties the Court was abolished. After a year or so, in which time the dockets of the trial courts of Cincinnati and Hamilton County became seriously congested, it was reëstablished. By this new act the Court was given greater dignity and importance, in that the number of judges was increased from one to three.

After serving the unexpired term of fourteen months, Taft stood for reëlection and defeated his opponent by a vote of 21,025 to 14,844. This overwhelming victory paid glowing tribute to Taft, proving that people realized his legal acumen, thoroughness and above all his fairness. To be sure, Taft was still comparatively inexperienced in applying the rules of equity and the law to a confused mass of evidence presented in court and in moulding, out of a disorganized mass of fact, a legal judgment. Moreover, the cases he decided at this time are insignificant in comparison to those which he later judged. But he was as indefatigable, as keen, in his examination of facts and his application of the law as he was when an occupant of the benches of the lower Federal Court and the Supreme Court. A constant procession of lawyers, eminent as well as unknown, some honest, others crafty, fought their legal battles in Taft's courtroom. The case of the Cincinnati, New Orleans and Texas Pacific Railway Company versus the Citizens' Bank was conducted by four leading members of the local Bar. Judson Harmon, assisted by William M. Ramsay, who had been senior counsel in the Campbell disbarment proceedings, represented the railroad, while E. W. Kitteredge, the other senior counsel in the Campbell case, aided by a Mr. Warrington, argued the cause of the bank.

By far his most important case, however, was the lawsuit of Moore's and Company versus the Bricklayer's Union et al . . . one of those cases which require a jurist, in making his decision, to create a precedent rather than apply it.

Taft came to the bench at just about the time that labor problems were first engaging the United States. In its beginnings, when the country relied chiefly upon agriculture and agrarian pursuits for its sustenance, there was no such thing as labor organization, and little strife between employers and employees. With the development of mining, manufacturing and industry, however, the scattered remnants of the guilds began to take on vitality. And in their strengthening was the inception of the American labor movement. From the first of the nineteenth century, small local labor unions had existed in America. And the increased influx of unskilled labor from abroad, the oppressive measures adopted by capitalists as they amassed huge fortunes, compelled American labor to form protec-

17

tive associations. Impetus was given to this movement by an early decision handed down by the Massachusetts Supreme Court, favoring such organizations, and also by the rapidly mounting scale of prices, which leaped up so much more quickly than did wages, that the working-man's struggle for existence became definitely harder.

In fact, unrest and agitation had so permeated the crafts that the increase in local labor unions, during the Civil War period, was startling. Up to 1886, however, there had been no concerted effort to foster any labor organization other than these local bodies and the groups formed in specialized industries. But in that year, the need of some organization to unite the widely differing elements of laboring men, engaged in remotely connected trades, was made apparent by the increasing economic pressure. The first effort in that direction—and at that time any such attempt involved enormous difficulties—was the National Labor Union, founded by W. H. Sylvis, chief of the iron-molders. Its specific purpose was to shorten the hours of labor and to increase wages. It fell to pieces, however, through lack of proper organization and because the local units which composed it were more interested in their own political success than the corporate welfare.

Out of this abortive beginning grew the Noble Order of the Knights of Labor. This association, based upon the alliance of working-men of every trade within one common group, instead of unions on trade lines alone, started with a secret society formed among the garment workers of Philadelphia. Aiming at one great union, and discarding secrecy, they called upon all laborers over sixteen years old (expressly excluding lawyers, bankers, saloonkeepers and gamblers!) to join them in "the organizing and directing of the power of industrial masses, to make industrial and moral worth, not wealth, the standard of individual and national greatness."

The Knights, once launched upon their brief but significant career, adopted aggressive methods. They resorted with increasing frequency not only to strikes, but also to picketing, boycotting and sabotage. A succession of victories, thus achieved, led the members of this organization to identify eternal principles of liberty and justice with their cause, and to believe themselves invincible. Enjoying this new sense of power, they made increasing demands and extended their activities into politics. But here, as in the case of the National Labor Union, their weakness became evident. It was, in particular, foreseen and understood by Samuel Gompers, of the Cigar Makers' Union. Visioning a strong and permanent Labor Party, Gompers undertook to unify the myriad laboring elements into one common association, in order to better conditions everywhere. And thus, eventually, the Knights were supplanted by the American Federation of Labor.

The year of its beginning, 1886, was significant and ominous. The number of strikes more than doubled, and eclipsed in violence those of any preceding year. The storm center of the labor agitation was the Middle West, particularly Chicago, where industrial trouble had been brewing for months. In persistent hope of fomenting a revolution, the Anarchist party, under the editorship of August Spies, was publishing two radical newspapers, the *Alarm,* published in English, and the *Arbeiter Zeitung,* in German. Both advocated violence. This unruly spirit among the laboring classes had spread to Cincinnati. The local labor unions were employing all the newly established policies of coercive strikes. They picketted, boycotted, destroyed property. Out of these disturbances came the case of Moore's and Company versus the Bricklayer's Union et al. The trouble began when Moore's and Company sold lime to Parker Brothers, after Parker Brothers had for some reason been blacklisted by the union. In reprisal, the union declared a boycott against Moore's and Company, and when the boycott caused an appreciable decline in their business, Moore's and Company sued the union for damages, and the case came up before Taft.

At the trial, the attorney for the union argued that every man may dispose of his labor to such persons and by such contract as he pleases; he may refuse to accept employment with any man or group of men, and furthermore is well within his rights if he declines to work for any man using the materials of any certain dealer. What he may lawfully do himself, he may lawfully announce his intention of doing; he may notify his possible employers of his intention to refuse to work for any man using materials of a certain dealer. And as these are all acts within his rights and lawful, he may combine with others to do them. Such combination, having as its purpose only the performance of lawful acts, is not a conspiracy, and therefore not actionable. In other words, the Bricklayer's Union had the lawful right to refuse to work for Moore's and for any one using Moore's line; its members had a right to announce their intention so to act, and Moore's and Company, if thereby injured, had no right of action against them.

Judge Taft, in his opinion, treated the issues exhaustively. He had very little, in the way of prior decisions, to guide him in determining the relative rights, under the law, of employer and employees in their dealings with one another. There were a few English cases in point, but most of them were based on the theory of criminal conspiracy, and contributed little to facilitate his task of determining what limitations should be placed on the right of self-assertion by employees in order that the rights of the employer should not be endangered. In his decision, Taft did not reject entirely the argument made by the attorney for the union, but he differentiated, drew distinctions, and said,

"We are dealing in this case with common rights. Every man, be he capitalist, merchant, employer, laborer or professional man, is entitled to invest his capital to carry on his business, to bestow his labor, or to exercise his calling, if within the law, according to his pleasure. Generally speaking, if in the exercise of such a right by one, another suffers a loss, he has no ground of action. Thus, if two merchants are in the same business in the same place, and the business of the one is injured by the competition of the other, the loss is caused by the other's pursuing his lawful right to carry on his business as seems best to him. . . . So it may reduce the employer's profits that his workmen will not work at former prices and he is obliged to pay on a higher scale of wages. The loss which he sustains, if it can be called such, arises merely from the exercise of the workman's lawful right to work for such wages as he chooses, and to get as high a rate as he can. It is caused

21

by the workman, but it gives no right of action. Again if the workman is called upon to work with the material of a certain dealer, and it is of such a character to make his labor greater than that sold by another, or it is hurtful to the person using it, or for any reason is not satisfactory to the workman, he may lawfully notify his employers and refuse to work it. The loss of the material man in his sales caused by such action of the workman is not a legal injury, and not the subject of action. And so it may be said that in these respects what one may do, many may do, and many may combine to do without giving the sufferer any right of action against those who cause his loss.

"But on this common ground of common rights where every one is lawfully struggling for the mastery, and where losses suffered must be borne, there are losses willfully caused to one by another in the exercise of what otherwise would be a lawful right from simple motives of malice."

Taft then cited a number of authorities to sustain his reasoning, and continued, "I have cited these authorities to show that in the exercise of common rights, like the pursuit of a business or trade, which result in a mutual interference and loss, such loss is a legal injury, or not, according to the intent with which it has been caused and the presence or absence of malice in the person causing it. . . . If then, defendants with intent to injure plaintiffs, had persuaded plaintiffs' (Moore's and Company) customers to withdraw custom from the plaintiffs, and so inflict a loss, not for any benefit to such customers for any reason connected with their trade, but simply to gratify defendants' (The Union) intent to injure plaintiffs, the defendants would be liable to the plaintiffs for their loss. . . .

"We do not conceive that in this state or country, a combination of workingmen to raise their wages or to obtain any mutual advantage is contrary to law, provided that they do not use such indirect means as obscure their original intent

22

and make this combination one merely malicious to oppress and injure individuals. . . . The peculiar form of oppression resorted to in the case at bar is known as boycotting, the essential feature of which is the exclusion of the employer from all communication with former customers and material men by threats of similar exclusion of the employer from all communication with former customers and material men by threats of similar exclusion to the latter if the dealings are continued."

Taft overruled the motion for a new trial and ordered judgment entered for Moore's and Company for twenty-two hundred and fifty dollars, which amount had been awarded them by verdict of the jury.

This opinion is significant in itself as being among the first relating to disputes between employers and employees. And it is significant in being highly characteristic of Taft's way of marshaling facts in the unfaltering white light of his intelligence, his ability to sift and differentiate and judge. It was not a popular decision; he was to hear echoes of it during his later career.

For new vistas of opportunity were opening before him. Judge Taft was to be superseded by Solicitor General Taft of the United States.

CHAPTER III

SOLICITOR GENERAL

WHEN Orlow W. Chapman died in January, 1890, after having served as Solicitor General of the United States for only seven months, Taft's influential friends immediately busied themselves in his behalf. Congressman Ben Butterworth, John Addison Porter, Taft's former classmate, then editor of the *Hartford Post,* and various members of the Cincinnati as well as the Ohio Bar, besought President Harrison to make Taft Solicitor General. Taft had served but a year and a half of his elected term when he received this appointment. On the fourth of February, 1890, he assumed his new duties as principal barrister for the government, which meant that he must represent the government in all cases which came before the Supreme Court; that in the absence or disability of the Attorney General he should assume that official's responsibilities; and that he should, whenever called upon to do so, prepare opinions for the President and Cabinet members. It was an opportunity exactly to his liking, and to which he was fitted by temperament and experience.

But on that cold, bleak, gray morning when he alighted at the Pennsylvania station in Washington, Taft must have entertained certain misgivings as to whether he had followed the proper course in accepting the appointment. The city looked dark and unwelcoming in the grim, early light of the cloudy, dismal February day. There was no porter in sight, and Taft, carrying his heavy bags, walked alone to the old Ebbit House. He had a cheerless, solitary breakfast, then called upon the Attorney General at the Department of Justice, took the oath of office and climbed three long flights of stairs to his by no means spacious office. It was, in fact, a small, dingy, single room, occupied also by his staff—one stenographer, who was not only secretary to the Solicitor General but telegrapher in the Chief Clerk's office as well.

Thus unceremoniously, Taft entered upon the laborious tasks which were to occupy him for two years. The day was not without cheer, however, for Taft found awaiting him a letter from Governor Foraker, which read:

"I congratulate not only you but the President and the whole country. My congratulations aren't, however, merely because you are to be Solicitor General. That is an important and conspicuous office that great men have greatly honored and any one might feel highly complimented to have the privilege of filling it. But the special feature of good fortune that I see in it lies beyond that office in the other position to which I think it clearly leads. As Solicitor General you will have an opportunity to finish and fully sound out the splendid qualifications you already have for a seat on the bench of the Supreme Court."

Also awaiting him was a letter from Major W. W. Peabody enclosing annual passes on the Baltimore and Ohio Railroad. Taft pondered this. He was by no means a rich man. As a public servant, he had received a comparatively small salary, and the passes would mean a tremendous saving to him, for he would have to travel much between

Washington and Cincinnati. But . . . there was the Interstate Commerce Law. Was he not infringing upon its
provisions by accepting favors from a corporation, favors
to which he felt he was not entitled? Taft had the judicial
mind—and he was inexorable in his scrupulousness! He
wrote to Major Peabody:

"I have your favor in which you enclose me annual passes
over the Baltimore and Ohio, and the Baltimore and Ohio
Southwestern Railroads. I want to say that I am greatly indebted to you for your kindness in forwarding these, and that
I fully appreciate that it is in the spirit of great friendliness to
me that you do so. They would be most convenient for me, because I shall have to make a number of trips to Cincinnati this
year. On thinking the whole matter over, however, I must decline to enjoy the opportunities thus afforded by you. I believe
that the provision of the Interstate Commerce Act, in its spirit,
was not intended to affect such friendly courtesies as by your
letter you tender me. It was really intended to prevent railroad
companies from making unequal charges for freight transportation by the use of free passenger transportation. I am aware,
too, that this regulation of the Interstate Commerce Law is
more honored in the breach than in the observance. But the
passes are within the letter of the law, and therefore I must
forego the pleasure I would otherwise have in accepting them. I
know you will understand the spirit in which I decline these,
and that I feel from your offer as much under obligation to
you as if I found myself able to accept it. Bear with my inconsistencies and believe me. . . ."

Among Taft's callers that first morning was the distinguished attorney, United States Senator William M. Evarts,
who presented himself by saying, "I knew your father. I
was in the class of '37 at Yale, and he graduated before I

entered; but he was there as a tutor in my time, and I valued his friendship very highly. Mrs. Evarts and I are giving a dinner tonight for my former partner and his wife, Mr. and Mrs. Joseph Choate. Mr. Choate is in Washington for a short time to argue a case before the Supreme Court. Now, unfortunately, one of our guests has sent word that he can't come and I thought, perhaps, considering my long standing friendship with your father, you might consent to waive ceremony and fill the place at our table at this short notice." [1] Taft accepted with alacrity—much too quickly, he afterward reflected, for the exacting conventions of Washington—and with the dinner, his first day as Solicitor General, begun so forlornly, ended happily.

It was during his first months in Washington that Taft came to know that picturesque personality who was so significantly concerned with much of his later life—Theodore Roosevelt, then Chairman of the Civil Service Commission. He used to rush into Taft's little office, teeth and eyeglasses flashing, and perch himself on the desk while they talked by the hour. Roosevelt crisp, incisive, vehement— Taft as quiet in manner as he was shrewd in comment, preceding his frequently humorous observations with a deep, rich chuckle that seemed to boil and bubble out of his huge frame, as they exchanged impressions and consulted one another about their respective problems. They soon became fast friends, the calm, deliberate, judicial man of law and the fiery, pugnacious, impulsive politician. Both sound men, each recognized and admired in the other

<hr>

[1] "Recollections of Full Years," by Helen Herron Taft. Dodd, Mead & Company, New York, 1914.

qualities he himself lacked; they complemented each other in a way which makes for affection and esteem.

These were toilsome and trying days for Taft, and his work so engrossed him that he occasionally forgot the social obligations by which official Washington sets such store—the payment of first calls. It was Taft's duty, for instance, to call upon his official superiors, and Mrs. Taft was required, by precedent, to visit their wives, as he felt constrained to remind her upon one occasion which resulted in an amusing boomerang. Mrs. Taft was a little tardier than punctilio demanded in calling upon the wife of Justice Gray of the Supreme Court. When she apologized, Mrs. Gray reassured her at once, understanding that with two small children it was not always easy to do as one liked, and added that she, for her part, would have gladly varied the usual procedure and paid the first call, had not one thing made it impossible—the fact that Mr. Taft had not yet called upon Justice Gray![1]

But if he forgot social precedent, sometimes, in absorption in his work, Taft, conservative that he was, deliberately contradicted numerous traditions in the conduct of his business whenever he believed that to do so would be a service to the government. For instance, it had been customary for the Solicitor General to leave the trial of cases in the Lower Federal Courts to the Federal attorneys of the district in which the case arose. In the Hat Trimmings cases, where decision involved the construction of certain

[1] "Recollections of Full Years," by Helen Herron Taft. Dodd, Mead & Company, New York, 1914.

28

sections of the Tariff Act, Taft departed from that practice.

The litigations had been instituted, by a firm of importers, against the Collector of the Port of Philadelphia, to recover an excess of duties which they alleged had been collected by him upon articles that they had brought into the country. The importers based their action on the theory that the articles imported were not silk goods, as the Collector had contended, and, therefore, should have been assessed only twenty per cent instead of fifty. The case consumed the better part of a month. Taft made the opening statement, examined witnesses, and argued points of law as to the admission or exclusion of evidence presented. The thoroughness with which the case was prepared, and Taft's lucid presentation of it, resulted in a victory which saved the Federal Government many dollars of revenue.

Another of Taft's signal successes as Solicitor General was the In re Cooper case which grew out of the Bering Sea Controversy. This difficulty dated back to 1867, when the United States had purchased Alaska from the Russian Government under circumstances of spectacular haste. The Russian minister offered Alaska to Secretary of State Seward one evening, explaining that Russia found Alaska too remote to govern properly. (He did not add that the Czar's government feared the seizure of Alaska by England, and hoped to unload a possession which had become more than a burden.) Seward at once accepted, and when the Russian Minister offered to return the next day to draft the treaty, replied, "Why wait until tomorrow, Mr. Stoeckl? Let us make the treaty tonight."

Charles Sumner, Chairman of the Foreign Affairs Committee of the Senate, was summoned; various secretaries were called in, and at four o'clock in the morning the completed treaty was signed.

This covenant was ratified over the protests of many members of our two legislative branches who were unable to understand why the United States desired to pay seven million dollars for a frozen wilderness in the distant northwest. The following year, in order to end the indiscriminate destruction of seals in Alaskan waters, Congress enacted a law against killing seals "within the limits of the Alaska territory, or in the waters thereof." Upon the theory that Russia had claimed and enforced exclusive jurisdiction over the Bering Sea, that all the rights enjoyed by Russia had passed to the United States, and that this claim of Russia had been acquiesced in by many maritime nations, including Great Britain, the United States Government undertook to seize and condemn, irrespective of nationality, vessels discovered killing seals in the Bering Sea.

These seizures were followed by legislation more carefully to define what was meant by "the waters of Alaska." In 1889, the House of Representatives passed a bill declaring that all the waters of the Bering Sea were embraced within the Alaskan boundary lines. But when the act got to the Senate, the Chairman of the Committee on Foreign Relations objected that it "involved serious matters of International Law . . . and ought to be disagreed to or abandoned and considered more carefully hereafter." Subsequently a compromise bill was passed, which did not specifically define what waters were included within the Alaskan territorial limits.

When Great Britain complained about the seizure of certain English vessels, Secretary of State Bayard, without yielding a single point, proposed an international agreement for the protection of seals from extermination. And when Benjamin Harrison became President, James G. Blaine succeeded Bayard as Secretary of State. Following the policy adopted by his predecessor, Blaine held a conference in Washington with the British and Russian Ministers, but this effort toward conciliation failed, and there ensued the notable correspondence between Lord Salisbury and Blaine, in which the latter vigorously defended America's position.

This left three possible courses open to President Harrison, and he had to select one of them without delay. First, he could abandon the American claim of the right to exercise exclusive jurisdiction over the Bering Sea, and pay Great Britain the damages claimed for the seizures and condemnations which had taken place under Cleveland. Second, he could ignore the protests of the British Government and continue the policy of seizure, which might, of course, result in the resistance of British cruisers to such seizure, or even the recapture of seized vessels, by force. Third, he could resort to arbitration.

This, briefly, was the status of the Bering Sea controversy when the *W. P. Sayward,* a Canadian sailing schooner engaged in the seal trade and owned by a British subject named Cooper, was seized by a United States revenue cutter. It was ordered forfeited and condemned. Cooper presented, through the British Foreign Office, a claim for damages. Blaine rejected the claim, and Great Britain proposed arbitration. Before any determination was reached, however, the British Government abandoned diplomacy and resorted to law. Hence the case of In re Cooper.

The distinguished and able Mr. Joseph H. Choate appeared on behalf of Cooper, assisted by Mr. Calderon Carlisle, appearing on behalf of Sir John Thompson, Attorney General for Canada. William Howard Taft, as Solicitor General of the United States, represented our Government.

The court refused the Writ of Prohibition that Cooper had prayed for, in agreement with Taft's argument that, "an application to a court to review the action of the political department of the Government upon a question between it and a foreign power, made while diplomatic negotiations were going on, should be denied."

CHAPTER IV

FIRST ENCOUNTERS WITH LABOR

During his two years as Solicitor General, Taft argued twenty-seven cases before the Supreme Court, and his renown, in consequence, became national instead of local. He had proved himself a formidable opponent, a valuable advocate, and a master of argument and presentation. Therefore when Congress, in March, 1892, enacted a law providing for the appointment of a new judge on each circuit of the Federal Circuit Court, Taft seemed the logical appointee for the sixth circuit. Members of the Cincinnati Bar telegraphed to President Harrison:

> "We earnestly recommend the appointment of Solicitor General Taft to the new judgeship for the Ohio Circuit. His service on the Superior bench here has shown that he possesses judicial qualities of the highest order. The Cincinnati Bar is practically unanimous in urging his appointment."

Senator John Sherman brought to the President a similar telegram from a number of prominent lawyers of the Ohio Bar:

> "We earnestly recommend the appointment of Honorable William Howard Taft Circuit Judge for this circuit. He has proved his ability in judicial service and has the confidence of the bar of the State of Ohio. We hope you will present him to the favorable consideration of the President."

33

President Harrison appointed Taft to the Court. He was then but thirty-five and this elevation represented the acme of success. Indeed it was, for the sixth circuit of the Federal Circuit Court was a court of rigorous and exacting traditions. Its jurisdiction in all Federal matters extended over the states of Kentucky, Ohio, Michigan and Tennessee. Thus a wide diversity of litigated questions was brought before its judges, and its incumbents had been and were men of exceptional talents and capabilities, who, by the rendition of innumerable able opinions, had demonstrated their singular fitness for the judiciary.

The growth of trusts and the marketing of highly inflated securities had turned the wave of prosperity into a slough of depression. Business was in chaos. More than four hundred banks had failed. President Cleveland proposed a tariff bill as a relief measure and, under the guidance of William L. Wilson, a former president of West Virginia University, it was presented to the House. But its progress was sluggish, and the ominous feeling of uncertainty among capitalists and business men became more widespread and pronounced. Mills and factories were closing, hence industrial disorders arose and these soon developed into bitter class conflict. Strikes and boycotts were increasing. In expression of the general discontent, marching groups of the unemployed were organized. One of these, under the leadership of a man named Frye, was "The United States Industrial Army;" another, under Kelley, had no particular title, but the most famous and picturesque was "Coxey's Army" or "The Army of the Commonweal of Christ," led by Jacob Coxey, a well-to-do manufacturer of Massilon, Ohio. Starting from various parts of the country, they all planned to march upon Washington and, by force of numbers, impress upon Congress the necessity for enacting relief measures.

And yet, despite these adverse conditions, labor persisted to demand increasingly large returns for its services. Thousands of workingmen were thus thrown out of employment in consequence, and the black days which followed became known as the "Panic of 1893." The organization of labor was still imperfect and in its formative state. As its purposes and methods were still comparatively undefined, they altered to fit various sets of circumstances, and obviously the strike and the boycott were favorite, because immediate, devices. And out of these disturbed labor and financial conditions developed two of the most important cases Taft was called upon to decide, after his elevation to the Federal bench. The first of these was the case of the Toledo, Ann Arbor and North Michigan Railway Company against the Pennsylvania Railway Company and others.[1] The controversy began when, in spite of the financial depression, the engineers of the Toledo, Ann Arbor and North Michigan Railroad demanded a raise in wages and threatened to strike if it were not forthcoming. P. M. Arthur, for thirty years Grand Chief of the Brotherhood of Locomotive Engineers, vainly endeavored to effect a friendly settlement of the differences, but the railroad officials refused the raise, and the strike was called.

After notifying the general managers of the railway systems that the members of the Brotherhood (it was by far

[1] 54, Federal Reporter, 730.

35

the strongest of the labor organizations) would decline to handle freight to and from the Ann Arbor road, Arthur acted to put Rule Twelve of the Union into effect. This rule, "any member employed on a railroad running in connection with or adjacent to the offending road, must refuse to handle property belonging to the said railroad system," was intended, obviously, to hamper the company with which the Brotherhood was at issue in its dealings with other roads, until the demands of the employees had been granted. Upon motion by the railroad, Taft, after hearing the evidence produced, issued a temporary injunction restraining P. M. Arthur from putting Rule Twelve into effect. He did not decree, as was popularly supposed at the time, that a man was compelled to remain in the service of his employer against his will, nor did he decree that, in any labor dispute, a man in the employ of another could be enjoined from striking. This was reported, mistakenly, to be the effect of the opinion rendered by Taft, and he was bitterly denounced as having by his judicial misinterpretation of the law subjected the workingman to the whims of employers.

The second crucial labor case, and a much more significant one than the Ann Arbor litigation, was that known as In re Phelan.

In order to combat labor's demands, the employers were forming powerful combinations, and the strongest of these was the General Managers' Association, composed of capitalists and officials of railway systems serving the city of Chicago. President Cleveland's commission found it to be "an example of the persistent and shrewdly devised plan of corporations to over-reach their limitations and to usurp indirectly powers and rights not contemplated in their charters." This arbitrary group, whose methods were pitiless and ruthless, discharged workmen without just cause and then blacklisted them so that they were unable to procure employment elsewhere.

A leading spirit of the General Managers' Association was George Pullman, president of the Pullman Car Company. In May, 1894, he appreciably lowered the wages of his employees. A committee representing the workers had called upon him and lodged a protest against this reduction, soliciting Pullman to continue the old wage scale. The following day, three members of this committee were summarily discharged. This unjustifiable action caused much indignation among the employees, and they voted a strike.

The employees of the railroad, in order to combat the General Managers' Association, had formed the American Railway Union, under the organizing leadership of Eugene V. Debs. When the Pullman difficulty arose, Debs, because a large number of Pullman employees were members of the American Railway Union, appointed a committee which sought, in vain, an appointment with Pullman. Numerous civic bodies in Chicago also entreated Pullman to arbitrate. To one of these Vice President Wickes of the Pullman Company declared, "The Pullman Company has nothing to arbitrate."

There was a painful silence, then Alderman McGillen of the Committee said, "Am I to understand that the Pullman Company refuses this slight request, made at so grave an hour and upon which so much depends?"

"The Pullman Company had nothing to arbitrate," reiterated Mr. Wickes.

Mr. McGillen said, "Mr. Wickes, your company demands the police protection of the Federal Government, the State of Illinois, the County of Cook, and the city of Chicago, and yet you utterly ignore a fair request made by the city . . . a request the fundamental idea of which is the preservation of the peace. We have come to you as conservers of the peace, and you have assumed a grave responsibility in thus refusing the request we make . . . a responsibility greater, perhaps than even you are aware of."

"There is a principle involved in this matter," replied Mr. Wickes, "which the Pullman Company will not surrender. It is that employers must be permitted to run their business in their own way, and without interference from the employee or anyone else."

At the failure of these conciliatory efforts, the officers of the American Railway Union issued an ultimatum, to the effect that if their demands were not met and a satisfactory agreement reached, the members of the union, who numbered approximately two hundred and fifty thousand and were distributed throughout every state in the Union, would be instructed to decline to handle any Pullman car on any railway system in the country! On June twenty-first, the order was issued.

Accompanied by rioting, terror and bloodshed, the strike assumed mammoth proportions, and almost immediately railway traffic was paralyzed. President Cleveland was forced to call out the United States regular troops. At this, the usual prudence of Debs failed him. He is reported to have said,

> "The Pullman Company is responsible for any blood that may flow from now on. If honest labor is not entitled to recognition, the worker cannot be blamed if he tries to commit some acts of violence against the man who spurned him."

And Debs sent his lieutenant, Frank M. Phelan, to Cincinnnati, to further the attempt of the union to tie up the railways of the country. Phelan began his activities by urging the men "to quit work and coax other men to go out, and if this was not successful, to take a club and knock them out!"

One of the railroads affected by Phelan's propaganda was the Cincinnati Southern Railroad which, by action of the Federal District Court, had gone into the hands of a receiver, Samuel W. Felton. Declaring that he was impeded in his operation of the railroad by Phelan's acts, Felton came before the court and secured an injunction restraining Phelan from "inciting, encouraging or ordering a strike on the Cincinnati Southern Railway." A few days later Felton appeared again, and moved that Phelan be committed to jail for contempt of court in having violated the injunction. Thus the case of In re Phelan came before Taft.

For the better part of a week testimony was taken. There was no doubt, of course, that Phelan had come to Cincinnati with the avowed purpose of extending the boycott instituted by the union. The evidence was clear on that point. The question before the court, however, was, had Phelan

39

by his actions violated the terms of the injunction? During the days of the hearings, the lawless element made a decided effort to intimidate Taft. The court room was always crowded with strikers, who, despite repeated warnings that the court room would be cleared if quiet were not maintained, gave noisy vent to their approval or disapproval of testimony as it was elicited. After the argument, Taft announced that he would render his decision at a specified time, four days later. To compile, to prepare, and to dictate an opinion as lengthy as the one rendered in the Phelan case, in the short time which Taft alloted himself, was an enormous task.

But short as this interval really was, it seemed interminable to the anxious factions awaiting Taft's judgment. The situation was tense and ominous. On one side, the strikers, with their hot sense of injustice, seeing nothing beyond the fact that a sentence against Phelan meant a persecution of labor. On the other, capital and business, angry and uneasy at the disturbance of their functioning, the encroachment upon their power. And the watchful public, aghast at a state of affairs which stopped the trains and filled the streets with rioters, a public which objected mainly to the interference with its routine, and saw the strikers either as abused and righteous underlings, or as dangerous rowdies, according to their predilections! And the eyes of all were fixed upon Taft. In the center of the storm, calm with the detachment and the impersonality which only intense concentration upon a principle can give a man, Taft himself was concerned with but one thing—the interpretation of the law. Undisturbed and undeflected by the emotions that

40

beat upon him from without, as indifferent to the opinion of capital as he was to the menacing notes sent him by the strikers, he set himself to assembling and sifting the facts.

On the day set for the public reading of his finding, the court room was packed. The strikers filled the chairs, aisles and passageways, their badges conspicuously displayed. Huge, impressive, imperturbable, in his official robes, Taft entered, mounted the dais, swept the crowded court room with his eyes, then fastened them upon his foolscap, and read:

"The punishment for contempt is the most disagreeable duty a court has to perform, but is one from which the court cannot shrink. If the orders of the court are not obeyed, the next step is into anarchy. It is absolutely essential to the administration of justice that courts should have the power to punish contempts and that they should use it when the enforcement of their orders is flagrantly defied. But it is only to secure present and future compliance with its orders that the power is given, and not to impose punishment commensurate with the crimes or misdemeanors committed in the course of contempt, which was cognizable in a different tribunal or in this court by indictment or trial by jury. I have no right and do not wish to punish the contemner (Phelan) for the havoc which he and his associates have wrought to the business of this country, and the injuries they have done to labor and capital alike, or for the privations and sufferings to which they have subjected innocent people, even if they may not be amenable to the criminal law therefor. I can only inflict a penalty which may have some effect to secure future compliance with the orders of this court and to prevent unlawful constructions thereof."

41

Taft raised his eyes and looked sternly at the strikers. Continuing, he said:

"After much consideration, I do not think I should be doing my duty as a judicial officer of the United States without imposing upon the contemner (Phelan) the penalty of imprisonment. The sentence of this court is that Frank W. Phelan be confined in the county jail of Warren County, Ohio, for a term of six months. The marshal will take the prisoner into custody and safely convey him to the place of imprisonment. . . . When you leave this room, I want you to go with the conviction that if there is any power in the army of the United States to run these trains, they shall be run."

Rising, Taft left the bench, and the great throng filed out silently.

Taft's opinion is quoted at length below because it so clearly reveals his mind in action, shows so perfectly the way he cut through obscuring circumstances to reach essential truths.

"The employees of the Receiver have the right to organize into or join a labor union which should take joint action as to their terms of employment. It is of benefit to them and to the public that laborers should unite in their common interest and for lawful purposes. They have labor to sell. If they stand together, they are often able, all of them, to command better prices for their labor than when dealing singly with rich employers, because the necessities of the single employee may compel him to accept any terms offered him. The accumulation of a fund for the support of those who feel that the wages offered are below market prices is one of the legitimate objects of such an organization. They have the right to appoint officers who shall advise them as to the course to be taken by

42

them in their relation with their employer. They may unite with other unions. The officers they appoint or any other person to whom they choose to listen, may advise them as to the proper course to be taken by them in regard to their employment, or, if they choose to repose such authority in any one, may order them, on pain of expulsion from their union, peaceably to leave the employment of their employer because any of the terms of the employment are unsatisfactory. It follows, therefore, that if Phelan had come to this city when the Receiver reduced the wages of his employees by ten percent and had urged a peaceable strike, and had succeeded in maintaining one, the loss to the business of the receiver would not be a reasonable ground for recovering damages, and Phelan would not have been liable to contempt even if the strike much impeded the operation of the road under the order of the court. His action in giving the advice, or issuing an order based on unsatisfactory terms of employment, would have been entirely lawful.

"But his coming here, and his advice to the Southern Railway employees, or to the employees of the other roads, to quit, has nothing to do with the terms of their employment. They were not dissatisfied with their service or their pay. Phelan came to Cincinnati to carry out the purpose of a combination of men, and his act in inciting the employees of all Cincinnati roads to quit service was part of that combination. If the combination was unlawful, then every act in pursuance of it was unlawful, and his instigation of the strike would be an unlawful wrong done by him to every railway company in the city, for which they can recover damages, and for which, so far as his acts affected the Southern Railway, he is in contempt of court.

"They proposed to inflict pecuniary injury on Pullman by compelling the railway companies to give up using his cars, and, on refusal of the railway companies to yield to compul-

43

sion, to inflict pecuniary injury on the railway companies by inciting their employees to quit their services, and thus paralyze their business. . . .

"One purpose of the combination was to compel railway companies to injure Pullman by breaking their contract with him. The Receiver of this court is under contract to Pullman, which he would have to break were he to yield to the demand of Phelan and his associates. The breach of a contract is unlawful. A combination with that as its purpose is unlawful and is a conspiracy. But the combination was unlawful without respect to the contract feature. It was a boycott. The employees of the railway companies had no grievance against their employers. Handling and hauling Pullman cars did not render their services any more burdensome.

"They came into no natural relation with Pullman in handling the cars. He paid them no wages. He did not regulate their hours, or in any way determine their services. Simply to injure him in his business, they were incited and encouraged to compel the railway companies to withdraw custom from him by threats of quitting their service, and actually quitting their service. This inflicted an injury on the companies that was very great and it was unlawful, because it was without legal excuse. All the employees had the right to quit their employment, but they had no right to combine to quit in order thereby to compel their employer to withdraw from a mutually profitable relation with a third person for the purpose of injuring that third person, when the relation thus sought to be broken had no effect whatever on the character or reward of their services. It is the motive for quitting, and the end sought thereby, that make the injury inflicted unlawful, and the combination by which it is effected, an unlawful conspiracy. The distinction between an ordinary lawful and peaceable strike entered upon to obtain concessions in the terms of the striker's employment and a boycott is not a fanciful one, or one which

44

needs the power of fine distinction to determine which is which. . . .

"The gigantic character of the conspiracy of the American Railway Union staggers the imagination. The railroads have become as necessary to life and health and comfort of the people of the country as are the arteries of the human body, and yet Debs and Phelan and their associates proposed by inciting the employees of the railways of the country to suddenly quit their services without any dissatisfaction with the terms of their employment, to paralyze utterly all the traffic by which the people live, and in this way compel Pullman, for whose acts neither the public nor the railroads are in the slightest degree responsible, and over whose acts they can lawfully exercise no control, to pay more wages to his employees.

"The merits of the controversy between Pullman and his employees have no bearing whatever on the legality of the combination effected through the American Railway Union. The purpose, shortly stated, was to starve the railway companies and the public into compelling Pullman to do something which they had no lawful right to compel him to do. Certainly the starvation of a nation cannot be a lawful purpose of a combination, and it is utterly immaterial whether the purpose is effected by means usually lawful or otherwise."

Of course this opinion reaped a whirlwind of denunciation. Labor leaders declared that Taft had used his high office to deprive the laboring man of his just rights. And in the minds of many people, Taft had definitely aligned himself with capital as against labor—in more emotional terms, had sided with the rich against the poor. Yet Taft's judgment was merely the application of established legal principles to facts brought out in open court, principles sustained by precedent and practice throughout centuries

45

of the law. In making it he was concerned, as always, with justice and with justice only.

Taft was distressed, of course, by complaints that he had been unfair to labor. When he addressed the American Bar Association in Detroit, the following year, he chose for his topic a defense of the Federal judiciary against charges that it had assumed jurisdiction not only to protect corporations and to perpetuate their abuses, but also to oppress and destroy the power of organized labor. He said in part:

"On the whole, when the charges made against the Federal courts of favoritism towards corporations are stripped of their rhetoric and epithet, and the specific instances upon which the charges are founded are reviewed, it appears that the action of the courts complained of was not only reasonable, but rested on precedents established decades ago and fully acquiesced in since, and that the real ground of the complaint is that the constitutional and statutory jurisdiction of the Federal courts is of such a character that it is frequently invoked to avoid some of the manifest injustice which a justifiable hostility to the corrupt methods of many of them incline legislatures and juries and others to inflict upon all of them."

In discussing the complaints made by labor leaders, he reiterated the opinion he had so frequently declared:

"The capitalist and laborer share the profit of production, the more capital in active employment, the more work there is to do, and the more work there is to do, the more laborers are needed. The greater the need of laborers, the better pay per man. It is clearly in the interest of those who work that capital shall increase more rapidly than they do. Everything, therefore, having a legitimate tendency to increase the accumulation of wealth and its use for production will give the workingman

46

a larger share of the joint result of capital and labor. . . . But while it is in the common interest of labor and capital to increase the fruits of production, yet in determining the share of each, their interests are plainly opposed. . . . The organization of capital into corporations with the position of advantage which this gave in a dispute with a single laborer over wages, made it absolutely necessary for labor to unite to maintain itself. . . .

"The fact that many railroads have been operated by Federal Receivers, the non-residence of the railway companies in the states where the strikes occur, and the interstate commerce feature of the business have brought some of these violations of property and private and public right within the cognizance of the Federal courts. Because the participants in such contests have been spread more widely over the country than in similar contests with which the states had to deal, the action of the Federal courts in these cases had attracted more public attention and evoked more bitter condemnation by those who naturally sympathize with labor in every controversy with capital.

"The efficiency of the processes of a court of Equity to prevent much of the threatened injury from the public and private nuisances which it is often the purpose of the leaders of such strikes to cause, has led to the charge, which is perfectly true, that judicial action has been much more efficient to restrain labor excesses than corporate evils and greed. If it were possible by the quick blow of an injunction to strike down the conspiracy against public and private rights involved in the corruption of a legislature or a council, Federal and other courts would not be less prompt to use the remedy than they are to restrain unlawful injuries by labor unions. But I have had occasion to point out that the nature of the corporate wrong is almost wholly beyond the reach of the courts, especially those of the United States. The corporate miners and sappers of public

47

virtue do not work in the open but under cover; their purposes are generally accomplished before they are known to exist, and the traces of their evil paths are destroyed and placed beyond the possibility of legal proof. On the other hand, the chief wrongs committed by labor unions are the open, defiant trespass upon property rights and violations of public order, which the processes of the courts are well adapted to punish and prevent.

"As a matter of fact there is nothing in any Federal decision directed against the organization of labor to maintain wages and to secure terms of employment otherwise favorable. The courts so far as they have expressed themselves on the subject recognize the right of men for a lawful purpose to combine to leave their employment at the same time, and to use the inconvenience this may cause to their employer as a legitimate weapon in the frequently recurring controversy as to the amount of wages. It is only when the combination is for an unlawful purpose and an unlawful injury is thereby sought to be inflicted that the combination has received the condemnation of the Federal as well as the state courts. . . . But whatever fate betide the Federal judiciary, I hope that it may always be said of them, as a whole, by the impartial observer of their conduct, that they have not lacked in the two essentials of judicial moral character, a sincere desire to reach right conclusions and firmness to enforce them."

And it was Taft who struck the first blow for the Anti-Trust Law and paved the way for the prosecution continued under Roosevelt, and in his own administration. The tendency of American business to consolidate had brought about a relief from competition, a command of greater capital, and the advantage of a market control which enabled the trusts to force out smaller competitors and raise prices at will and beyond all reason. These monopolies were

48

resented not only by the smaller businesses, thus crowded to the wall, but by the public, who finally sought, through political channels, to curb the trusts.

When Congress met for its fifty-first session, on the fourth of December, 1889, Senator Sherman introduced the first Anti-Trust Act—to "declare unlawful trusts and combinations in restraint of trade and production." It met with immediate opposition, but, after many amendments and considerable political jockeying, was finally passed on the second of July, 1890. Then for several years it lay dormant, and no effort was made to vitalize it, until a group of corporations engaged in the manufacture and vending of cast-iron pipe entered into a combination to raise the price of pipe in a number of states. Thereupon the Attorney General, on behalf of the Federal Government, filed a petition against the corporations charging them with a combination and conspiracy in unlawful restraint of interstate commerce, in violation of the Anti-Trust law. This case, which came to be known as the Addyston Pipe Case,[1] was dismissed in the lower court and appealed to the circuit court; there Taft delivered the opinion.

Answering the argument made on behalf of the corporations, that the association would have been valid at common law, and that the Federal Anti-Trust law was not intended to reach any agreements that were not void and unenforceable at common law, Taft said:

> "From early times it was the policy of Englishmen to encourage trade in England, and to discourage those voluntary restraints which tradesmen were often induced to impose upon

[1] 85, Federal Reporter, 271.

themselves by contract. Courts recognize this public policy by refusing to enforce stipulations of this character. . . .

"After a time it became apparent to the people and the courts that it was in the interest of trade that certain covenants in restraint of trade should be enforced. It was of importance as an incentive to industry and honest dealing in trade that, after a man had built up a business with an extensive good will, he should be able to sell his business and good will to the best advantage, and he could not do so unless he could bind himself by an enforcible contract not to engage in the same business in such a way as to prevent injury to that which he was about to sell. . . . For the reasons given then, covenants in partial restraint of trade are generally upheld as valid when they are agreements, first, by the seller of property or business, not to compete with the buyer in such a way as to derogate from the value of the property or business sold; second, by a retiring partner not to compete with the firm; third, by a partner pending the partnership not to do anything to interfere by competition, or otherwise, with the business of the firm; fourth, by the buyer of property not to use the same in competition with the business retained by the seller; and fifth, by an assistant servant or agent not to compete with the master or employer after the expiration of his time of service. Before such agreements are upheld, however, the court must find that the restraints attempted thereby are reasonably necessary to the enjoyment in the first, second and third cases, by the buyer of the property, good will or interest in the partnership bought, or in the fourth case, to the legitimate ends of the existing partnership, or, in the fifth case, to the prevention of possible injury to the business of the seller from use by the buyer of the thing sold. . . . It would be stating it too strongly to say that these five classes of covenants in restraint of trade include all of those upheld as valid at common law, but it would certainly seem to follow from the tests laid down for determining the validity of such agreement, that no conventional restraint of trade can be enforced unless the covenant embodying it is merely ancillary to the main purpose of a lawful contract and necessary to protect the covenantee in the enjoyment of the legitimate fruits of the contract, or to protect him from the dangers of an unjust use of those fruits by the other party. . . .

"This very statement of the rule implies that the contract must be one in which there is a main purpose to which the covenant in restraint of trade is merely ancillary. The covenant is inserted only to protect one of the parties from the injury which, in the execution of the contract, or enjoyment of its fruits, he may suffer from the unrestrained competition of the other. The main purpose of the contract, such as the measure of protection needed, furnishes a sufficiently uniform standard by which the validity of such restraints may be judicially determined. In such a case, if the restraint exceeds the necessity presented by the main purpose of the contract, it is void. . . . But where the sole object of both parties in making the contract, as expressed therein, is merely to restrain competition and enhance or maintain prices, it would seem that there was nothing to justify or excuse the restraint, that it would necessarily have a tendency to monopoly and, therefore, would be void. In such a case there is no measure of what is necessary to the protection of either party, except the vague and varying opinion of judges as to how much, on principles of political economy, men ought to be allowed to restrain themselves. . . ."

Taft then proceeded to cite a number of authorities differentiating from or reconciling them to the rule as he had stated it. The opinion concludes:

"Upon this review of the law and the authorities, we can have no doubt that the association of the defendants, however reasonable the prices they fixed, however great the competition they had to encounter, and however great the necessity for grouping themselves by joint agreement from committing financial suicide by ill-advised competition, was void at common law because in restraint of trade and tending to a monopoly."

Taft's finding perpetually enjoined the companies from maintaining their combination.

CHAPTER V

TROUBLE IN THE PHILIPPINES

I T is highly probable that Taft would have been appointed to the presidency of Yale University, when Timothy Dwight resigned in 1898, had he not stated positively that he would not accept the post if it were offered to him. His brother, Henry Taft, had written him,

"I have just had a long talk with Buchanan Winthrop of the Yale Corporation in relation to the Presidency question. It seems as if all the sentiment of the liberal element in the corporation is centering upon you as the fit man for the place, and some of the men in the Corporation are very anxious to know definitely what your attitude will be. . . . The persons in the Corporation advocating your selection fear that you think the man selected should have the qualities which no man living could possess, or, in other words, that you have idealized the position beyond the possibility of realization. What they are striving to obtain is a broad man of affairs, of reputation and position in the country at large, of good presence and scholarly, though not professional, attainments, of executive ability, popularity and aggressiveness. . . .

"It is the belief of your friends in the Corporation that you possess in an eminent degree the qualities which a President, performing functions, like those mentioned above, should have, and they are anxious, before you reach a conclusion that you should consider the question from their standpoint."

In answering his brother to decline the possible honor, Taft wrote,

"There are insuperable objections to my accepting an election to the Presidency of Yale University. Its President should first of all be an educator. He ought to be the real presiding officer in each of the faculties that make up the governing and teaching bodies of the University. He must have broad culture and wide learning that he may be able to enter intelligently into the general discussions likely to arise in each faculty meeting. The profession of an educator is as distinct from that of the lawyer or that of a minister as those two professions are distinct from each other. . . . The President must represent the University to the world. The exalted position of independence and disinterestedness which is accorded to a President of a University like Yale gives him an influence and power for good in the discussion of public affairs and the guiding of public thought that can hardly be exaggerated. It is this opportunity of the President of Yale which most attracts me.

"I venture to think, however, that in our enthusiasm over the material advancements of our University and the pride we may feel in a President, who worthily represents our Alma Mater to the world and is a power in the nation that makes for righteousness, we may become unmindful of the fact that the prime object of the University is to maintain the highest educational standard and that the first duty of the head of a University is to see to it that the educational opportunities it affords are progressively higher from year to year. . . .

"The President should be one having wide learning, the liberal spirit of progress, the comprehensive grasp of the whole educational field to enable him to give the initiative, if it be necessary, to real progress in each department, and on the other hand, to restrain ill-advised changes proposed by one-sided enthusiasts. A man like myself who has had the benefit of only the usual academic education, who has occupied himself, since graduation, with the practice and study of a jealous profession like the law, and whose general reading and study have been

AT THE 222ND COMMENCEMENT EXERCISES AT YALE IN 1923

of a desultory character, is necessarily lacking in the wide culture, breadth of learning, and technical preparation in the science of education which are needed to discharge the duties that I have attempted to describe. He would make a great mistake, and injure both the University and himself were he to assume the high obligations of the office of President.

"For these reasons, I have no hesitation in saying definitely that were the Corporation of Yale to invite me to become President, I should decline the great honor."

This letter of Taft's conclusively ended the hope of securing him for president of Yale. But events in the Far East were shaping themselves to change materially the destiny of William Howard Taft in a manner of which he never dreamed.

The opening of the Suez Canal, in 1869, had sounded the death knell of the peaceful missionary era in the Philippine Archipelago. Two immediate results were evident. If possible, the already serious abuses practiced by the Spaniards in the islands were aggravated, and, secondly, the facilities for travel were so increased that more and more Filipinos visited Europe. Assimilating a knowledge of freedom and liberty, as they learned more about other places and other peoples, they became more embittered by the intolerable conditions to which the Spaniards were subjecting them. But the more these natives chafed against oppression, the more hostile became Spain to any form of liberalism.

One of the Filipinos to visit Europe was Jose Rizal, who had taken the degree of Doctor of Medicine in Madrid. He had traveled extensively, completing his education, broadening his views, and sharpening his already keen humanitarian instincts. He published a number of books, among them "Noli Me Tangere," which decried the insufferable conditions in the Philippines and raised him from comparative obscurity to the limelight of fame. This book, and his activity in the Young Filipino Party, incensed the local Spanish government officials against him. He was closely watched, his activities were catalogued, and after what the officials considered sufficient evidence had been gathered, orders were issued for Rizal's arrest on the charge of conspiracy to incite insurrection. Warnings reached him, however, in time to permit his hasty departure for Europe. He unwisely returned, when the Spanish Governor General promised him personal safety and immunity from arrest. And as soon as he arrived in Manila he was seized, his luggage was searched and found (according to report) to contain seditious literature. Although he ably defended himself when on trial, he was exiled for four years to the desolate north shore of the Island of Mindanao.

Rizal was a charming, cultivated man, socially and intellectually. His dignity and patience won the respect and admiration of the local authorities under whom he remained in exile. And having been already respected by the natives, his banishment caused his name to be hallowed as a martyr to the Filipino cause. His popularity grew with every day of his exile, and when, depressed to the point of ennui from inactivity, he sought service as a physician with the Spanish armed forces operating in Cuba, government officials considered it expedient to seem to grant his plea. But as soon as he embarked for Barcelona he was again arrested, returned to Manila, accused of treason and found guilty. The trial was a farce, a mockery of justice, with subornation coloring the evidence, perjury rife and hearsay testimony freely admitted and accepted. The eight captains who sat as his judges solemnly condemned him to the ignominious death of a traitor.

At sunrise on the thirtieth of December, 1896, Rizal was led from his cell to a hollow square on the beach, formed by two thousand heavily armed Spanish troops. He walked to his doom with courageous calm, and knelt, facing the shore. An officer stepped forward and shouted, "In the name of the King! Whosoever shall raise his voice to crave clemency for the condemned shall suffer death." [1] Four rifles were fired and Rizal fell forward dead. The immense crowd that had gathered were stupefied. Rizal, their leader, had been killed, and on that day the Filipinos resolved that their independence from Spain must be achieved by other than pacific endeavor.

After this execution, the unrest which had long permeated the islands flamed into open rebellion when the hitherto docile Filipinos, under the leadership of Emilio Aguinaldo, the son of a farmer from the province of Cavite Viejo, rebelled against Spanish authority. For a time the revolution was restricted to that province, but gradually it spread through the Archipelago. Madrid, though her seasoned troops were in Cuba, dispatched ten thousand raw levies to be quartered on the islands.

With superior generalship, the European troops were successful, driving the insurrectionists to the mountains of the

[1] "The Philippine Islands," by John Foreman. Chas. Scribner's Sons, New York, 1899.

interior. Though not exactly a master of military strategy, General de Rivera, who had succeeded General Polavieja as the Spanish commander, was keen enough to realize that if he pressed the temporary advantage that he had gained, guerilla warfare would ensue. Knowing also that this would prolong the struggle indefinitely, he chose the more insidious plan of discrediting the insurrectionist leader with his own people. He offered Aguinaldo a general amnesty for himself and his followers and promised that reforms would be instituted in regard to the laws, religious orders, taxation and native participation in affairs of government if Aguinaldo would leave the islands. Aguinaldo agreeing, the Treaty of Biacnabato was signed on the twelfth of December, 1897, after which he and his followers sailed for Hong Kong, where he continued to work for Filipino freedom by becoming a member of the Filipino Revolutionary Committee in that city.

CHAPTER VI

THE SPANISH WAR AND AFTER

THE tyrannous and repressive measures adopted by Spain in Cuba had greatly incensed the American public, increasing the popularity of the Cuban cause in the United States, and this, in turn, implanted in the minds of the Filipinos the belief that war between Spain and America was imminent. On the third of November, 1897, Rounceville Wildman, American consul at Hong Kong communicated to the State Department,

"Since my arrival in Hong Kong, I have been called upon several times by Mr. F. Agoncilla, foreign agent and High Commissioner of the new Republic. Mr. Agoncilla holds a commission signed by the president, members of the cabinet and General in Chief of the Republic of the Philippines, empowering him to conclude treaties with foreign governments.

"Mr. Agoncilla offers on· behalf of his government alliance offensive and defensive when the United States declares war on Spain, which, in Mr. Agoncilla's opinion will be very soon. In the meantime he wishes the United States to send to some port of the Philippines, twenty thousand stand of arms and two hundred thousand rounds of ammunition, to be paid for on the recognition of his government by the United States." [1]

The Department of State reprimanded Wildman and ordered him to discontinue his conferences with Agon-

[1] "William McKinley," by Charles S. Olcott. Houghton Mifflin Company, Boston, 1916.

59

cilla. But with the destruction of the American battleship *Maine* in Havana harbor, during February, 1898, hostilities became inevitable, and war was declared on the twenty-third of April. The war was, as Theodore Roosevelt, an Assistant Secretary of the Navy, termed it, "the war of America the unready."

All the European states, except England, were unfriendly. Looking upon our army as an untutored mob, composed of mercenaries, and our fleet as unskilled hirelings, they jeered contemptuously at our efforts to mobilize. The English, skeptical of our ability, felt just a little sorry for the United States. A critic, in one of their technical magazines, wrote,

> The three thousand Swedish sailors who form a part of the complement of the United States Navy might be excellent material if fighting in defense of their own hearth and homes, but naval warfare of today is no pastime, it is a grim and ghastly reality, swiftly executed, and no hirelings of an alien state are liable to come out of such an ordeal. In point of fact, we do not believe that the Yankees thoroughly understand the spirit of mischief that they seemed determined to evoke.

Admiral George Dewey was commander of the American Asiatic fleet. On February twenty-fifth, 1898, he had received this cablegram from the Assistant Secretary of the Navy:

> "Order the squadron to Hong Hong. Keep full of coal. In the event of war with Spain, your duty will be to see that the Spanish squadron does not leave the Asiatic coast and then offensive operations in the Philippine Islands." [1]

[1] "Theodore Roosevelt, An Autobiography." Chas. Scribner's Sons, New York, 1919.

Dewey accordingly remained at Hong Kong until war was declared, then moved on to Mirs Bay.

Here he received dispatches from E. Spencer Pratt, American consul in Singapore, urging him to permit Aguinaldo to accompany him, in order to arrange for co-operation between the Americans and the Filipinos in their attack upon Manila. Pratt, whose friendliness to the Filipino cause was well-known in the far East, had conferred with Aguinaldo at a meeting arranged by an English newspaper man, Howard W. Bray, who acted as interpreter.

Hostilities had commenced. A Spanish merchantman, the *Buena Ventina,* had been stopped by a shot from the *U. S. S. Nashville.* Admiral Sampson, in command of three vessels, had bombarded Matanzas. On April twenty-fifth Dewey received his battle orders, to "proceed to the Philippine Islands. Commence operations against the Spanish fleet; capture vessels or destroy." [1] And in Manila the Philippine Patriotic League issued the following proclamation:

> "A nation which has nothing good can give nothing. It is evident that we cannot depend on Spain to obtain the welfare we desire. . . . Spain will need much time to shake off the parasites which have grown upon and cling to her. . . . Do not fall into the error of taking Spain to be a civilized country. Europe and America regard her as the most barbarous of the century. . . . Spain is always more ready to promise than to perform. . . . Providence will aid the Americans in their triumph, for the war is a just one, for the nation elected to lead

[1] "Theodore Roosevelt and His Time," by Joseph Bucklin Bishop. Chas. Scribner's Sons, New York, 1920.

us to the goal of our liberty. Do not rail against the designs of providence; it would be suicidal. Aid the Americans!" [1]

When word of the threatened attack reached Manila, people stampeded madly to remove themselves from the scene of the impending conflict. Many sought refuge up the river Pasig, near the Lake of Bay. Others, paying three and four times the customary passage, swamped the steamship *Esmeralda,* bound for Hong Kong. The bay front swarmed with life, the forts humming with activity as soldiers made them ready. Painters, suspended on rope seats over the sides, hurriedly made the white vessels of the Spanish navy a dull gray to look like the American ships. The Spanish officers of one native regiment, suspecting their men of disaffection, demanded the names of the ringleaders of a supposed plot. When the soldiers failed to comply, six corporals were indiscriminately selected and executed. That night the whole regiment, with rifles and accoutrements, went over to the rebels.

In hope of conciliating the Filipino people, Governor General Augusti issued this proclamation:

"Spaniards, between Spain and the United States of North America hostilities have broken out. . . . The North American people, composed of all the social excrescences, have exhausted our patience and provoked war with their perfidious machinations, with their acts of treachery, with their outrages against the Law of Nations and International Treaties. . . . A squadron manned by foreigners possessing neither instruction nor discipline is preparing to come to the Archipelago with the blackguard intention of robbing us of all that means life, liberty and honor. . . ." [1]

[1] "The Philippine Islands," by John Foreman. Chas. Scribner's Sons, New York, 1899.

Setting sail from Mirs Bay on the twenty-seventh of April, the American fleet entered the Bay of Manila on the night of April thirtieth. As one inspired song writer put it—

"Dewy was the morning,
Upon the first of May,
And Dewey was the Admiral
Down in Manila Bay."

Just at daybreak, as the early rays of the sun gleamed on the long line of low, red tile roofs, the white domes and towering spires of convents and monasteries, the first shots of the battle rang out. And to an incredulous world which expected word of Spain's victory, was flashed the news that "America the unready" had burned half the Spanish fleet and sent the rest to the bottom of the bay.

Dewey declared Manila blockaded, established military authority over the bay, cabled to Washington that he could take the city of Manila if he had troops to occupy it, and asked instructions. The jubilation which greeted Dewey's dispatches was tempered, in official circles, with consternation. McKinley observed that when Dewey sank the ships at Manila as he was ordered to do, it was not to capture the Philippines. It was to destroy the fleet of a nation with whom we were waging war. Conquest of the Philippines had been a very remote idea, to both the president and his cabinet. But Dewey was ordered to remain.

Both General Anderson, commanding the first relief expedition of American troops, and Admiral Dewey, treated the Filipinos as colleagues. Then Aguinaldo announced

63

that Pratt had promised him, during their conference in Singapore, that the United States would grant the Philippines independence and recognize their government. On the fifteenth of July, after he had expended much effort in organizing the Filipino Republic, Aguinaldo issued two decrees stating that he had selected his cabinet, and that it was his intention to remain on terms of peace with the North American Republic.

Ten days later General Wesley Merritt arrived to assume command of the American troops in the Archipelago and to establish, without regard to Aguinaldo, a provisional government. And when Manila was captured, Aguinaldo and his forces were refused any part in its taking. After the formal surrender of Manila, the insurrectionist chief requested dual occupancy of the city but this also was denied.

In late August, General Merritt was succeeded by General Otis, who immediately replaced the Spanish officials in the Civil Government with American Army officers. This meant, of course, a gradual concentration of power in the hands of the Military Governor. This was a necessary and timely, though drastic, action, for matters were in a chaotic state. The American blockade had paralyzed trade and commerce, and the food supply of Manila was rapidly becoming exhausted. Spanish military prisoners were a source of constant trouble. Large numbers of Chinese were being smuggled into the islands. Sporadic guerilla outbreaks brought atrocious outrages in their wake—murder, rapine, robbery and every sort of cruelty. Clerics were seized, tortured and killed, one being saturated with oil and

64

burned on a bamboo pole thrust like a spit through his body.

The hopelessly confused state of affairs in Manila, a natural consequence of the American attempt to reconcile their own policy of occupation with the already complicated Spanish form of government, forced the commanding general to entrust the city's government to the Military Provost General. This officer became the focal point of the American administration in the Archipelago, for, in addition to his other duties, he deposited all the funds collected from whatever source, and withdrew, from the public treasury, the money which had to be spent.

Meanwhile, argument raged in the United States as to the disposition of the Philippines. Public opinion was divided into two groups, Imperialists and anti-Imperialists. At the outset, President McKinley did not declare himself, although he stated in a memorandum, "While we are conducting war, and until its conclusion, we must keep all we get; when the war is over, we must keep all we want." [1] But since the question of annexation became seriously and acrimoniously debated immediately after Dewey's victory in Manila Bay, the President was faced with the vexatious problem of determining what the majority of American people wanted.

The Imperialists contended that the islands presented unlimited commercial possibilities, that our natural prestige was commensurate with the size and number of the domains over which we exercised control, and that by annexing the Philippines we would enhance our prestige as a

[1] "William McKinley," by Charles Olcott. Houghton Mifflin Company, Boston, 1916.

world power. Others, and they were many, adopted the missionary attitude which considered it our duty to acquire the Archipelago in order to impart to the Filipinos our Western ideals.

The anti-Imperialists, on the contrary, presented many forcible reasons why we should not take over the Archipelago. They stressed the perils of Oriental diplomacy and duplicity. Even assuming, they argued, that we could acquire the Philippines, could we retain and develop the islands? Would it not lead to further expansion and the need for a larger military force? The dissimilarity of climatic and racial conditions was also cited as an excellent reason why we should not attempt to impose our political philosophies upon the Filipinos.

Judge Taft aligned himself with the anti-Imperialists. Although he did not take part in the debates concerning acquisition as against non-acquisition, he favored granting the Filipinos their independence. He held that our government could not effectively control the islands, and that the only result of acquisition would be an increase in our responsibilities. He felt that America was already confronted with too many vital problems consequent upon the Spanish War, problems social as well as economic, which claimed our attention, and believed that the benefits accruing from annexation would not be commensurate with the detriments. But, considering the question distinctly to be in the province of the political department of the government, he devoted little study to the Philippine problem, being far too busy with legal matters.

Hostilities with Spain ceased on August the twelfth,

66

with the signing of a protocol by which Spain ceded Porto Rico to the United States and agreed to evacuate Cuba. The disposition of the Philippines was delayed until the Commissioners of the two countries met in Paris to draft the peace treaty.

To conduct the peace negotiations with Spain, President McKinley designated an exceedingly able body of men. They included William R. Day, who resigned the post of Secretary of State to accept the appointment, Cushman K. Davis, United States Senator from Minnesota, Senator William P. Frye of Maine, Senator George Gray of Delaware, and Whitelaw Reid, a journalist. John Bassett Moore, of the Department of State, accompanied the delegation as Secretary and counsel.

When they departed for France, the Commissioners were not definitely instructed as to what disposition was to be made of the Philippines. Public opinion had not clarified sufficiently to permit McKinley to promulgate a definite policy. Therefore in his original instructions the President merely mentioned the cession of the Island of Luzon as the least which the United States would accept. Day had expressed himself as favoring the annexation of some of the larger islands in order to control the entrance into the China Sea, but he did not believe that we should demand the entire Archipelago. Commissioners Davis, Frye and Reid wished to take the entire group of islands, whereas Senator Gray did not want to take any of them.

But when the negotiations had begun, President McKinley concluded that the majority of the American people believed that, even assuming that we had by implication promised independence to the Filipinos, we could not with-draw and leave them to put their own house in order, for with the passing of time it became increasingly evident that they were unfitted for this tremendous task. Accord-ingly, he ordered the American emissaries in Paris to de-mand the cession of the entire Archipelago. The retaining of the Philippines represented an entirely new departure in our statecraft; it meant that we were departing from our traditional isolation to enter upon a policy of inter-tropical colonization.

Meanwhile, in the Philippines, the natives had followed the peace negotiations closely and with increasing bitter-ness. They had been alienated the preceding August by General Merritt's action, and although their attitude had bordered upon open hostility, they had avoided armed con-flict with the Americans. The Paris negotiations being concluded on the tenth of December, the completed treaty was sent by the President to the United States Senate for consideration on the fourth of January. And on February fourth, 1899, the Filipinos attacked the American troops holding Manila. Repulsed, they were sent reeling back into the interior of the Island of Luzon.

Despite the armed resistance of the Filipinos, President McKinley proceeded with his plans for the pacification of the Archipelago. He appointed the First Philippine Com-mission, its members being Jacob Gould Schurman, presi-dent of Cornell University, Major-General Elwell Otis, ·ranking officer in the Philippines, Rear Admiral George Dewey, in command of the American fleet in the Far East, Colonel Charles Denby, for fourteen years United States

Minister to China, and Professor Dean C. Worcester, of the University of Michigan.

President McKinley desired that the First Philippine Commission should work without interfering with the military régime, though he wished them, at the same time, to ascertain what amelioration in the condition of the inhabitants, what improvements in the public order, were practicable. He instructed the Commission to endeavor to lessen the burden of taxation, to establish, in so far as possible, industrial and commercial prosperity, and to provide for the safety of persons and property. He reminded them that they were on a good will errand, that they were to have due regard for the ideals and institutions of the people, and to treat all local customs with respect. They were to study the existing forms of the local governments, the administration of justice, the collection of the customs, the levying of the taxes and, after due consideration, were to make a report to the President summarizing the results of their investigations. This report was to incorporate their recommendations and include any information they might consider important and beneficial to the United States in its future administration of the Archipelago.

The First Philippine Commission completed its work in March, 1900. Formulated with the conviction that President McKinley had acted wisely in adopting the course he did, the report read, in part:

"Should our power by any fatality be withdrawn, the Commission believe that the government of the Philippines would speedily lapse into anarchy, which would excuse if it would not necessitate the intervention of the other powers and event-

69

ual division of the islands between them. Only through American intervention, therefore, is the idea of a free, self-governing and united Philippine Commonwealth conceivable. The indispensable need from the Filipino point of view of maintaining American sovereignty over the Archipelago is recognized by all intelligent Filipinos, and even by those insurgents who desire an American protectorate. The latter, it is true, would take the revenues and leave us the responsibilities. Nevertheless, they recognize the indubitable fact that the Filipinos cannot stand alone. Thus the welfare of the Filipinos coincides with the dictates of national honor in forbidding our abandonment of the Archipelago. We cannot from any point of view escape the responsibilities of government which our sovereignty entails; and the Commission is strongly persuaded that the performance of our national duty will prove the greatest blessing to the people of the Philippine Islands."

CHAPTER VII

THE SUMMONS TO THE PHILIPPINES

IN his message to Congress on the fifth of December, 1899, McKinley declared that the pacification of the Philippines was not far distant, and that he believed we should proceed with the installation of a civil government in the Archipelago. For this work he determined to appoint a Second Commission. He hoped to procure the men who had served with the First Philippine Commission, but all of them, except Worcester, rejected the offer of reappointment. These refusals made the President's task more difficult. It necessitated the appointment of a man who, unfamiliar as he would be with the Philippine situation, was endowed with the requisite statesmanship, tact and ability to direct the establishment of a civil government.

McKinley consulted Elihu Root who, as Secretary of War, would supervise the actions of the appointees, and his intimate friend and fellow-Ohioan, General H. C. Corbin. It happened that the previous autumn Corbin had returned to his native state from Washington for the election, and, on his return, by chance, had taken the same train that carried Judge Taft to Cleveland. They struck up an acquaintance, and Corbin became so enthusiastic about the young Federal judge that when McKinley consulted him, Corbin at once suggested Taft for the presidency of the

Second Philippine Commission. And one day early in February, 1900, when Taft was sitting in the consultation room of the United States Circuit Court in Cincinnati, he received this telegram,

"I would like to see you in Washington on important business within the next few days. On Thursday if possible.
WILLIAM McKINLEY.[1]

He hastened to respond to the summons without having the slightest idea why he was wanted.

When President McKinley informed Taft that he intended to establish a civil government in the Philippine Islands; that he was appointing a Commission to undertake the task of creating such a government, and that he wanted Taft to head the Commission, the judge was dumbfounded.

"Why, Mr. President," he exclaimed, "that would be impossible. I am not in sympathy with your policy. I don't think we ought to take the Philippines. They are sure to entail a great deal of trouble and expense."

"Neither do I," replied McKinley, "but that isn't the question. We've got them. What I want you to do is to go there and establish a civil government."

Taft protested that his training had not been of a nature to qualify him for such work. He said that he knew nothing about colonial government, that he had had no experience in the administrative field, had never held an executive position, and that he felt that the President could

[1] "Recollections of Full Years," by Helen Herron Taft. Dodd, Mead & Company, New York, 1914.

certainly find a man more competent than he for the task. The President replied that he had given due consideration to Taft's qualifications for the post, and considered him eminently suited for such work. Still Taft protested. Then McKinley summoned Root, because, as he said, the immediate supervision of all Philippine affairs would be under the direction of the Secretary of War.

Root told Taft that while he did not rejoice in our taking over the administration of Philippine affairs, the situation demanded that the United States govern the Archipelago until the natives had learned the difficult task of governing themselves.

Root said, "The work to be done in the islands is as great as the work Livingston had to do in Louisiana. It is an opportunity for you to do your country a great service and achieve for yourself a reputation for the finest kind of constructive work. You have had a fortunate career. You are only over forty and you have had eight years on the Federal bench, three years on the state bench, and two years as Solicitor General. These places you have filled well but they have involved no sacrifice on your part. Here is a field that calls for risk and sacrifice. Your country is confronted with one of the greatest problems in its history and you, Judge Taft, are asked to take immediate charge of the solution of that problem seven thousand miles away from home. You are at the parting of the ways. Will you take the easier course, the way of least resistance, with the thought that you had the opportunity to serve your country and declined it because of the possible sacrifice, or will you take the more courageous course and risking much, achieve much? This work in the Philippines will give you an invaluable experience in building up a government and in the study of laws needed to govern a people, and such experience cannot

73

but make you a broader, better judge, should you be called upon to serve your country in that capacity." [1]

Root, possessing keen discernment, had advanced an argument to which the judge was most vulnerable. Still Taft held off. He disliked relinquishing his judicial position, and the Philippines, of all places, attracted him least at the time. He asked a few days to talk things over with his family, before deciding, and left for Cincinnati without giving an answer. From there he wrote his brothers, Horace and Henry Taft,

"The President said that he sent for me to induce me to accept an appointment as a member of the Philippine Commission which he expected to reappoint to visit the Islands, and to organize a civil government, and prepare a provisional code adapted to the present circumstances. He said that he did not think that President Schurman, of Cornell University, was going back again, and in that case, he wished to make me President of the Commission.

"I told him I was very much opposed to taking them, that I did not favor expansion, but that now we were under the most sacred duty to give them a good form of government. I explained that I did not agree with Senator Hoar and his followers that the Filipinos were capable of self-government, or that we were violating the principles of our government, or the Declaration of Independence as far as they were concerned; that I thought we were doing them great good but that I deprecated our taking of the Philippines because of the assumption of a burden by us contrary to our traditions at a time when we had quite enough to do at home; but, being there, we must exert ourselves to construct a government which would be

[1] "Recollections of Full Years," by Helen Herron Taft. Dodd, Mead & Company, New York, 1914.

74

adapted to the needs of the people so that they might be developed into self-governing people.

"I said, however, that I am not a Spanish scholar, and did not feel I could render the service that he could secure from others. He said he had selected me, that Hay, Root, Long, had all said 'I must go,' when my name was suggested. I asked him whether he expected me to resign my judicial office. 'Well,' McKinley responded, 'all I can say to you is that if you give up this judicial office at my request you shall not suffer. . . .'

"I took a week in which to decide. The President is evidently very anxious to have me accept, and if I do, and the opportunity arises, I have no doubt that promotion would follow. If it does not, I should have to go back to the practice after the service terminates. . . . The question, of course, is 'Am I willing and ought I to give up my present position for what is offered *In Presenti* and *In futuro?'*

"The opportunity to do good and help along in a critical stage in the country's history is very great. Root especially urged this view. I am still young as men go, and I am willing and not afraid to go back to the practice though I confess I love my present position. Perhaps it is the comfort and dignity and power without worry, I like. Ought I to allow this to deter me from accepting an opportunity thrust upon me to accomplish more important and more venturesome tasks with a possible greater reward. . . . ?"

Both brothers urged Judge Taft to accept the President's offer. Horace Taft wrote to him:

"Of course, you must accept. I take it for granted that the position is for President of the Commission. Harry (Henry Taft) wrote me that he had advised you to accept, if this were the case, but from your letter, it does not seem to me that there is any doubt that this is so. You can do more good in that position in a year than you could on the bench in a dozen, much

75

as I honor and appreciate judicial work. They can't get a better man than you. My old prejudices in that respect have never wavered. If you get stuck I can give you a place in the school (Taft School). . . . Seriously, without any promises from the President at all, you must feel the absurdity of being troubled about your future."

While Taft still debated the proposal, McKinley sent him a letter saying that it would probably not be necessary for the Commission to remain in the Archipelago more than nine months at the most, and that Taft could take an extended leave of absence from the court. Taft, however, believed that the building of a government in the Philippines would take years and not months. So did Root, who advised his resignation from the court if he accepted the post. The more Taft hesitated, the more determined McKinley became to have him accept. When Judge William R. Day wrote the President that he was going to Cincinnati, McKinley hurriedly dispatched this letter to Day.

"Indeed, on some accounts, I am rather glad you are going to Cincinnati, because Judge Taft will consult you about a matter which I have brought to his attention. I want him to go to the Philippines on a commission to establish civil government in the provinces where there is peace. I have had him down here, have gone over the whole ground with him. He took a week to reply. This morning a letter comes that he wants a little more time, that he may consult with his brothers on next Monday. I want you to appreciate, Judge, that this is a very important matter, and I invoke your aid to get the consent of Judge Taft to go. It is a great field for him, a great opportunity, and he will never have so good a one again to serve his country. I think he is inclined to accept. You must not make it harder for him to accept.

"The Commission which I shall send will have large powers and a wide jurisdiction. They can accomplish great good and help me more than I can tell you in the solution of the important problems of the East. Besides, a Commission made up of men of the character of Judge Taft will give repose and confidence to the country and will be an earnest of my high purpose to bring to those peoples the blessings of peace and liberty. It will be an assurance that my instructions to the Peace Commission were sincere and my purpose to abide by them." [1]

Taft's unwillingness to go to the Philippines is understandable enough. He loved the Federal judgeship. If ever a promotion meant a sacrifice, this promotion did. To bring order out of the chaos in the Archipelago was a Herculean job in itself, and would have been so even to a man who felt attracted to administrative work. And to Taft it meant giving up a life in which his labors were a constant source of joy, for the acceptance of a post the tenure of which depended upon the whims of public opinion. It meant undertaking a gigantic and precarious task for which he did not feel himself well-fitted. But he realized that he could not decline what he considered to be a doubtful honor. He accepted the appointment and resigned from the Federal Court.

His period on the bench had been much more stormy than the average, because of the type of cases he was called upon to decide. It coincided with the troublesome transition period for organized labor and, as some of his decisions restricted and placed limitations upon the scope of

[1] "William McKinley," by Charles Olcott. Houghton Mifflin Company, Boston, 1916.

their actions, the workingmen branded Taft as unfair to them, a charge which was manifestly unjust. During his seven years as a judge, Taft penned over two hundred and sixty opinions. He worked hard. His secretary has said that "on many and many a night he would return to his office after dinner and dictate until twelve and one." He spent six weeks of this type of intensive labor, for instance, on his opinion in the Addyston Pipe Case. His associates on the circuit bench during those seven years were William R. Day, Howell E. Jackson, Horace H. Lurton and Henry F. Severens. Three of these four, Jackson, Lurton and Day, served as Justices of the United States Supreme Court.

CHAPTER VIII

THE SECOND PHILIPPINE COMMISSION

WHEN McKinley received Taft's acceptance, he summoned him to Washington for a conference concerning the details and personnel of the Commission. At this meeting, Taft, feeling that every effort should be made by the civil authorities to avoid unnecessary conflicts with the military, requested the President to draft written instructions carefully outlining the jurisdiction of the Commission and defining its duties. This precaution was a wise beginning, as later events proved.

McKinley delegated to his Secretary of War the task of drafting these instructions. Root's enunciation of the Commission's powers and duties, elucidating our policy of colonization, proved to be an astonishing revelation to the European states. Political and social conditions had compelled these governments to colonize and expand in order to find an outlet for their too-rapidly increasing population. It followed that their practice had been to ignore the political development of the dependent colony, and to deal with the economic only in so far as it benefited the metropolitan state. The United States differed from these governments both in the theory and practice of colonizing, accepting as axiomatic that the good of the colony was the main concern of the mother country, that the aspirations of the natives for independence and self-government were

79

perfectly natural and therefore proper. We proposed to aid rather than obstruct, and this theory became our practice in the Archipelago.

Accordingly the instructions directed the commissioners to acquaint themselves thoroughly with the condition of affairs in the Archipelago. Three months were allotted for study and investigation, and on the first of September, 1900, the military, who had been exercising both the legislative and executive functions of the Philippine Government, were instructed to relinquish to the Commissioners the legislative duties, while retaining and continuing their discharge of executive responsibilities.

Among the functions delegated to the Commissioners were the appointment of the officials for the judicial, the educational and the civil service systems; the making of rules and regulations to raise revenue by taxation, customs and imposts; the appropriation and expenditure of public funds; and the organization of the municipal and provincial governments, along the lines of American city and state governments, with distribution of authority among the legislative, executive and judicial departments. These instructions represented a point of view and policy theretofore unheard-of in the Philippines. Upon the Commission, as upon the military, was imposed the imperative injunction, embodying all the principles set forth in the Bill of Rights, that

"no person shall be deprived of life, liberty or property without due process of law; that private property shall not be taken for public use without just compensation; that in all criminal prosecutions the accused shall enjoy the right to a speedy and public trial, to be informed of the nature and cause of the accusation, to be confronted with the witnesses against him, to have compulsory process for obtaining witnesses in his favor, and to have the assistance of counsel for defence; that excessive bail shall not be required, nor excessive fines imposed, nor cruel and unusual punishment inflicted; that no person shall be twice in jeopardy for the same offence or be compelled in any criminal case to be a witness against himself; that the right to be secure against unreasonable searches and seizures shall not be violated; that neither slavery nor involuntary servitude shall exist except as a punishment for a crime; that no bill of attainder or ex post facto law shall be passed; that no law shall be passed abridging the right of free speech or of the press; that no law shall be made respecting the establishment of religion or prohibiting the free exercise thereof, and that the free exercise and enjoyment of religious profession and worship, without discrimination or preference, shall forever be allowed."

No limit, of course, was placed by government officials upon the period of time during which it would be necessary for us to remain in the Archipelago. That the future had to determine. By defeating Spain, we had acquired responsibilities which had to be conscientiously discharged. Our principles of colonization assumed that eventually the Filipinos were to be free and self-governed, and therefore the Commission must have for its primary object the well-being of the natives. There must be no exploitation of the Filipinos. Any measures adopted were to conform to their habits, their customs and even their prejudices, in so far as it was possible to do this and at the same time create a stable government. The Secretary of War also stressed the importance of coöperation between the civil and the military authorities of the United States operating in the Philippines. Root said that, in his opinion, if the military and civil officials worked in harmony, an enduring government, insuring a faithful, just administration of Philippine affairs, could be established. He cautioned the Commissioners to have due regard for the lack of educational background of the Filipinos. They were instructed to extend and expand the system of education already adopted by the military, with the object of developing eventually an organization of schools which would beget an educated electorate, making thereby for a strong government. He further advised them to begin with the simplest forms of municipal and provincial governments and, in so far as feasible, to have the officials of these governments elected by the natives.

The men who composed the Second Philippine Commission were rich in mental equipment and ability, possessing qualifications for every line of work in practical government and research. McKinley had re-appointed Professor Dean C. Worcester; Professor Bernard Moses, General Luke Wright and Judge Henry C. Ide were the other members of the Commission. Three of them were attorneys—Taft, Wright and Ide. Each had been eminently successful, Taft as a jurist, Wright as a practitioner at the Bar, and Ide in combining business with law.

Wright, a Tennesseean by birth, had enjoyed a large and lucrative law practice. A scintillating sort of man was Wright, and a gifted raconteur.

Born and bred in New England, Ide was in many ways a typical Yankee. His extensive banking connections in

Vermont and New Hampshire had given him an excellent business training; having served as Chief Justice of Samoa, where he exercised judicial, consular and diplomatic functions, he was well-equipped for the work which confronted him in the Philippines.

Worcester, a large, powerful man, rather abrupt in manner, was the only member of the Second Philippine Commission who possessed any special knowledge of the customs and habits of the people of the Archipelago, having spent some time in the Philippines even before he served on the First Commission.

Professor Bernard Moses, who left his native Connecticut to accept the chair of History and Political Science at the University of California, was well-equipped as an economist, historian and political student.

Such a group augured well for American success in the Philippines, and the press commended McKinley's selections. The *Washington Star,* which knew him best, thus singled out Taft,

> "Judge Taft's sacrifice in leaving his judicial post for the more arduous service in Manila testifies, like the case of General Wood, to the high public spirit to be found in men of high moral and intellectual grade at a time when such men are so much in demand."

Said the *Chicago Tribune,*

> "The Commission seems to be a judicious combination of the practical and theoretical elements necessary for the solution of the difficult problems that may arise in creating good political and judicial systems for the Philippines."

After this conference Taft returned to Cincinnati. He was much feted by his multitude of friends and shortly before his departure a farewell banquet was arranged in his honor. In his address that evening, Taft said,

"Circumstances beyond our control, the sequel of the Spanish War, have thrust on us the responsibility for the future of the government of the Philippines. I have now to deal with the situation as it is and whatever the cause of it, the question now is, 'What are we to do to meet the present needs?'"

Taft explained that he had been an "anti-Imperialist," but that circumstances had altered his belief and demanded his departure for the Archipelago. He continued,

"The high and patriotic purpose of the President in the present juncture is to give the people of the Philippine Islands, the best civil government which he can provide with the largest measure of self-government consistent with stability. He seeks only the welfare of the Filipino, and the betterment of his condition. The incidental benefits of the trade of this country arising from this new relation must be made subservient to the interest of those who have become our wards. With this purpose thus defined I have the deepest sympathy. A strict merit system must be devised to prevent the machine politicians whether of this country or of those distant islands . . . from making use of the offices needed to serve the public wants, to reward their henchmen, or to perpetuate their power. One of the glaring defects of Spanish colonial government in those islands was the making of useless offices in order to fill them with favorites. The spoils system was allowed to have full effect with all the abuses that follow in its wake. If we are not to give the islands a civil service free from this cancerous growth, our claim that we have taken and kept the Philippines

84

for the good of their people is a hollow and unworthy pretense."

After a round of festivities in Cincinnati, Taft hastened once again to Washington to complete preparations for the departure of the Commission. From Washington he proceeded to San Francisco, whence the Commissioners were to sail for the Philippines.

William Jennings Bryan happened to be on the train which carried Taft from Los Angeles to San Francisco. As the Philippine question was certain to be the major political issue of the 1900 campaign and as Bryan was the most likely Democratic candidate for the Presidency, the Commoner, apparently believing that he might secure a statement from Taft which he could use on the stump against the Republicans, pressed a conversation. Irritated by the Democrat's catch-penny phrases, the spirit which actuated him, and his persistence, Taft finally asked Bryan why he insisted on talking with him; whether he thought he could convince him, or whether he thought that he, Taft, might convince Bryan. The Commoner answered no, neither, all that he wished to get was Taft's views on the situation in the Far East.

The Western people had favored the acquisition of the Archipelago. Their point of view, in contrast to the sentiment that had prevailed in the East, was based upon the belief that there was great profit to be derived from trade with the islands. And they greeted the Civil Commission with characteristic heartiness. So lavish was the entertainment, in fact, that Taft, just before sailing, wrote in a per-

85

sonal letter, ". . . the people of California are boisterous in their hospitality and I shall reach the ship tomorrow with a feeling of intense relief that I can give my stomach a rest when I tackle the ship's fare. . . ."

At noon, on a brilliant, golden, sunlit day, the seventeenth of April, 1900, the United States Army Transport *Hancock*, with the Second Philippine Commission on board, pulled away from the crowded dock, while handkerchiefs waved, whistles shrieked farewell, and the air rang with cheers. The boat had hardly cleared San Francisco harbor when the Commissioners, retiring to a cabin which had been specially fitted for the conducting of business conferences, held the first session of the Second Philippine Commission.

For none of the Commissioners, least of all Taft, failed to appreciate the fact that their task was truly colossal. The physical character of the islands, the nature of the people, the problematical social and political conditions, made the work of tranquillizing the Philippines and establishing a civil government extremely difficult. And since the Philippine venture was America's first attempt at colonization, there were no precedents to guide them in their undertaking. The entire voyage to Manila was devoted to mapping out a program which might be sufficiently flexible to meet the myriad complex problems which were certain to obstruct their progress.

Stops were made at Honolulu, Yokohama, Hong Kong. At each port the Commissioners were lavishly entertained. When the *Hancock* docked at Hong Kong, several Chinese came to the boat and announced that they had been

86

engaged as servants to Mr. Taft. When Taft expressed surprise, one of them handed him a letter from Flag Lieutenant John H. Shipley, of the *U. S. S. Brooklyn,* which enclosed a note to Ah Sing, steward of the Brooklyn, from Ah Man, Admiral Dewey's servant.

"It is a new Governor General coming out to Manila. His name is Mr. William H. Taft and is going to sail from here on the first of April. The Admiral asked me to write to you and ask if you please find some good Chinese servants for Mr. Taft. He like a very, very good cook, just like myself, the Admiral said, and two men to wait on table, butler and second man, just like you. Now would you be so kind as to try and find some very nice people that will take good care and understand their business."

CHAPTER IX

BEGINNINGS OF A GREAT EXPERIMENT

O<small>N</small> the third of June, a blistering, hot, tropical day, the *Hancock* anchored in Manila Bay and the Commissioners, freely perspiring, retired to their cabin to await the arrival of the military commander. But General Mac-Arthur did not present himself, which was his initial contribution to the coöperative unity President McKinley so much desired. He sent, in his stead, Colonel Crowder, who tactfully presented the General's compliments and stated that he had come to make arrangements for a formal ceremony to take place the following day. After Crowder's departure, interesting and interested visitors thronged the boat to pay their respects. The "Americanistas," those Filipinos who sympathized with American control, particularly charmed the Commission with their politeness and cordiality. Deploring the turbulent conditions existing in the Archipelago, they assured the Commissioners that, with patience and diplomacy, the hostility of the natives could be overcome.

The Commission formally went ashore the next day, escorted by innumerable small boats, with whistles screaming and flags flying. They alighted at the mouth of the River Pasig, where long lines of artillerymen, stretching from the landing to the government building—General

MacArthur's headquarters—stood at attention. The reception, however, was merely perfunctory, for, as Taft said later, when they were escorted into the presence of the commanding general, MacArthur's greeting was so frigid that he stopped perspiring. After the formal introductions, General MacArthur told the Commissioners bluntly that he considered their appointment a reflection upon his ability to cope with the situation and that he was not in sympathy with the administration's plan to install civil government in the Islands. He bitterly resented their presence, calling them "an injection into an otherwise normal situation." [1] Taft assumed a conciliatory attitude. He explained that the Commission proposed to assume only legislative duties and to train the Filipinos for civil government; that the Military Commander would retain the executive functions. He also called MacArthur's attention to the fact that the General was in command of the largest military unit assembled by the United States since the Civil War, and that that alone was a responsibility of much dignity.

"Yes," MacArthur said, "that would be all right if I hadn't been exercising so much more power than that before you came." [1]

Exasperated by the discourtesy of the military man, Taft finally reminded the General that since his authority in the Philippines dated back only a month (he came on the fifth of May) and expressed the hope that the General's brief enjoyment of his position would not hinder his apprecia-

[1] "Recollections of Full Years," by Helen Herron Taft. Dodd, Mead & Company, New York, 1914.

tion of the exalted post he would continue to hold, despite the arrival of the Commission.

This letter to Annie Roelker of Cincinnati happily records Taft's first impression of the Philippines.

"We had a very successful trip. We stopped four days at Honolulu and saw a great deal of the Island of Oahu. . . . From there we went to Yokohama which we reached in about twelve days and there everything was most interesting. . . . During our stay of five days in Yokohama we were all presented to the Emperor and Empress of Japan. The incident was an interesting one, of course, to look back upon. . . . We came on through the inland sea to Hong Kong, where we spent four or five days in the midst of the plague, and then, without contracting that disease, came over to Manila, reaching here on the second of June. . . .

"I have succeeded in getting a very good house on the Bay of Manila in the suburb of Malate, to the south of the city. The house stands about forty feet back from the waves, from which it is protected by a sea wall. There is a porch or gallery on the second floor, and one on the first floor, with a tile pavement seventy-five feet long by twelve or fifteen feet wide, and covered with a roof, and with glass windows and a place for awnings. On that porch which had a roof sufficiently thick to prevent it being hot in the daytime we usually find a very pleasant breeze from the sea. . . .

"The city of Manila has beautiful possibilities. The wall of the walled town is the best specimen of . . . fortifications in the world, I presume. The Luneta and Botanical Garden present opportunities very beautiful, which have not been improved since the Spaniards left, because they destroyed everything in the nature of large trees and beautifying shrubs before leaving. The walled town is full of ancient old convents, churches and public buildings. The Americans have put the streets in good order and have done a great deal towards sanitation. The situation politically and from a military standpoint is distinctly better than I had been led to suppose. . . . The Friar question, I think, will work itself out. . . ."

Secretary Root, realizing that it would be necessary for the Commissioners to familiarize themselves with conditions in the Islands and to study the characteristics and habits of the natives before they could do very much, had inserted in his instructions a provision that the period between the arrival of the Commission and September first was to be spent in acquiring such knowledge. The allotted period was all too short, but in order to make as thorough an investigation as possible under the circumstances, Taft assigned to each of the Commissioners certain problems to study individually. The results of their examination, and such recommendations as they cared to submit to the whole Commission, were to be summarized by each in a report.

Worcester was given municipal corporations, forestry, agriculture and public health. Moses was charged with problems relating to schools and taxation. Questions pertaining to the criminal code, police, franchises and public improvements were entrusted to Wright. Ide was to draft the new code of civil procedure for the courts and to study bank, currency and registration laws. Taft took upon himself the problems arising from the public lands, the civil service and the "Friar" situation.

It is no wonder that the Filipinos, ignorant of the English language and taught by the Spaniards to expect the worst, regarded Taft and his fellow-Commissioners, when first installed in the Ayuntamiento, with foreboding and hostile suspicion. Spain had been to them illiberal, restrictive and oppressive. The American military, declining to solve the multitude of problems with the disorganized and antiquated Spanish governmental machinery, had for the sake of expediency proclaimed martial law. Thus experience had turned the Filipinos against any form of alien government and left them bitter and antagonistic. Besides, social and political conditions had been greatly aggravated by famine and disease—the rinderpest, locusts, cholera and typhoons had all taken their toll. In hope of winning the confidence of the natives, the Commissioners set forth their aims in a printed document, the first they issued, which they distributed widely. It announced that they "intended to study the situation deliberately, consulting the Filipinos who would lend their help and eventually they hoped to secure to all Filipinos such a measure of popular control as would be consistent with stability and the security of law, order and property."

Although it was perhaps the last of all possible tasks he would have chosen, Taft took a certain pleasure in contemplating the problems which faced him. The Philippines were to be turned into a great experimental laboratory of practical government. Political, social and industrial tests were to be conducted at the offices of the Commissioners until a formula, in the shape of laws, was evolved to meet the needs of the Filipinos. The application of these laws would necessarily have to be delayed until the policy of the United States toward the retention of the Islands had been determined by the election of 1900. Unless McKinley were reëlected, the labor of the Commissioners might possibly be in vain.

Happily Taft was of an optimistic turn of mind. Even as the passing days revealed the extent to which Filipino society had been permeated by the corruption of the Spanish administration of every office, Taft did not lose his cheerfulness, nor was his confidence in the ultimate solution of the Philippine problem shaken. However, Taft, in his zeal to construct for the Philippine Islands a government which would render secure the rights of the individual, and harmonize and unite the heterogeneous races of the Archipelago, soon had disillusioning experiences. They are reflected in this interesting letter to Justice John Harlan.

"Manila is a hard city to get settled in. First, houses are hard to get; second, after you get them, they always need repairs; and, third, after your repairs are begun the slowness with which the workmen work tries one's patience exceedingly. I had cabled out from Washington for a particular house and had secured it. The house stands immediately on the sea shore and is separated from the beach only by a sea wall. This secures a constant breeze, and in the tropics the difference between a breeze and still air is most important. The house, while not quite large enough for my purpose, is roomy and will give us, I think, every comfort. It needs a good deal of repair and what would take in the States about two weeks will here probably consume all the time before Mrs. Taft arrives. I expect her on the first of September.

"The condition of things here is distinctly more favorable than I had been led to suppose. . . . A company of one hundred men could go from one end of the island to the other and not be disturbed by any force which they might meet, but a person without escort is liable to attack any place beyond the towns or places occupied by the United States troops.

"These people are a peculiar race. They are polite, appear light-hearted, but are not industrious. The great problem of the Philippine Islands is that of labor. They are wealthy beyond the dreams of avarice in everything which nature can afford, but capital will not find sufficient labor here of a constant character to justify an investment of a great deal of money, and whether we shall let the Chinese in or not, is one of the serious issues for our consideration. A large plantation owner, or sugar producer or owner, can gather five hundred to a thousand men, and secure a contract with them for a month's labor. They will not take a step until they are paid two weeks in advance. They may then work three or four days in the desultory manner in which they work in this country, and then more than half of them will quit with the advanced wage in their pockets. . . . They have an artistic temperament; they are musical; they are very superstitious and are the most gullible people in the world. . . .

"The question of a civil government is most perplexing. There is a small percentage of these people who are educated and are able to exercise the suffrage. The great mass of them are superstitious, ignorant and their leaders do not recommend universal suffrage, but quite a high qualification for it. . . .

"The Catholic church has implanted into the minds of most of the race a strong love of chastity. . . . Three hundred years of Spanish political rule has given them to understand that it is the legitimate function of every public official to be bribed, and a proper method for anyone having to do with them is to bribe them; that it is the legitimate part of the duties of an official, where he has the opportunity,—to 'squeeze' the citizens and get something more than the law requires from them. This is so general that it will be impossible for us to trust for a long

94

time the collection of money or the disbursing of it, to any considerable number of Filipinos. . . .

"They need the training of fifty to one hundred years before they shall even realize what Anglo-Saxon liberty is. Of the educated ones among them, most are profound constitutional lawyers, who will discuss with eloquence and volume American constitutional questions and who are most glib in running off the phrases, but they have not the slightest conceptions of the political questions. How taxes are to be levied, how to be collected, or from what source. Their liberty is a kind of liberty that entitles the speaker to complete license, and the person who differs with him to imprisonment or the loss of limb or head. The possibility of a majority rule in which the minority has indefeasible rights is something that is hard to bring to their minds."

CHAPTER X

THE HANDICAP OF POLITICS

Meanwhile the Democratic Party in the United States had made a political issue out of the acquisition of the Philippines.

> "We condemn and denounce the Philippine policy of the present administration," their platform read. "The Filipinos cannot be made citizens without endangering our civilization; we favor an immediate declaration of the nation's purpose to give the Filipinos first, a stable form of government; second, independence; third, protection from outside influence or rather interference."

There can be no doubt that the intensity and bitterness of the campaign in the United States prolonged the Philippine insurrection and impeded Taft's work. The natives followed the election with absorbed interest. In a letter to his brothers, Taft related the impossibility of sure progress till McKinley should defeat Bryan.

> "You can hardly believe the closeness with which the Presidential matters are being watched," he wrote, "and how they follow the speeches made against the Republican cause. General Smith away down on the island of Negros told me he had found speeches by Hoar and Bryan and other 'Anti-Expansionists' and 'Anti-Imperialists' in the most remote mountains of his district."

96

Under instructions from Washington, although doubting the wisdom of such a course, General MacArthur issued an amnesty proclamation. All natives in arms were granted ninety days within which they might present themselves and take the oath of allegiance to the United States, thus obtaining pardon. Among those who availed themselves of this opportunity was Pedro A. Paterno, canny, unreliable, clever in a Machiavellian way. Paterno had acted as the representative of the Insurrectos in negotiating the Treaty of Biacnabato with the Spaniards, which terminated the 1896 insurrection. Shortly afterward, writing to an official of the Spanish Government, Paterno showed his duplicity by saying,

"I, who, amidst inundations and hurricanes have assaulted and conquered the barracks and military posts of the enemy, causing them to lay down their arms to Spain without bloodshed and at my command surrendered their chiefs and revolutionary government with their brigades and companies, I think I have good right to ask Spain if she wishes to show herself a mother to me, to give me as much as she has given other sons for lesser service.

"It is notorious that I have worked so grandly that no one can now ask me to sink into insignificance.

"To conclude, I want a title of Castile, that of Prince or Duke, if possible, and to be a Grandee of the First Class." [1]

Now, Pedro A. Paterno proposed a three day grand fiesta, with music, marching, speeches, fireworks, flags and a banquet, in honor of the Military Governor, a celebration which should eclipse in grandeur any previous fiesta ever

[1] "The Philippine Islands," by John Foreman. Chas. Scribner's Sons, New York, 1899.

held. Although he knew Paterno's guile, MacArthur, hoping that the fiesta might promote friendly relations between the American authorities and the natives, assented to the celebration, with the provision that all the addresses should be censored. Invitations to attend the banquet were extended to the Military Governor, who declined, and to the Commissioners, who accepted. Arches were erected—with pictures of McKinley and Aguinaldo side by side in a double frame of greens! This caused Taft to investigate. He found that the speeches to be delivered were seditious in character in that they promised American evacuation of the Archipelago and independence to the Filipinos. Taft accordingly declined to attend the dinner, and by way of reprimand wrote this to Paterno:

"No one having any authority to speak for the United States has ever said one word justifying the belief that a protectorate such as this speech promises will be established. It is impossible. The discussion of a protectorate as a possibility involves misrepresentation which may induce submission to the authorities of the United States by deceit. The members of the Commission cannot be parties to any such misrepresentation."

As the Military Provost General had ordered that no speeches were to be made and as General MacArthur had ordered that no banquet was to be held unless one of the Commissioners was present, the stage was all set for the discrediting of Paterno. Rushing to Taft's residence, the Filipino threw himself upon his knees before the Judge and implored him to attend the banquet. Finally Taft assented, but as the guests had been kept waiting for two hours, and no speeches were permitted, the fiesta was a failure.

Other Filipino politicians continued their efforts to commit the Commissioners to a program of evacuation and independence. A former lieutenant of Aguinaldo's, Apolinario Mabini, then in jail, requested an interview with the Commission. He was brought before Judge Taft, and launched into a vociferous dissertation on freedom, liberty and equality. The old Filipino was obsessed with the idea that "because all people are endowed with certain primary and admitted rights any attempt to regulate the exercise of those rights by others was unjustifiable." Taft endeavored vainly to confine the discussion to the application of those theories to conditions then existing in the Archipelago.

"Suppose, Senor Mabini," Taft asked, "the Americans should withdraw and this freedom of which you speak be granted you, what then? Your country is composed of many scattered islands, some of them inhabited by savages, and all of them by people speaking different dialects and without any cohesion of ideas or experience in government. You occupy an exposed and coveted position in the path of world commerce, and would doubtless be called upon very soon to defend your nationality.

"You have many foreigners living here, for whose lives and property you would be held accountable not only from outside interference, but from the ambitions and jealousies of your own people. To protect your country from these dangers you would need an army of considerable strength and at least the nucleus of a navy. All these things together with the necessary expenses of government, would cost a great deal of money. Your country and your people are poor and your industries paralyzed. Waiving all question of your ability to govern yourself, I would ask you how you propose to raise the revenue necessary to preserve and administer such a government?"

Mabini simply shrugged his shoulders and replied, "The question of revenue is a mere detail." [1]

But little by little Taft's prestige increased among the Filipinos. He worked day and night studying the conditions presented for his consideration, and his knowledge of Philippine problems became more and more apparent. And the intelligent little brown people began to know that this vast, deliberate American, whose eyes twinkled narrowly above branching mustachios in a wide, impassive face, could be trusted. He questioned and questioned, he studied and studied, he acted with firmness, he was not after anything for himself, he cared above all for the truth. Above all, he was patient. Here is testimony from one Juan de Juan, who wrote the following editorial in a Manila newspaper.

> "Before the *Hancock,* bearing this statesman, had anchored in Manila Bay, the echo of his reputation and the radiation of the brilliant aureole which his success in the judiciary of his country had imposed upon him . . . and we underline the word imposed because the characteristic trait of Mr. Taft is his modesty . . . had reached the Philippines. The Filipinos awaited him with the same pleasing curiosity with which a child opens a toy with a concealed surprise. . . .
>
> "Mr. Taft leaves his home every morning at eight and as unostentatiously as a clerk, proceeds to become a part of his chair in the Ayuntamiento. There his first occupation is glancing over the American press, and what is of interest in the

[1] "The Odyssey of the Philippine Commission," by Daniel R. Williams. A. C. McClurg & Company, Chicago, 1913.

Spanish papers. Then the show begins. Paterno, Macabulos, Montenegoro, some envoy from Cebu, for example, who come to sound him, as the slang saying goes, arrive. Mr. Taft has the same respectful smile for all, the same courtesy, and addresses them all in the same terms, while his athletic secretary, Mr. Ferguson, repeats in Spanish with the gravity of a Sphinx, and the fidelity of a phonograph. When the matter warrants it, Mr. Peppermann, the chief stenographer of the Commission, enters the office and proceeds to take notes of the interview.

"In this way the Americans are forming a luminous record which, united to what were in our archives, which they preser，e through the terms of the Treaty of Paris, will guide them well in the administration of the Philippines. Later, Mr. Taft becomes engulfed in the examination of the bills which the other members of the Commission present for him to study; he discusses their text with his colleagues, listens to all their observations, and judging them by a standard most favorable to the interests of the Philippines, the most liberal within the instructions from Washington—it is proper to say that Mr. Taft is the most democratic element of the Commission—he expresses his opinions, generous, calm and noble, which assuredly, in view of his personal prestige, must carry great weight in the framing of the bills. . . ." [1]

After three months of preliminary investigation and study, Taft forwarded to Root an exhaustive report, summarizing the Commission's conclusions. Feeling that the hostility against the Americans had originally been aroused by absurd falsehoods, the Commissioners reported that the distribution of the military in small detachments throughout the Islands was dispelling this hostility and improving

[1] "Recollections of Full Years," by Helen Herron Taft. Dodd, Mead & Company, New York, 1914.

the temper of the native people. They attributed the continuance of the insurrection and the sporadic outbreaks of guerilla warfare to uncertainty concerning the future policy of the United States.

Advocating the immediate establishment of a native constabulary and militia, which would end the terrorism to which the Filipinos had been subjected under the Spaniards, the report said that such an organization would restore normal business conditions and permit an early and material reduction of the American Army in the Archipelago. The report recounted, at some length, the many reforms the Commission proposed and stated that the near future would see the creation of a central government, similar in many respects to the one in Porto Rico, which would bring to the people of the Philippines "contentment, prosperity, education and public enlightenment."

It was all very uphill work, however. In order to provide the best opportunity for public consideration of proposed laws, the Commission set aside Wednesdays and Fridays of each week for public hearings. But the irresponsible population of the Islands, watching the electoral campaign in the United States and imagining that freedom would follow a Democratic victory, were, much to Taft's disappointment, apathetic. And further to obstruct the Commissioners' plans, General MacArthur, with exasperating regularity, objected to the proposals of Taft and his associates. To conciliate him, Taft had made it a rule that no law was to be passed, except in cases of dire emergency, without first being submitted to the Military Governor for consideration and comment. Upon the Commanding General's approval, each proposed Act was published in the newspapers, and a specific date set for a public hearing. In this way Taft hoped not only to pacify MacArthur but to give the Filipinos the opportunity of being present and making suggestions concerning the measures at hand.

Among the first and most important acts made law by the Civil Commission was the Civil Service Bill, drafted by Taft. In presenting this Bill to the consideration of the Commissioners, Taft explained that he had sought to make it malleable, so that it might expand with the growth, progress and requirements of the Archipelago government, and exclude all possibility of favoritism and politics. The Commissioners read the Act with growing amazement. It included every official and employee of the Government from the heads of departments down to the lowest grade of laborers! It provided for the creation of a Civil Service Board, whose sole function it would be to handle the details of its administration. Entrance to the Civil Service was restricted to those persons between the ages of eighteen and forty who were citizens of the United States, natives of the Archipelago, and persons who, by reason of the Treaty of Paris, had acquired the political rights of natives. The Bill established an efficient civil service which had as its basis a merit system with competitive examinations as the only reason for promotion.

Other early legislative enactments were bills appropriating sums of money to improve the means of communication. When the Second Civil Commission first arrived, transportation facilities were extraordinarily primitive. There was but one railroad, the Manila Railway Company

Limited, which operated about one hundred and twenty miles of "Oriental gauge" track from Manila to Dagupan, and the public roads were nothing more than foot-paths, impassable during much of the year.

Difficult to construct and more difficult to maintain, the roads presented a very serious problem to the Commission. Labor was unskilled and scarce. Road building machinery had to be transported from the United States. The topography of the country necessitated abstruse engineering investigations and calculations. And after the roads were built, all too often the torrential rains would wash out the bridges, wreck the surface and destroy the road beds. Taft and his associates determined to leave the problem of the railroads to private persons or corporations, and to devote themselves exclusively to the building and maintenance of highways. And their first bill for expenditure was one appropriating two million dollars Mexican for that purpose.

Other acts passed during early September established three Government Bureaus, Forestry, Mining and Statistics.

CHAPTER XI

FRIARS' LANDS AND THE CRIMINAL CODE

IN reserving for himself what was popularly known as "The Friar Question," when he distributed problems that confronted the American Civil authorities, Taft retained one of the most vexing and difficult questions presented by the Philippines. Its origin was rooted in the early history of the Islands.

The Spanish conquest in the Far East had opened a virgin missionary field for the Roman Catholic church. Zealous Spanish friars of many orders had followed the military, and vied with one another in sowing the faith of their church on prolific soil. Introducing new methods of agriculture, founding a college, and, half a century before the advent of the Pilgrims into New England, establishing a hospital for the care of the Filipinos, they did much toward bettering the physical condition of the natives. With real missionary ardor the priests preached to these Oriental people, and their efforts were amply rewarded. Centuries passed, and practically the entire population of the Archipelago, except the Moros in the Southern Islands and certain wild tribes of savages dwelling in the fastnesses of the mountains on the Island of Luzon, were converted to Catholicism.

Churches, schools and monasteries sprang up everywhere. The ecclesiastical power of the friars increased with the years and four of the orders, the Recoletos, the Augustinians, the Franciscans and the Dominicans, had had their authority extended by the Spanish Government to include civil affairs. The Spanish Government, finding it increasingly difficult to attract young men into its colonial service, filled the gaps by giving civil power to these religious leaders, who collected the taxes, drafted men for military service under the Spanish arms, and directed public affairs, generally. The friars thus came to be charged with the enforcement of many unreasonable and arbitrary demands made upon the Philippines by the Spanish government. It followed that they became in the eyes of the natives the embodiment and symbol of all that was looked upon as tyrannical and oppressive.

The friars of these four orders were in charge of three hundred and forty-six of the five hundred and ninety-six parishes in the Philippines. The Dominicans, the Augustinians and the Recoletos (the Franciscans were prohibited by the rules of their order from owning real estate) had acquired either by grant from the government or by purchase from the Filipinos, some four hundred thousand acres of the best agricultural lands of the Archipelago, a fact not at all relished by the natives. The landlord-tenant relationship thus created between the religious orders and the Filipinos, when, unable to cultivate all of their holdings themselves, the priests leased portions of it to the natives, caused considerable friction, and implanted in the minds of the natives a dissatisfaction which subsequently grew into hatred.

Therefore, when the Filipinos rebelled against Spanish

106

authority, they naturally identified the wealthy orders with all that they detested in the Spanish régime, and made them the special objects and victims of retaliation. In the insurrection of 1895, more than forty priests had been tortured and killed, and when the First Philippine Congress met at Malolos, its first official act had been to pass a law confiscating all the land holdings of the religious orders.

Most of the friars had fled to Manila to save themselves from the insurrectionists, and there they were, awaiting the restoration of order, when the United States superseded Spanish dominion over the Archipelago. To prevent further violence, the American army officials, as a military measure, had prohibited the clerics from returning to their parishes or collecting their rents from the land. In preserving the status quo the military had acted upon President McKinley's direction, for the friar problem was a civil, not a military problem, and it was not until the Second Philippine Commission had been appointed that the President determined to effect a settlement of the difficulty.

"It will be the duty of the Commission to make a thorough investigation into the titles of the large tracts of land held or claimed by individuals or by religious orders," the President had written in his instructions, "into the justice of the claims and complaints made against such landlords by the people of the Islands, or any part of the people, and to seek by wise and peaceable measures a just settlement of the controversies, and redress of the wrongs, which have caused strife and bloodshed in the past. In the performance of this duty the Commission is enjoined to see that no injustice is done; to have regard for substantial right and equity, disregarding technicalities so far as substantial right permits."

Taft came to realize more and more that unless the friar problem was adjusted to the satisfaction of the Filipinos, armed resistance was inevitable. So deep-seated was the hostility of the natives toward the clerics of those four orders that, as Taft knew, if they were allowed to return to their parishes the Filipinos would believe the American Government was following in the footsteps of its predecessor. On the other hand, all property rights had been expressly guaranteed by the United States, under the Treaty of Paris.

It could not be disputed that these religious orders possessed valid titles to the land, which promised them protection in the enjoyment of their property. It was equally evident that the friars were patiently awaiting the reëstablishment of order and the reorganization of the civil courts before enforcing their rights.

But the real problem lay in the necessity of dispossessing the friars without offending or infringing upon the rights of a religious body, for, after all, the disposal of the clergy was a matter of church policy and one over which the American Government could exercise no control. Failing to understand the impossibility of any immediate solution of the problem, the people were flooding Taft with letters and petitions protesting against the return of the churchmen, and demanding that the new Government prohibit the restoration of their civil rights. The matter of the friars' lands thus became a question of policy rather than one of law, for, as the Commission had reported, the return of the friars to the Philippines would have had the same effect as "the return of General Weyler under an American Commission as Governor of Cuba would have had on the people of that island."

What Taft hoped to do was to purchase the vast estates of the religious orders and then sell the land back to the natives on easy terms. In this way, he believed, the friction between the people and the friars could be eliminated. Accordingly, in order to acquaint himself further with the situation, he interviewed heads of the various religious orders and prominent Filipinos. He also conferred with Archbishop Chappelle of New Orleans, who, by direction of the Vatican, had come to Manila to assist the United States in working out the friar problem. It was much later that he finally solved and closed it, and while these negotiations were gradually bringing Taft nearer to the settling of the friars' question, he also participated daily in the public sessions held by the Civil Commission.

Another imperative necessity confronting them was the revision of the civil and criminal codes. The Filipinos who came before the Commission to register complaints revealed a maladministration of justice which astonished its members. One native, for instance, explaining that under the Spanish code there was a provision which permitted the successful party in a litigation to tax his attorney fees as part of the court costs, related this misadventure. He had instituted a law suit, praying for a judgment of five hundred and seventy-nine dollars. A finding had been made for the opposing party, upon demurrer, and his opponent's attorney had fixed the fee at six hundred and twenty-four dollars—forty-five dollars in excess of the amount sued for! Under the Spanish code, this would have exacted the payment of approximately eight hundred dollars as court costs, nearly three hundred dollars more than he prayed for! Upon his objection, the court referred the matter to two members of the Manila Bar for an opinion. Declaring the fee was just, these lawyers assessed the Filipino an additional fifty dollars each for their services, which assessment the court approved, and he was compelled to pay the whole amount!

An even more flagrant abuse under the old Spanish code was brought to the Commission's attention by a prominent member of the Manila Bar, Senor Don Felipe Calderon, appearing on behalf of another Filipino. Calderon explained that the son of this old native had been in prison for over six years without even having a charge brought against him, much less of coming to trial. Directing Calderon to prepare a Writ of Habeas Corpus, Taft told him to proceed likewise on behalf of any other Filipinos thus unjustly incarcerated, and nearly a hundred were thus released.

Outraged by such iniquitous persecutions, Taft proposed to make sweeping changes in the personnel of the judiciary. He determined to bring from the United States a tried, capable, honest group of Americans to supplant the jurists of the Archipelago. Among others, he wrote to Judge Erskine M. Ross as follows:

"One of the most difficult problems we have is the establishment of a satisfactory judicial system. Such Filipino lawyers as there are have been trained in the Spanish school and under a Spanish judiciary which was as venal as the executive administration, so it is that it is impossible for us to find, with one or two notable exceptions, any Filipino lawyers capable and honest enough to administer justice as we understand that term in an Anglo-Saxon country.

"We cannot, therefore, make satisfactory courts unless we appoint American judges in most cases in order that by example these people may be shown what Anglo-Saxon justice means. I write to ask you whether you can recommend to me good, upright lawyers with at least ten years of experience, who would make good judges, who have the moral courage and the sense of fairness necessary to make a good judge, and who have sufficient knowledge of Spanish to enable them by one or two months practice to carry on a court in that language."

In the meantime, the courts presided over by Filipino and Spanish judges, trying to interpret both the Spanish code and the legislative enactments of the Commission, were grinding out a confused body of law. And, in spite of the fact that they had suffered outrageously from the greediness of the Island judiciary, the Philippine press, when Taft made public his intentions, protested violently against the substitution of American judges. They demanded the filing of specific charges of incompetency, setting forth the particulars in which each judge was deficient. They argued that the native judiciary had stood by the Americans during their period of trial, and that to oust these Filipinos without formal preferment of charges would be a great injustice.

Obviously, to file charges against each judge and to try each case would have required years, delayed the Commission's work indefinitely, and might even have jeopardized the eventual establishment of a civil government. Having considered all this before making the announcement public, Taft ignored the deluge of abuse to which he was subjected.

For eight months the Commissioners conducted open hearings on both the Judiciary Act and the Code of Procedure. The Commission urged the College of Advocates (as the Filipino Bar was called) and the American lawyers practicing in the Philippines, to attend these sessions and coöperate with them in the framing of the Acts, but these overtures were received with passive, if not active, opposition. The apathy of the American lawyers was due to Taft's unwillingness to substitute English for Spanish as the official court language, a change which the Americans had proposed. Taft pointed out, in rejecting this proposed amendment, that if Spanish were replaced by English as the official court language, every Filipino attorney, by reason of his inability to understand and speak English, would be eliminated from the practice of law.

As it was, the judicial machinery was practically paralyzed, and the Commission finally passed the Judiciary Act and the Code of Procedure, without assistance from the native and American attorneys. These new rules, governing the commencement of actions, process, trial and judgment, thus displaced the archaic Spanish Prodecural Code. By the Judiciary Act, the Islands were divided into fourteen judicial districts and, in each district, courts of first instance, municipal courts and Justice of the Peace courts were established. No provision for a jury system was made because Taft and the other Commissioners, knowing that so many of the natives were illiterate, believed them as a whole unfit for such service, and that the installation of a jury system would imperil rather than aid the efforts they were making to remove corruption from the administration of justice. The act did, however, provide for the appointment of assessors, upon the application of either party to a litigation, who should sit with the court and render a finding of fact.

Besides setting up trial courts in each judicial district, the new law created a Supreme Court of the Archipelago, to consist of seven members, a Chief Justice (a Filipino) and six Associate Justices, three of whom were to be Americans and three Filipinos. The judges were to be appointed by the Governor General of the Islands, subject to confirmation by the Commission, and to hold office during good behavior. Power of removal of any judge was vested in the Governor General, with the consent of the Civil Commission.

CHAPTER XII

THE MUNICIPAL CODE AND PROVINCIAL
GOVERNMENT

FURTHER to educate the Filipinos for active participation in their own Government, Taft had helped prominent natives to organize the first Philippine political party, known as the Federal Party, its object being to promote a speedy restoration of civil authority and to gain, ultimately, not independence, but admission to the Federal union as a state. The Federal Party, composed of leading citizens of the Archipelago, early made its influence felt. Branches were established throughout the Islands, to hasten the surrender of the insurrection leaders and to convince the Philippine people that the American Government wished them well.

Conditions were improving, on the whole, and Taft wrote to Samuel Dickson of Philadelphia:

"The insurrecto leaders are very tired and time is curing most of the lawlessness. In the Southern islands, it is true that there are small organized bands that give trouble. The troops are spread over all the islands in the principal towns and are not able to mass themselves for fear that should they leave a town the small bands of ladrones and insurrectos in the neighborhood would kill all those who have been favorable in any way to the Americans. . . . The method the insurrectos have at present of fighting is to cut a telegraph line and then sit down in ambush

114

and wait until the two linemen come along and kill them. It is difficult to meet this kind of warfare. . . .

"As a sample of the ignorance that we have in these islands, let me repeat to you what Captain Bandholtz, the Governor of Tayabas, told me of a ladrone and religious fanatic or fakir named Rios in Tayabas; Rios was a blacksmith and an officer of Zurbano, one of Cailles Colonels, who had committed a murder and was afraid to surrender when Zurbano surrendered. He therefore took to the woods and announced that he had supernatural powers. He hid in a tree and had a lot of people called about him and came down out of the tree announcing he had come from God. He brought with him a handsomely carved box, on the top of which was marked 'Independencia.' He then told the people that they all wanted independence and that it was a good thing and said,

" 'I have it here in this box and if you will organize into a band and enable me to spread my government here, I will take it out of the box and give it to you,' and he succeeded in this way in organizing a band of ladrones. . . . They were at length scattered. Later one of the ladrones was asked what they were fighting for. He answered, 'They were fighting for independence; that their captain had gone to Cebu to get it and he was going to bring it back with him.' "

November sixth brought tidings of President McKinley's reëlection. This news probably contributed more to the success of the Commission than any other single factor. The period of uncertainty was ended.

The Commission had divided the Islands into Provinces and Municipalities, through which governmental units they proposed to test the qualifications of the Filipinos for self-government. The relation of each Province to the Insular Government was not unlike that of each American state to the United States; and the Filipino municipalities were to the provinces what the American cities are to the states. In fact the Commissioners had modeled the Provincial Government Law and the Municipal Government Act upon the constitutions of the American states and the charters of American cities and villages. There were, however, conspicuous differences, owing to the nature, background and training of the people. Eager as they were to grant the Filipinos a degree of popular control that amounted to independence, the Commission had been constrained, by the natives' lack of experience in self-government and consequent disregard of the significance and responsibility of governmental duties, to draft laws containing many checks and restrictions. These two acts, after months of labor, the Provincial Government Law and the Municipal Government Act, were finally passed in early January, 1901.

By the Municipal Code the natives were for the first time granted an opportunity to control their own affairs. Believing that the exercise of suffrage would be a first step toward political education, Taft included a provision for the election, by the people, of all Municipal officials except the Treasurer. And the suffrage was confined to persons possessing prescribed qualifications. The offices of President, Vice President were created, as well as a Council, and the duties of each carefully defined. These were to be filled by Filipinos. A Secretary and Treasurer, both Americans, were to be appointed by the President, with the consent and approval of the Council. The Councillors were to be elected on the theory of ward representation, their numbers to be decided by the size of the village population. Following the ancient Spanish custom, the Commission specified that the Municipal officers should carry canes, as badges of office.

Under the Provincial Government Bill, each Province corresponding roughly to our state, was governed by five officials, Governor, Secretary, Fiscal, Treasurer and Supervisor. The Provincial government functioned not only as an independent unit, but also exercised supervision over the Municipal authorities, with power to suspend any officer charged with malfeasance or nonfeasance in the duties of his office. The legislative body of the Province was "The Provincial Board," composed of Governor, Treasurer and Supervisor. Temporarily, the Commission intended to appoint the Governors of each Province, but eventually these were to be selected by the councilors of the Municipalities, when they met at the Provincial capitals.

The Fiscal was the legal official of the Province, while the Supervisor's duties were those of an engineer, including the construction, repair and maintenance of roads and bridges. Realizing that the Filipinos, owing to their training under the Spaniards, had not grasped the sacredness of public funds, the Commissioners concluded it best to appoint only Americans to the office of Provincial Treasurer. This official was to collect all taxes, Municipal as well as Provincial, excepting the minor fees accruing to the local governments, which were to be collected by their own financial officials.

Having completed the Provincial Law, the Commissioners decided to give its first application their personal supervision, and to establish direct and friendly contact with the people of the Provinces by making a tour. San

Fernando, some fifty miles distant from Manila, in the Province of Pampagna, was their first destination. They started out on the morning of the twelfth of February, 1901, in special coaches which Taft had ordered to be attached to the Manila-Dagupan train. It was quite a triumphal tour in a way. All along the route, at Bocaue, Guiguinto, Malolos (where the Insurgent Congress first met) and Calumpit, they were greeted by throngs of people, seas of brown upturned faces, innumerable bands, and always a reception committee, attired in morning black and silk hats.

The same ceremony was repeated at each village along the route. A few leading citizens stepped forward from the respectful group, one of them made an address of welcome, Taft responded, and the train started on again, amid a clamor played by the native bands, in which strains of "A Hot Time" mingled with those of "The Star-Spangled Banner" and swelling shouts of "Vivas" for "La Comision Civil." As the railroad cars had no facilities for platform speaking, the members of the Commission had to lean out of the car windows in order to be heard. The cars were small, the windows smaller, and Taft was a very large man, so that it was something of an achievement to get even part of his upper portion through the inadequate aperture. And although Taft himself and the other Commissioners thought it funny, the grave, always polite Filipinos gave no sign of amusement. Plainly, they liked Taft, his directness, his chuckle, his expansive, disarming smile.

At San Fernando, a whole procession of carriages waited to transport the Commissioners through a town bedecked as for a fiesta. The streets were spanned by elaborate arches of bamboo and palms. Paper lanterns bobbed about everywhere, nondescript flags with an intermingling of stars and stripes waved and fluttered from every house, eager Filipinos lined the roadways. After a short stop at San Fernando, the party went on to Bacolor where the Provincial convention was to be held.

Here the Commissioners were lavishly entertained. Tiffin, consisting of six meat courses, fruits and wines, was served at noon. That evening a banquet was held at the Provincial building, in a hall brilliantly lighted with Japanese lanterns and lavishly decorated with palms and flags— a banquet so sumptuous that Taft prefaced his address by saying that no town of like size in the United States could duplicate such overflowing hospitality. When Taft and his party came to the Provincial building, where the meeting to organize the Province was to be held, they found an immense expectant crowd, besides the representatives of twenty-five municipalities. It was a skeptical and disillusioned throng, for many times had they been promised participation in the Government; each time had they been disappointed. But they were willing to try, if not to hope, once more. The roll of towns was called and each delegate rose to respond. At the completion of the roll call, Taft stepped to the front of the platform and, speaking into an awesome silence, outlined the purposes of the American Government in the Philippines and explained how the Commission, as an instrument of that Government, proposed to carry these objects into effect.

Taft's speech elucidated, minutely and simply, the provisions of the new Provincial Law. He said that the American officials expected to bestow a greater measure of self-government upon the natives as time passed and they demonstrated their ability to govern themselves. When Taft had finished, Arthur Fergueson, Secretary of the Philippine Commission, who stood beside Taft at the front of the platform, translated the address into Spanish. As Fergueson proceeded, the respect with which the Filipinos listened became less apathetic and more animated. This did not seem to be merely a speech. It had the simplicity and the explicitness of sincerity. They could not but believe him. When Taft invited the delegates to offer suggestions and such amendments to the Provincial Law as local conditions might demand, many responded. And because Taft received their suggestions thoughtfully and graciously, the Filipinos spoke more freely until, as the meeting went on, a general discussion took place.

Of course many of these proposals had to be considered by the Commissioners in private session but they were, whenever possible, put into effect. That afternoon the special act applying the new Provincial Law to that Province was passed, and the Commission selected the town president of Bacolor to serve as Governor. And thus simply a new epoch was launched in the government of the Philippines—a new milestone was passed in American colonial government!

Early the next morning the Commission departed for Dagupan in the Province of Pangasinan. There, in the village theater, three hundred and fifty delegates from thirty-one different pueblos awaited the arrival of the Commission. The procedure at Dagupan followed that of Bacolor except that, upon roll call, each delegate, as his name was called, rose and walked before the stage where the Commissioners sat. After the enactment of the law creating the Province of Pangasinan, the Commissioners returned South to Manila, stopping on the way to organize the Province of Tarlac.

The lavish entertainment and hospitality shown to the Commission by the Filipinos made almost as much impression upon the guests as the new Provincial Law did upon the natives. And upon his return to Manila, Taft wrote to Secretary Root that "some sort of pension should be provided for the widows and orphans of the men who fell in action before the powerful onslaughts of native hospitality."

Hand in hand with the political progress made by the Commissioners, went their efforts in the cause of education. The Spaniards, considering the education of the common people quite unnecessary, for years made no effort to establish schools. But toward the latter part of the nineteenth century, the yearning for education among the lower classes of the Archipelago so definitely asserted itself that a primitive system of public primary instruction, with courses in reading and writing, had been established. Instruction continued to be sporadic, however, for from the beginning of the insurrection in 1896 to the American occupation a few years later, most of the schools had been closed and the buildings used for barracks, prisons and hospitals. On August 13th, 1898, seven schools were reopened in the city of Manila, under the supervision of Father W. D. MacKinnon, the Catholic chaplain of the First California Regiment, officers and soldiers acting as volunteer teachers. This situation continued until June, 1899, when Lieutenant George Anderson was detailed by the military commander to be city superintendent of schools in Manila.

When the Second Philippine Commission took the place of the military in the work of education, they established a Department of Public Instruction, comprising a General Superintendent, eighteen Divisional Superintendents, and many local school boards. Common schools were founded in each community and every child was to be taught arithmetic, reading and writing. English was prescribed as the medium of communication, because the Filipinos did not have a common language. This necessitated the bringing of teachers from the United States, and in the summer of 1901, after a month of recruiting, six hundred teachers sailed from San Francisco for Manila. Regarded apathetically at first, the schools soon gained new interest, became crowded, and added many new courses to their curricula.

In fact, such remarkable success had attended the efforts of the Commission that the complete pacification of the Islands did not seem far distant. There were occasional insurgent outbreaks by a few guerilla bands still operating in remote sections, but they were almost immediately suppressed. And on Washington's birthday, 1901, an extraordinary celebration took place in Manila, in recognition of the achievement of the Civil Commission. Ten thousand natives, with scores of bands, marched through the city to the Luneta, where, from a platform especially erected for the occasion, General Luke Wright addressed them.

President McKinley acknowledged the Commission's

success by signifying his intention of appointing Taft Governor General of the Islands, to supersede the military commander as chief executive. Whereupon the recalcitrant MacArthur began to display a willingness to coöperate and offered his assistance in arranging for the second trip which Taft was planning, this time for the purpose of installing a civil régime in the Southern and less peaceful territory. Another and most important obstacle was removed from the path of the Commission by the capture of Aguinaldo. For almost a year he had been playing hide-and-seek with the American army, some seventy thousand strong, scattered in small detachments through the Archipelago. They were marched hither and thither in search of him, but always in vain, and America know that so long as he was at large the insurrection would have some vitality.

Finally, in early February, messages giving a clue to his whereabouts were intercepted, and Colonel Frederick Funston, leader of the so-called "suicide squad," after an exciting march over dangerous jungle trails and across a river, made a spectacular capture of Aguinaldo and took him to Manila as prisoner of war.[1] The tranquillizing effect of this feat upon the Philippines has never been properly appreciated. The insurrection might have continued indefinitely, with wasteful expenditure of lives and money, had it not been for the daring of Funston and his squad.

[1] Aguinaldo has been living in Manila, where he took the oath of allegiance to the United States, prosperously and quietly ever since. And within the past year he made one of his few public statements. "It is absurd and ridiculous," he declared, "to demand independence when we could not possibly maintain a government without the help of the United States. A handful of Filipino politicians have formed an oligarchy and are wasting the money of the Filipino people. They want independence so that they can waste more. We don't need independence. We need common sense."

CHAPTER XIII

THE SOUTHERN JOURNEY

L ATE in February, Taft had created the Provinces of Bataan and Balacan, and was there greeted with the same enthusiasm which he had encountered in his tour through Pampagna, Tarlac and Panganisan. Now he planned an expedition among the Southern Islands, to begin at Lucena in the Province of Tayabas, proceed across the inland waters and the Sulu Sea as far as Jolo, and, after winding around the southern point of the Island of Mindanao, return to Manila, with stops at Iloilo in Panay, and at Cebu. On Sunday morning, March 10th, his party left Manila on the transport *Sumner*. The group included the Commissioners and their wives, a number of prominent Filipinos, members of the newly formed Federal Party, and some newspaper correspondents.

At Lucena they were welcomed by friendly throngs and two bands in resplendent costume. After the preliminary meeting in the school-house, where Taft explained the Provincial Act, he and Mrs. Taft, in a flower-decked victoria, and the other members of the party in a somewhat nondescript collection of vehicles, made progress through the town, one band preceding the victoria and playing "A Hot Time in the Old Town," another following with "Ta-ra-ra-boom-de-ay," and still another, farther back in the procession, contributing "Won't You Come Home, Bill Bailey."

124

"The road wound its way for the entire distance through an immense cocoanut grove. Looking backward or forward you saw a vista of these beautiful trees with their chiseled stems and tufted tops, and from every elevation they spread a sea of waving plumes to the horizon,"

says Daniel R. Williams in his "Odyssey of the Philippine Commission."

The banquet at Lucena was almost as overpowering as the one which the Commission had to attend in Cebu a few weeks later, when the following thirty-four courses were served:

(1) Oyster soup
(2) Roast turkey
(3) Roast beef
(4) Roast pork
(5) Boiled tongue
(6) Chicken, French style
(7) Oyster pie
(8) Baked fish
(9) Boiled ham in jelly
(10) Veal pot pie
(11) Beef steak
(12) Pork chop
(13) Veal cutlet
(14) Fried chicken
(15) Roast chicken
(16) Chipped ham
(17) Fried pigeons
(18) Cream pie
(19) Apple pie
(20) Peach pie
(21) Pineapple pie
(22) Chocolate cake

(23) Raisin cake
(24) Jelly roll cake
(25) Apple pudding
(26) Minced potato
(27) Fried potato
(28) Shoe string potatoes
(29) Sweet corn
(30) Stewed beans
(31) Asparagus
(32) Raw tomatoes
(33) Green onions
(34) Radishes [1]

At the ball which followed the "banquete," the first dance was the old Spanish quadrille, which the Philippines called the "rigodon," an extremely complicated affair, requiring no little skill. At the first bars of the rigodon music, Taft rose, gallantly led the wife of the local Presidente out on the floor, and to the evident astonishment of his fellow Commissioners and the delight of the Filipinos, went through the intricate steps with perfect ease. Anticipating just this social emergency, he had taken the time and trouble to learn the dance before starting out from Manila.

The next stop was Boak, across the Bay of Tayabas, on the Island of Marinduque. Thence the Commissioners proceeded to Masbate, on south to the Archipelago's second city, Iloilo, where they left the *Sumner* to take the small coastwise vessel across the dangerous straits to Bacolod, in the Island of Negros. After Negros they visited Jolo. Mrs.

[1] "The Odyssey of the Philippine Commission," by Daniel R. Williams. A. C. McClurg & Company, Chicago, 1913.

THE CHIEF JUSTICE AND MRS. TAFT, WITH THEIR
CHILDREN AND GRANDCHILDREN, SEPTEMBER, 1929

Moses, the wife of Commissioner Moses, thus describes the reception at Jolo:

". . . By breakfast time dozens of little boats came alongside the *Sumner* with fruit, hats, shells and curios for sale. At half past nine the officers of the garrison came aboard. Following them was a double row of native boats, gayly decorated. There were seventy-five boats and barges, and they circled around the transport beating tom-toms and playing on other barbaric musical instruments, making the weirdest noises imaginable. From every boat a continuous fusillade of firecrackers added to the din. Besides the small boats, decorated with American and Moro flags, there were three or four large barges containing the most important Moros. These were covered with colored canopies or great parasols to protect the officials from the hot sun. In the prow of each boat there were half-naked men, wearing gay colored turbans and brilliant loin cloths, dancing a weird Malay dance accompanied by singing and handclapping. . . . It was like a scene in an opera. The flotilla sailed around the transport several times, and thus gave us a full view from all points. Then it divided, making a double guard of honor; and the Sultan was seen coming from the shore in a launch.

"It was only with great difficulty and after much diplomacy that the Sultan was persuaded to come aboard the transport. He was afraid that it might compromise his dignity, but after he was convinced that he must come, he donned a gold embroidered suit, and allowed himself to be escorted to the ship. A salute was fired, the marines were drawn up on the deck; and the Commissioners received him with due solemnity. Following the Sultan was a motley crew of half-naked Moros, who acted as his suite. They wore gay turbans and sashes, with barongs, or large knives, sticking in their belts. Several wore light trousers of silk, but others wore simple costumes of bath

towels. After the speeches of welcome the Sultan was introduced to us. . . ." [1]

Bailan, Jolo and Mindanao were chiefly inhabited by
Moros, a savage, piratical, fanatically religious Moham-
medan people, not sufficiently civilized to take any part in
government matters. Capable of any duplicity, they were
so incapable of self-government that the American military
maintained a strict surveillance over them. Taft had included these islands in his Southern tour for the purpose
of studying conditions there, rather than with any idea of
granting them even a restricted form of independence.

After two days in Jolo, Taft went on to Bailan, then to
Zamboanga and Cotabato. At Cotabato, two powerful
Moro chieftains, Datto Piang and Datto Ali, who ruled
that section of the Island of Mindanao, came on board the
military launch when it anchored. Taft questioned Piang,
the more intelligent of the two, concerning the Moro population, its customs, domestic and religious, and inquired
particularly about the gutta percha industry. Piang replied
that he was a large dealer in gutta percha, and explained to
Taft how the gum was gathered, by the Moro method,
which destroyed any number of trees annually without any
thought for conservation. Taft offered to send an expert in
tree culture to the islands, and urged the Datto to enforce
whatever regulations he might lay down for conservation.

"Suppose the United States should desire to lay a cable from
San Francisco to the Philippines," said Taft, "One of the greatest items of expense would be the gutta percha."

[1] "Unofficial Letters of An Official's Wife," by Edith Moses. D. Appleton & Company,
New York, 1908.

Piang's face glowed with pleasure, so delighted was he at this possible chance to prove his friendship for the United States. He told Taft that he would make the United States Government a present of all the gutta percha required for a Pacific cable, if the Government would tell him how much was needed. And at the close of the interview, Datto Piang assured Taft that he and his men held the American officials in such high esteem that they would certainly follow, if the Commission left the Philippines for America.[1]

"America would be glad to welcome you," replied Taft.

Reassured, Piang continued, "After the American troops come here, a Colonel of the Spanish army arrived here and he says to me,

'What did you do with the cross and ribbon and band that I gave you?'

'Pooh,' he, Piang, retorted, 'I threw them into the river.'

And he, the Spanish Colonel, says, 'What did you do that for?'

And he, Piang, replied, 'When the American troops come here, they give me the American flag and that is all I wanted, and everything the Spaniards gave me, I threw into the water.'

He, the Spanish Colonel, says, 'He, Piang ought not to have thrown the cross and band into the river because the American Government was just as bad as the Spanish Government.'

And he, Piang, says, 'No, the American Government, when they come here, have treated me like a brother . . . When the Spanish Government come it raised hell and fight us all the time.' "

Leaving Cotabato, the Commissioners went on to Antique, Cebu and Marinduque.

[1] "Recollections of Full Years," by Helen Herron Taft. Dodd, Mead & Company, New York, 1914.

An amusing contretemps interrupted the harmony of one of the Provincial meetings, when Taft facetiously remarked that "if the appointees failed to behave, their official heads would be removed." Incredulous dismay suddenly clouded the Filipino faces before him, which a moment ago had beamed with gratification. They believed they heard the affable-seeming President of the Civil Commission, representing the American Government, threatening to behead such Provincial officers as failed to justify their appointment. Sensing the mistake at once, Taft talked desperately for half an hour to convince his audience that he had not meant actual decapitation.

CHAPTER XIV

GOVERNOR GENERAL OF THE PHILIPPINES

U PON his return to Manila on the third of May, Taft found himself swamped with work. He was to be formally inaugurated as Governor General of the Philippines on the Fourth of July, and much had to be done before that. Under the new régime, the administrative work of the Insular Government was to be conducted through four departments—the Interior, Commerce and Police, Finance and Justice, and Public Instruction. Each of these was to be in charge of a Secretary, chosen from the Civil Commission. General Luke Wright was made Secretary of Commerce and Labor; Henry C. Ide was Secretary of Finance and Justice; Dean Worcester became head of the Department of the Interior, and Bernard Moses was Secretary of Public Instruction. After many conferences it was decided that the Commission, continuing as the legislative body of the Philippines, should include three Filipino members, Dr. T. H. Pardo de Tavera, Don Benito Legarda and Don Jose Luzuriaga, all men of exceptional ability who had rendered inestimable service in the work of pacification.

During the Spanish occupation the Governor General had always lived in the Palace of the Malacanan. And when the Americans captured Manila, the Commander of the Army had established himself there. The Filipinos had thus grown accustomed to regarding the resident of the Palace as the head of the Government. Therefore, believing it unwise to disregard the Filipinos' ideas of propriety whenever he could conform to them, Taft suggested that General MacArthur relinquish the palace to him. The Military Commander was not hospitable to this idea, and consented, in fact, only after orders from Washington. Shortly afterward, however, General Chaffee succeeded General Mac-Arthur, and another minor cause of friction was eliminated.

The ceremony of Taft's inauguration was very simple in itself, but the setting lacked nothing of picturesqueness and color. The procession proceeded from the Ayuntiamento across the square to the Cathedral Plaza, amid throbbing drums and blaring trumpets. Long before the ceremony began, the Plaza swarmed with a bizarre assemblage —small, kinky-haired Negritoes, Moros with bracelets and brass rings gleaming against their brown skins, Visayans from Romblon, "dog-eating" Igorrotes of Benguet in gay-colored tunics and elaborately beaded knee breeches, a sprinkling of Spaniards and Chinamen, with plenty of tall American soldiers in khaki and sailors in white duck.

And as Mrs. Moses recounts it:

"Promptly at the specified time, across the broad central path of the plaza the procession passed, the Americans in white duck suits, the Filipinos and Europeans in black. . . . First came the 'diplomatic corps' as some one called them, in array more or less gorgeous, as business had been dull or lively during the year, for the 'diplomatic corps' consists principally of merchants of Manila acting as consuls or agents of foreign governments, very few of them being natives of the country they represent. The consul for Spain, however, is a Spaniard, and he headed the corps in a uniform gorgeous with brass buttons and gold lace. He had a proud and haughty air. Behind him came the German consul in a duck suit not quite immaculate, belted in so tightly that he recalled the traditional pillow with a string tied about the middle, but on his broad breast glittered seven medals, and a black cocked hat made him almost as imposing a figure as the Spanish consul. The representatives of countries less conspicuous wore everyday clothes, but the Chinese consul, in bell hat and button and yellow silk robe, lent a picturesque note to the corps, while the French consul was in full evening dress. . . . They did not pretend to march two by two, or even in single file, but flocked along anyhow after the Spanish consul. The second division of the procession consisted of the representatives of justice in the Philippines, and was headed by the Chief Justice of the Islands, who was apparently dressed in a robe. As for the judges, they wore the traditional black frock coat of the variety one recognizes as Oriental, with a collection of tall hats, including the opera style, I have not seen equaled since I left Japan.

". . . First came General MacArthur with Judge Taft, followed by General Chaffee. Behind them, two by two, the four Civil Commissioners, and then a long line of Colonels and Majors comprising all the staff officers in Manila. . . . General MacArthur introduced Judge Taft without any special ceremony. Judge Arellano administered the oath of office, and then Governor Taft made his inaugural address. It was to the point, and not too long.

"The procession returned to the Ayuntamiento after the inauguration, where they entered carriages and escorted General MacArthur to the office of the captain of the port, where he embarked in a launch for the transport." [1]

The extraordinary results achieved by Taft in directing the Civil Commission during that first year had attracted

[1] "Unofficial Letters of An Official's Wife," by Edith Moses. D. Appleton & Company, New York, 1908.

133

much attention and favorable comment in the United States. His friend Theodore Roosevelt, now Vice President of the United States, stated in a magazine article.

"A year ago a man of wide acquaintance both with American public life and with American public men remarked that the first Governor of the Philippines ought to combine the qualities that would make a first class President of the United States with the qualities which would make a first class Chief Justice of the United States, and that the only man he knew who possessed all those qualities was Judge William H. Taft. The statement was entirely correct. Few more difficult tasks have devolved upon any man of our nationality during our century and a quarter of public life than the handling of the Philippine situation at this time; and it may be doubted whether among men now living another could be found as well fitted as Judge Taft to do this incredibly difficult work. . . .

"But, I think that almost all men who have been brought in close contact personally and officially with Judge Taft agree that he combines as very, very few men can combine, a standard of unflinching rectitude on every point of public duty and a literally dauntless courage and willingness to bear responsibility. With the knowledge of men, and a far-reaching tact and kindliness which enable his great abilities and high principles to be of use in a way that would be impossible were he not thus gifted with the capacity to work hand in hand with his fellows.

"When Judge Taft was sent out as the head of the Commission appointed by the President to inaugurate civil rule in the Philippines he was in a position not only of great difficulty but of great delicacy. He had to show inflexible strength and yet capacity to work heartily with other men and get results out of conflicting ideas and interests. . . . The way has been cleared for civil rule; and astonishing progress has been made. . . ."

After he became Chief Executive of the Archipelago, Taft did not relinquish his post as President of the Civil Commission, but still devoted much time to the preparation and study of prospective legislation. One of the most vexatious problems now facing him was the creation of a native constabulary, for the Municipal police were worse than useless. The Islands swarmed with guerilla bands which preyed upon the smaller communities. This ladronism, a legacy from the Spaniards, had been spread by the war, and since the Municipal police were unable to suppress these disorders and it was undesirable to employ the military to aid in civil work, a Provincial or Insular police force, under the supervision of the central Government, was badly needed. Besides, the Commissioners were convinced that an early recall of the military was most desirable. The military failed to share this point of view, or to recognize the need of an Island constabulary. General MacArthur had contended that it would be the height of folly to trust the native with arms, and General Chaffee adopted the same attitude.

General Luke Wright, at Taft's request, called upon Chaffee to ask him why he objected to an island constabulary.

"I am opposed to the whole business," Chaffee said, "It seems to me that you are trying to introduce something to take the place of the military."

"Why, so we are," replied General Wright. "We are trying to create a civil police force to do the police work which we understand the army was anxious to get rid of. You have announced your intention to concentrate the army in the interests of economy, and to let our civil governments stand alone to see what is in them, and we consider it necessary to have a constabulary, or some such force, to take care of the lawless characters that are sure to be in a country after four years of war, and especially in a country where the natives take naturally to ladronism. The municipal police as now organized are not able to meet all the requirements in this regard."

"There you are," said General Chaffee, "you give your whole case away."

"I have no case to give away," responded General Wright. "We are trying to put our Provincial governments on a basis where they will require nothing but the moral force of the military arm and actually to preserve law and order through the civil arm. The people desire peace, but they also desire protection, and we intend through the civil government to give it to them." [1]

General Chaffee was finally prevailed upon to withdraw his opposition, and on April 18th, an act was passed, providing for the arming, equipping and drilling of a Filipino constabulary force. This law decreed the appointment of a Chief of Constabulary and four Assistant Chiefs, each in charge of a separate district. It restricted the enlistment in the constabulary to a number not exceeding one hundred and fifty natives to each Province, all residents of the territory in which the constabulary was to serve, and provided for the appointment of three Provincial Inspectors of Constabulary, two Americans and one Filipino.

In addition to the Constabulary Bill, an Act for the Postal Service, an Act incorporating the city of Manila, an Act for the reorganization of the Forestry service and an Act

[1] "Recollections of Full Years," by Helen Herron Taft. Dodd, Mead & Company, New York, 1914.

creating a Board of Health, were passed during July. The last in particular was a badly needed measure, for the officials of the Spanish occupation had paid little or no attention to such matters, and the Filipinos themselves had small respect for sanitation. There were no sewage systems, no building restrictions, no pure food laws, not a single decent operating room in the whole Archipelago, and as a result conditions became shocking. Leprosy was common, tuberculosis almost universal, and the death list, from curable maladies alone, numbered into the thousands yearly.

On the first of September, 1901, the Commission terminated its first year in the Philippines. Their main purpose in devising a policy had been the elimination of the United States as a factor to be considered, and this had been accomplished in the face of seemingly insuperable difficulties. The Commission had passed during that first year two hundred and forty-eight laws, all of which had to be thoroughly considered and discussed before enactment. Thus they had slowly constructed out of chaos a functioning governmental machine. And to Taft in particular, to his patience, his integrity, his tact and indefatigability, and above all to his far-sightedness, must go the greater credit for the success of the Second Philippine Commission during that first long crucial year.

CHAPTER XV

THE COMMISSION TO THE VATICAN

GOVERNMENT affairs in the Philippines seemed to be moving along with surprising smoothness when suddenly they were thrown into jeopardy by the assassination of President McKinley in Buffalo. A few days later, an outbreak occurred at Balangiga, in the Province of Samar, which also threatened the tranquillity of the Archipelago. Company C of the Ninth Infantry had been assigned for duty in that village, and the soldiers had apparently established friendly relations with the natives, when one morning while they were at breakfast the church bells pealed, and out of the hills surrounding the town swarmed hundreds of Insurrectos. They knifed the sentries and attacked the soldiers, who were unarmed. Only a few survivors fought their way clear of the encircling bolos and guns. This incident so disturbed the general calm that men openly carried weapons to and from business.

There was an uneasy feeling among the Filipinos because Theodore Roosevelt, who succeeded McKinley, had not revealed his prospective attitude toward the Philippines, and the American military had not announced what reprisals would be made for the Balangiga affair. Retaliation, however, was not even considered, and it was not long before President Roosevelt announced that he intended sedulously to follow the policies of his predecessor, a

declaration which alleviated much of the prevailing unrest. But before the situation in the islands had resumed
normalcy, Taft developed an illness which physicians first
diagnosed as dengue fever. He was carried from the Palace
of the Malacanan to an army hospital and there, after two
weeks of treatment and many consultations, it was discovered that he had an abdominal abscess which called for
an immediate operation. For a time his recovery was uncertain. While Taft was recuperating slowly and transact-
ing business from his bed, General Funston, the captor of
Aguinaldo, was in the hospital recovering from an operation for appendicitis and often came into Taft's room to
chat. One day, when Manila was shaken by a severe earth-
quake, Funston rushed into Taft's room in the midst of
the vibrations.

"We must carry out the Governor," shouted Funston,
who was no more than five feet three, but made up in
spirit what he lacked in size. "We must carry out the
Governor."

"But how are you going to do that, General?" exclaimed
Taft, amused in spite of the uncomfortable fact that he expected the roof to collapse momentarily.

"Oh, I have my orderly with me," replied Funston,
dauntless in any emergency, grasping the bed, while
through the door rushed a private soldier somewhat smaller
than the General.[1]

Taft slowly convalesced through the fall and early
winter, but really needed a change of climate in order to

[1] "Recollections of Full Years," by Helen Herron Taft. Dodd, Mead & Company,
New York, 1908.

get fully well. President Roosevelt knew this, but felt sure that Taft might decline to leave the Philippines if his leave of absence was based upon that ground alone. Some other reason must be found. It happened opportunely that a Senate Committee, which had been appointed to formulate a legislative policy for the Philippines, decided to hold sessions for the purpose of enlightening themselves on conditions in the Islands. Therefore the President, anxious to have Taft present to the country a statement on the Philippines, directed Secretary Root to grant Taft a much-needed leave of absence so that he would attend these sessions.

When it was announced in Manila that Taft was returning to the United States, rumors and false alarms overspread the Islands. His success in improving their conditions of living, his resolute refusal to permit any exploitation, had convinced the Filipinos that Taft was their friend. He was extremely popular with them, more popular, perhaps, than he ever became with his own countrymen. For the American public is free to demand from its public men a certain ingratiating histrionism, whatever his more solid qualities, before they take him to their heart. But a subject people cannot be thus concerned with externals; and it cannot be fooled concerning the caliber of the man in charge of its destinies. The Filipinos, being at Taft's mercy, knew his mettle, just as a man is most accurately known by the people for whom he daily works. He was just, and they knew it. He cared nothing for self-aggrandizement, and they knew it. He was honest, and they knew it. He was wise in the making of law, and that they knew!

A Chinese servant of Commissioner Moses told him that

"market man he say gobnor no come back, everybody all same fighty bimeby." And the coachman told Mrs. Moses that "if El Gobernador did not come back, he would return to his native town to the north." [1] The public announcement of Taft's departure brought scores of deputations and committees to the Palace, to be reassured by the Governor's own promise that he would return to the Archipelago after his business in the United States was completed.

The Tafts sailed from Manila for San Francisco on Christmas Eve, 1901. After a brief stop in Cincinnati, Taft hurried on to Washington, to testify before the Senate Committee on the Philippines. For three weeks he remained, as guest of Secretary and Mrs. Root, while in a Senate Committee room he was subjected to a most searching examination and cross-examination as to affairs in the Archipelago. In testifying, Taft said it was the duty of the United States to establish in the Philippines

> "a government suited to the present possibilities of the people, which shall gradually change, conferring more and more right upon the people to govern themselves, thus educating them in self-government, until their knowledge of government, their knowledge of liberty, shall be such that further action may be taken either by giving them statehood or by making them a quasi-independent government like Canada or Australia or, if they desire it, independence."

The problem of the friars' lands especially engaged the Senate Committee. In response to many questions, Taft told the Senators:

---

[1] "Unofficial Letters of An Official's Wife," by Edith Moses. D. Appleton & Company, New York, 1908.

"I think it may be said generally that the title of the friars to those lands is, as a legal proposition, indisputable. . . . The most distinguished lawyer who is engaged in opposition to the friars, Senor Don Felipe Calderon, admitted that under any law of Prescription or statute of limitations of which he knew, the title to the friars' lands, speaking generally, of course making allowances for special cases, was unimpeachable. . . . If we can buy those lands and make them government property, and in that way separate in the minds of the tenants the relation of the friar to the lands and say to the tenants, 'We shall sell you these lands on long payments, so that they will become yours', I believe that we can satisfy the people and avoid the agrarian question which will arise when our government is appealed to to put into possession of those lands the people who own them. . . ."

During a conference between President Roosevelt, Taft and Root, Taft impressed upon the President the desirability of a speedy settlement of this question. Because Taft considered it so important, Roosevelt determined that he should stop at Rome on his journey back to Manila,

"for the purpose of reaching, if possible, a friendly understanding with the authorities having control of the disposition of the property of the religious orders, and other church property in the islands. . . . Of course, nothing can be done until Congress acts. But, as the Committees of both Houses have acted favorably on the Commission's recommendations for the purchase of the friar lands, it is thought best not to lose this opportunity afforded by Governor Taft's presence in Europe to begin negotiations and make as much progress as possible, so that they may be readily closed up after Congress has acted, if it does act favorably. . . .

"The object of this conference is to secure separation of

church and state, and it would seem to be a condition precedent to such a result. Governor Taft's mission is not in any sense a diplomatic mission. It is simply a business transaction with the owners of the property. Any agreement effected for the purchase of the lands is subject to the ratification of Congress which must provide the necessary legislation."

To assist Taft in his negotiations with the Vatican, President Roosevelt appointed Bishop O'Gorman, of the Roman Catholic diocese of South Dakota, Judge James F. Smith, a Catholic and a member of the Philippine judiciary, and Major John Biddle Porter, to accompany the group as secretary and interpreter. A storm of denunciation greeted Roosevelt's announcement of this project. The *Boston Watchman* (a Baptist publication), said, "However defensible the measure taken by the President may be, it indicates in a most unmistakable way the new influence which Rome is acquiring in the United States."

Other denominational papers were opposed to Governor Taft's going to Rome, contending that the Vatican should send a mission to Manila. Still others suggested that Taft, by going to Rome, would sacrifice his personal dignity and destroy the prestige he enjoyed in the Orient. The Catholic newspapers rather made light of the matter, one of them declaring, "It is the lands that we are interested in, and the question has nothing to do with church and state."

Shortly before they sailed, the Commission to the Vatican were instructed to remember that there was a complete separation of church and state in the United States; that there must be a readjustment of the old order in the Philippines; that the landed proprietorship of the religious

143

orders in the Archipelago should cease; that provision should be made for the ascertaining of rental to be charged for the convents and the church property occupied by the American forces on the Islands during the Insurrection, and that the errand undertaken by the Commission was in no sense to be construed as diplomatic, but purely a business endeavor, for the purpose of negotiating and purchasing the friars' lands and settling the land titles.

Arriving at Rome, the Commission at once arranged for an audience with the Pope, concerning whom Judge Smith later wrote,

> "My recollection of the Holy Father is that his face was like transparent parchment, that he had brilliant eyes of a young man, and that he was wonderfully alert in his mind although bent over by the weight of years." [1]

Taft, after presenting his personal respects, spoke briefly on the Philippines and pointed out that the United States believed in the entire separation of church and state, a belief which indicated no hostility toward any church. The Pope informed the Governor that a committee of cardinals would have to go into the matter and that "the issues would be presented in a most anxious spirit to reach a settlement satisfactory to all parties." The audience lasted for the better part of an hour, and afterward Taft delivered his instructions to Cardinal Rampolla, the Papal Secretary of State.

Concerning the interview, Taft wrote to his brother Charles, "The Pope came down from the dais on which

---

[1] "Recollections of Full Years," by Helen Herron Taft. Dodd, Mead & Company, New York, 1914.

he sat and asked for the pleasure of shaking my hand, a privilege which I very graciously accorded him."

The Pope also indulged in a few mild jokes about Taft's monumental proportions, saying he understood Taft had been very ill, but saw no effects of anything serious.

A committee of Cardinals, including Vives y Tuto, reputed to be the most liberal of the Spanish prelates, Vannutelli, Gotti, the Carmelite monk, the Jesuit Steinhuber, and Rampolla, was appointed to consider the American proposals, and instructed by the Pope that he desired an amicable understanding with the representatives of the United States. A week later an answer to the American proposals was delivered to Taft, an answer, which as he said,

". . . agreed generally with all the proposals stated in the letter of instructions, including among other things the purchase of the friars' lands by our government. . . . The answer further proposed that further negotiations be had between the Apostolic Delegate and myself in Manila."

Conciliatory in tone, the reply assured the American government,

"the Vatican is aware of the entire separation of church and state in the United States, but hopes that the Washington Government will take into consideration the contrary conditions in the new territory now under their jurisdiction."

Taft in reply suggested that the Pope agree to submit the questions at issue to an arbitration tribunal, which should consist of two American representatives, two ecclesiastics appointed by the Vatican, and a fifth member to

145

be selected by the Viceroy of India, this tribunal to meet
in the city of Manila not later than the first of January,
1903, to consider and examine the land and the witnesses,
the conclusions of a majority of its members to constitute
the finding of the tribunal. He further promised that any
damages assessed against the American Government by
this group would be paid by the United States in Mexican
dollars, one-third down, one-third in nine months, and the
balance in eighteen months. The proposed contract also
provided for the withdrawal of the four religious orders,
the Dominicans, the Recoletos, the Augustinians and the
Franciscans, from the Philippines within two years' time,
and that only secular and non-Spanish members of the
regular clergy should act as parish priests.

Shortly afterward Taft received the Vatican's answer
to his note. The Cardinals composing the Vatican Committee agreed to sign the contract, provided the stipulation
for withdrawal of the friars be stricken out. Cardinal
Rampolla said that otherwise the Vatican would offend
Spain, and that since the withdrawal of the friars related
solely to the administration of religious matters, it could
not be made a matter of commercial contract. He agreed,
however, to recognize the church government in the Archipelago and promised to devote the money realized from
the sale of the lands to the development and welfare of
the church in the Philippines.

Because the Vatican was unwilling to guarantee the removal of the friars from the Islands, Secretary Root, for
the American Government, declined to enter into a contract obligating the Philippine Government and the Gov-

146

ernment of the United States, to pay an indefinite sum, the amount of which had to be later determined. Taft delivered Root's message to Cardinal Rampolla, who agreed with Taft that further negotiations should be suspended until an Apostolic Delegate should arrive in Manila.

Taft then requested a farewell audience with the Pope which Cardinal Rampolla set for July the twenty-first. At this audience the Pope presented Taft with a gold goose-quill, of exquisite workmanship, with Leo's coat of arms on the feather. The Pope told Taft, "I will see that orders be given the Apostolic Delegate as to his work over which I will personally watch." [1] Later that day, Taft, accompanied by Judge Smith, left Rome for Naples, whence they sailed for Manila.

It was reported in the United States almost immediately after Taft's departure from Rome that the Pope was dissatisfied with the results of the negotiations. Archbishop Ireland of St. Paul took pains to refute these reports when he said in an address, "The Pope was greatly satisfied with the Taft mission. He said that he had the highest esteem for the American methods of treating church matters."

Certain of the American Catholic newspapers then attacked Governor Taft as being prejudiced against the Church. Once again, the St. Paul prelate defended the Governor of the Philippines, disproving the allegations made by publishing a letter written by the Reverend Father W. D. McKinnon, a Catholic priest then residing in Manila. "I can assure you that nothing can be more unjust

[1] "Recollections of Full Years," by Helen Herron Taft. Dodd, Mead & Company, New York, 1914.

than the criticism of Governor Taft in some of the Catholic papers. Governor Taft has not a particle of bigotry in his makeup. In all his acts here I defy anyone to say that he has shown himself prejudiced in the least."

The exact status of Taft during these negotiations raised interesting questions both inside and outside the Vatican during his stay in Rome and after his departure for Manila. His position was, and to some extent still is, considered anomalous. His credentials gave him powers as great as those of a diplomat, if not greater. He followed diplomatic precedent and called upon the accredited ambassadors to the Vatican from Austria, Spain, France and Portugal, just as any newly appointed representative might have done. He dined and entertained in the manner of a diplomat and by these actions placed himself upon an equality with foreign ministers and yet, at the same time, he scrupulously followed the tenor of his instructions and conducted himself in a tactful, unobtrusive way. It was a delicate situation, and he handled it superbly.

Later that fall the Apostolic Delegate, Monseigneur Guidi, Archbishop of Staurpoli, arrived in Manila and negotiations for the purchase of the friars' lands were at once re-opened. It soon became evident that a compromise purchase figure would have to be set, and finally, after much discussion, $7,200,000 was finally decided upon as the sum to be paid the Vatican by the Philippine Government for the land, with the stipulation that a portion of this sum would be expended for the benefit of the church in the Islands. This was eventually done. The Spanish friars of the four orders were never returned to their parishes, and in some cases American priests were sent from the United States to replace them.

The amount paid to the Vatican attracted considerable criticism. But, as Governor Taft said, the Government had not

"entered upon the purchase of these lands with a view to a profitable investment, but it is knowingly paying a considerable sum of money merely for the purpose of ridding the administration of the government of the islands of an issue dangerous to the peace and prosperity of the people." [1]

And its payment solved a problem which had harassed the Philippines for decades.

Taft was congratulated heartily on his successful settlement of the "Friar Lands" question. These felicitations came not only from the Filipinos, but, also, from members of the Roman Catholic hierarchy. Archbishop John Ireland, of St. Paul, writing him, said,

"I have obtained from Bishop O'Gorman fullest news about your visit to Rome. I cannot but admire the dignity and tactful diplomacy which marked your course during the negotiations. . . . What advices I have had from Rome give me the conviction that the Holy Father and Cardinal Rampolla were delighted with you and are in the best possible sentiments in your regard. . . .

"I was very much gratified with the announcement in the papers that in your address on your arrival in Manila you were able to state that the money derived from the sale of the Friar's lands was to be held in the Philippines for the use and benefit of the Catholic church in the Islands. In my opinion this is one

[1] "The Philippines," by Charles B. Elliott. Bobbs-Merrill Company, Indianapolis, 1917.

of the most important results that could have come from your negotiations with the Vatican."

The Vatican went even farther than the agreement called for, and later sent American bishops to the Islands. One of those whose work there was most successful and conciliatory, Bishop Dougherty of Jaro, was promoted to the archbishopric of Philadelphia and created Cardinal.

CHAPTER XVI

THE SUPREME COURT OFFER

TAFT returned to Manila to find the Filipino people wild with joy at his arrival. They came down the Bay in small boats to meet him, they climbed to the roofs and leaned from the windows, lined the river banks and crowded the city walls to salute him. When he disembarked at the landing near the customs house, an impromptu parade escorted him, through streets lined with cheering natives, to the Ayuntiamento.

He also found his officials much harassed by all sorts of difficulties. Everything from locusts and cholera to bandits and ladronism, balked them and troubled the islands. He did, however, note improvement in the constabulary, as he wrote President Roosevelt:

"The reception which has been accorded me by the Filipino people, especially the 'gente' or common people, has been a source of the utmost gratification to me and I think much of it has been due to the fact that I went to Rome as the representative to intercede for them with regard to the friars. We have now a work requiring the utmost patience, full of small disappointments, not only in the honesty and efficiency of the Filipinos appointed to office but also in the honesty and efficiency of Americans. The truth is that we are short of good Americans. . . .

"The constabulary is doing good work. . . . It is made up as you know of Filipinos. We have usually pursued the policy of

151

having a force of constabulary selected from the Province which it operates. This has not always been possible where we needed a larger amount than one hundred and fifty, and where members of the constabulary of one Province have been introduced into another, it has required the greatest supervision to prevent the looting and abuse of the people by members of the constabulary when not under the eye of an American Inspector, and this looting has not been confined either to the constabulary from other Provinces. Reports of abuses come occasionally from Provinces in which only domestic constabulary are employed. It is an evil that must be reckoned with in dealing with the native police. We investigate every case and try to punish it but of course the work of discipline is a slow work. We have had to centralize the constabulary in order to secure efficient action and in a sense made them independent of the Governors of the Provinces though subject to the call of such Governors. This creates friction sometimes between the Governors and the constabulary and so I have to listen to tales of treachery or sympathy with ladrones against the Governor by the constabulary, and of cruelty charged by the Governor against the constabulary and try and smooth over the differences. . . ."

The currency and coinage problem of the Archipelago also troubled the American officials. Under the Spanish administration until the latter part of the nineteenth century, the Philippines had possessed no currency of their own, the gold and silver they used having been brought from Spain, South America and Mexico. Gradually, however, the silver Mexican dollar became the common medium of exchange and this was universally employed throughout the islands when the American army took over Manila. But the fluctuating nature of silver and its gradual downward trend, due mostly to a decreased demand in China, had made it necessary to adopt a new currency for the Archipelago. Taft and his associates wanted to supplant the silver with a gold standard and a silver coinage, which the Government would stand behind by guaranteeing a parity, but feared that a sudden and immediate change might seriously disturb business in the Philippines. When he testified before the Senate Committee, Taft emphasized the gravity of the situation and the need for quick relief. But nothing had been done.

Therefore one of the first things he did upon resuming his labors was to write to Senator Henry Cabot Lodge of Massachusetts,

"The coinage situation here is becoming worse and worse. Silver is falling so that by my last proclamation I fixed the rate at two hundred and forty for one gold dollar. . . ."

and to Henry H. Cooper,

"the enactment into law of the House plan for a gold standard in these Islands is only second in importance to provision for a legislative assembly. . . ."

But before this and countless other problems had worked themselves out to Taft's satisfaction, he was interrupted—and at once pleased and disturbed—by the following cable from President Roosevelt, which came to him in October, 1902.

"On January first there will be a vacancy on the Supreme Court to which I earnestly desire to appoint you. . . . I feel that your duty is on the court unless you have decided not to

153

adopt a judicial career. I greatly hope you will accept. Would appreciate an early answer. THEODORE ROOSEVELT." [1]

Secretary Root also telegraphed Taft, expressing reluctance to have him leave his post as Governor of the Philippines, but urging that he accept the President's offer.

And the President soon followed his cable with a letter:

"On the first of January Judge Shiras is to resign, and on the whole it seems to me that it would be wise for you to go on in his place. Frankly I confess I am a little puzzled. No one can quite take your place where you are. I think I shall put in Wright, and then we would have Smith as second string, if after a year or two, Wright's health gave out; and from what I know of these two men I believe they would do the work well; but they could not do it as well as you and I would not feel quite as much at ease as I do while you are where you are.

"Of course, there is no telling how long your health will last in the Islands, nor whether there will be another chance for me to put you on the Supreme Court, and moreover, I feel that we do need you on the court . . . always, providing, that you feel that you wish a judicial career and do not intend to go into active political life in which I am certain you could do signal service. . . .

"So my own feeling is that you had better take the judgeship. Nothing can be more important than to strengthen in every way the Supreme Court. But I have immense confidence in your judgment and in your knowledge of the situation in the Islands and of the men who can take your place, and shall accept your decision as wise whichever way it comes."

Of course, the ambition of Taft's life had been to become a Justice on the United States Supreme Court, and yet his

[1] "Recollections of Full Years," by Helen Herron Taft. Dodd, Mead & Company, New York, 1914.

JUSTICES OF THE SUPREME COURT IN 1928   *Copyright by Harris and Ewing*

Seated: McReynolds, Holmes, Taft, Van Devanter, Brandeis   *Standing:* Sanford, Sutherland, Butler, Stone

first opportunity to achieve it could not but find him reluctant to accept. Conditions in the Philippines were just then disquieting and far from satisfactory. The cholera still raged. The carabao, which were the only draft animals in the Islands, were either dying or being rendered useless by the dread rinderpest, with a loss of almost ninety per cent. This and the ladronism which had not been wholly stamped out, required the maintenance of a constabulary force of over twelve thousand men, entailing an enormous expenditure of course, and that, aggravated by a steady decrease in the revenue of the Insular government, made the political situation a serious one. And Congress had failed to relieve the depression by acting upon the currency problem. Accordingly, Taft felt that it would be a grave mistake to change Governors just then. He believed, and rightly, that if he accepted the Supreme Court appointment it would greatly weaken the confidence of the Filipinos in America, for they would misconstrue his departure as the sign of a change of policy. Yet so sorely was he tempted to go that he consulted, confidentially, Mr. Benito Legarda and the Mr. Arellano, Chief Justice of the Archipelago, hoping they could together work out some way by which he might conscientiously accept the offer.

But after viewing the situation from every possible angle, Taft regretfully cabled the President:

"Great honor deeply appreciated but must decline. Situation here most critical from economic standpoint. Change proposed would create much disappointment and lack of confidence among people. Two years now to follow of greater importance to development of Islands than previous two years.

Cholera, rinderpest, religious excitement, ladrones, monetary crisis all render most unwise change of Governor. These are sentiments of my colleagues and leading Filipinos consulted confidentially. Nothing would satisfy individual taste more than acceptance. Look forward to the time when I can accept such an offer, but even if it is certain that it can never be repeated I must decline. Would not assume to answer in such positive terms in view of words of your dispatch if gravity of situation here was not necessarily known to me beter than it can be known in Washington."

But Roosevelt was determined to have Taft accept the Supreme Court appointment. He was preparing to test the legality, under the Sherman Act of 1890, of many business combinations, and he wanted a man of the highest legal qualifications and whose integrity was above reproach.

"I am disappointed, of course," Roosevelt replied, therefore, "that the situation is such as to make you feel it unwise for you to leave, because as no man can quite do your work in the Islands, so no one can quite take your place as the new member of the court. But, if possible, your refusal on the ground you give makes me admire you and believe in you more than ever. I am quite at a loss whom to appoint to the bench in the place that I meant for you. Everything else must give way to putting in the right man; but I can't make up my mind who is the right man."

Believing the incident definitely closed, Taft once more turned his whole attention to the administration of the Philippine Government. But the question was not closed. The President cabled for Taft's views of several men whom he had in mind for the place. Taft suggested Horace

Lurton, judge of the Federal Circuit Court of Appeals for the Sixth Circuit.

A month elapsed. No one was appointed. Then, on December first, the President again wrote to Taft.

"I am sorry, old man, but after faithful effort for a month to try to arrange matters on the basis you wanted I find that I shall have to bring you home and put you on the Supreme Court. I am very sorry, I have the greatest confidence in your judgment; but, after all, old fellow, if you will permit me to say so, I am President and see the whole field. The responsibility for any error must ultimately come upon me, and therefore I cannot shirk this responsibility or in the last resort yield to anyone else's decision if my judgment is against it. After the most careful thought, after the most earnest effort to do what you desired and thought best, I have come, irrevocably, to the decision that I shall appoint you to the Supreme Court in the vacancy caused by Judge Shiras's resignation. . . .

"I am very sorry if what I am doing displeases you, but, as I said, old fellow, this is one of the cases where the President, if he is fit for the position, must take the responsibility and put the men on whom he most relies in the particular positions in which he himself thinks they can render the greatest public good. I shall, therefore, about the first of February, nominate you as I have suggested." [1]

Concluding from the tone of this letter that Roosevelt's decision was final, Taft began preparations for leaving the Philippines. But the news of his leaving created a furore. Everywhere in Manila were posted placards, "We Want Taft." A monster demonstration was staged, with a parade in which thousands of Filipinos and innumerable bands,

[1] "Recollections of Full Years," by Helen Herron Taft. Dodd, Mead & Company, New York, 1914.

marched to the Palace of the Malacanan, where native orators eulogized Taft and implored him to remain.

The labor agitator, Dr. Gomez, called Taft "the saint who had the power to perform the great miracle." Pedro A. Paterno burst into the eloquent declaration that "as Christ converted the cross into a symbol of glory and triumph, so had Governor Taft turned a dying people to the light and life of modern liberties." And one Senor del Rosario compared Taft to a ship's rudder in his ability at "avoiding shallows" and bringing the ship of state into port.

So many cablegrams of protest were forwarded to the President that his office was fairly swamped with them. Taft, although he believed further protest was futile, cabled Roosevelt once again, asking that he be permitted to remain in the Islands until his job was completed. His cable read,

"Recognize soldier's duty to obey orders. Before orders irrevocable by action however I presume on our personal friendship even in the face of your letter to make one more appeal, in which I lay aside wholly my strong personal disinclination to leave work of intense interest half done. No man is indispensable; my death would little interfere with program, but my withdrawal more serious. Circumstances last three years have convinced these people, controlled largely by personal feeling, that I am their friend and stand for a policy of confidence in them and belief in their future and for the extension of self-government as they show themselves worthy. Visit to Rome and proposals there assure them of my sympathy in regard to friars in respect to whose far-reaching influence they are morbidly suspicious. Announcement of withdrawal pending settlement of church questions, economic crises, and formative political period when opinions of all parties are being slowly molded for the better, will, I fear, give impression that change of policy is intended because other reasons for action will not be understood. My successor's task is thus made much heavier because any loss of the people's confidence distinctly retards our work here. I feel it is my duty to say this. If your judgment is unshaken I bow to it and shall earnestly and enthusiastically labor to settle questions friars's lands before I leave, and to convince the people that no change of policy is at hand; that Wright is their friend as sincere as they think me, and that we both are but exponents of the sincere good will toward them of yourself and the American people."

Roosevelt's answer was short and incisive, "Taft, Manila. All right stay where you are. I shall appoint someone else to the court." [1] Shortly thereafter the President appointed William R. Day, of Ohio, to the United States Supreme Court.

[1] "Recollections of Full Years," by Helen Herron Taft. Dodd, Mead & Company, New York, 1914.

CHAPTER XVII

FAREWELL TO THE PHILIPPINES

THE arduous labors of Taft's three years in the Philippines, during which the outlook had alternately brightened and clouded, showed definite results for the better early in 1903. Economic and agricultural conditions were vastly improved. The Insular Government functioned more perfectly. There was still one considerable fly in the ointment—the apparent impossibility of reconciling the Moros in the Southern Islands, to American, or for that matter to any, rule. In organizing the non-Christian provinces, Taft felt that "to win the support and confidence of the Moros there must be a union of the civil and the military—that is, the force behind the government must be visible all the time."

Ancient racial and religious antagonisms made necessary the adoption of a special act, somewhat unlike the laws of organization that had already been applied to the other Provinces of the Archipelago. That part of the Philippines where the non-Christians lived, the Islands of Jolo, Mindanao and their neighboring smaller islands, were designated, by the law establishing for them a form of government, as the Moro Province. After this law was passed, dividing the territory into five districts, with subordinate local governments for each of these districts, to coöperate further with Taft in his efforts to pacify the inhabitants of these islands,

President Roosevelt despatched General Leonard Wood to the Philippines to assume command of the military department, and act as Civil Governor of the Moro Province.

The policy adopted by the Commission for the internal development of the Philippines had included a system of interlacing highways covering the entire Archipelago. Purposing thus to open world markets to the Filipinos the Commissioners had planned extensive road building operations. By far the most important of all their projects was the Benguet road, extending into a mountainous region which might easily be converted into a health resort for people suffering from tropical diseases.

Because he planned to make Baguio, the capital of Benguet, also the summer capital of the Insular Government, Taft had ordered a survey of this proposed road when the Commission first arrived in Manila. Work was finally begun, but it progressed very slowly; neither the engineers nor the Commission realized how expensive and difficult it would be. Finally, the cost assumed such proportions that had it not been demanded for government reasons, the Commission probably would have abandoned the work.

While this road was still under construction, Taft decided to visit Baguio and see for himself how the work was progressing. Riding a magnificent saddle horse which General Chaffee had presented to him, Taft left Manila on a burning hot April day, and it was with relief and satisfaction that he finally found himself comfortably seated on a cool porch of a cottage at Baguio. He cabled to Root,

"Stood trip well. Rode horseback twenty-five miles to five thousand feet elevation. Great province this, only one hundred and fifty miles from Manila with air as bracing as Adirondacks or Murray Bay. Only pines and grass lands . . . fires necessary night and morning . . ."

Secretary Root immediately cabled in reply,

"Referring to your telegram from your office of the fifteenth, how is horse?" [1]

Just as the situation in the Philippines was beginning to clarify and improve to a decided degree, Fate again summoned Taft to leave. In February, 1903, Root announced his intention of resigning from the cabinet and Roosevelt immediately thought: why not Taft to succeed Root? He felt this to be a "bully" idea and, accordingly, he wrote to Taft:

"The worst calamity that could happen to me officially is impending, because Root tells me that he will have to leave me next fall. I wish to heaven that I did not feel as strongly as I do about two or three men in the public service, notably Root and you. But I *do*. I want to ask you whether, if I can persuade Root to stay until a year hence, you cannot come back and take his place. Root is, I think, genuinely reluctant to go, but feels he must; and he feels furthermore that the advantage of having you take up the reins of control over the army and the Islands would be so great that he would do his best to stay an additional six months if it meant that thereby you would become his successor. Of course, he has not said, and cannot say definitely that he will stay, but he wishes to make the effort.

"Now I want you to give this your very careful thought and

[1] "Recollections of Full Years," by Helen Herron Taft. Dodd, Mead & Company, New York, 1914.

I do not want you to mention it to a soul, American or Filipino, for I desire your decision in your own thought and on the proposition's merits by itself. As Secretary of War you will still have the ultimate control of the Philippine situation and whatever was done would be under your immediate supervision. It seems to me that from the standpoint of the interests of the Islands alone you could well afford to take the place, which involves the general regulation, supervision and control of the Philippine Government. I need not say what an immense help you would be to me. The ideal situation in the Islands is to have Root at the head of the War Department and you at the head of the Civil Government in the Islands. With Root out, the closest approach to the ideal is to have you at the head of the War Department. . . .

"If only there were three of you. Then I would have one of you on the Supreme Court, as the Ohio member, in place of Day; one of you in Root's place as Secretary of War, when he goes out, and one of you permanently Governor of the Philippines. No one can quite take your place as Governor; but no one of whom I can think save only you can at all take Root's place as Secretary."

When Taft received this letter he was torn by conflicting desires. The President's wish to have him in Washington, thus urgently expressed, was of course most gratifying. But he well knew how hard it would be to leave his Filipino friends and at the same time convince them that his resignation as Governor did not mean a change of policy on the part of the United States toward the Philippines. And yet the work was well under way; his successor could carry on with much less trouble, now that the machinery was working smoothly.

A second and more personal objection was that, as Secretary of War, he would have nothing, substantially, but his salary to live on, which would be appreciably less than he received as Governor-General of the Philippines, and he believed that as a member of the cabinet, he would incur burdening and costly obligations which he would be unable to fulfill without financial loss. Besides, he rather dreaded political entanglements. This opportunity attracted him far less than the Supreme Court offer had, and yet by an irony of fate it came at a far easier time for him to accept!

A month elapsed and Roosevelt had received no answer from Taft. Root offered to stay on longer than he had planned, to accommodate the Governor, if that would make a difference. It was nearly six weeks after Taft had received Roosevelt's offer that Taft's letter of acceptance was received at the White House. It read, in part,

"I therefore accept your tender and thank you for it; of course, you will understand the pros and cons of the matter and I am sure appreciate the reason for my not wishing to accept unless I can stay here until next spring. It will take until that time I think to complete a good deal of the legislation which must be completed before we can be said to have finished the foundation work; that includes the criminal code, the criminal code of civil procedure, the internal revenue act, the land regulations for the settlement and the sale of the lands, the districting of the Islands for the legislative assembly, the settlement one way or the other of the purchase of the friar lands and the devising of a plan and its execution for the expenditure of the three million to relieve the agricultural crisis. Of course, I cannot hope to leave everything done, but these things I have mentioned and some others of very considerable importance will make a long step. . . ."

Taft's willingness to come into his cabinet as Root's successor delighted Roosevelt.

"You don't know what weight you have taken off my mind," he wrote. "I think that from the standpoint of the public interests it was of the utmost importance that when a man like Root went out of the Cabinet he should be succeeded by a man like yourself; and as in each case the individual named was in a class by himself, this meant that I deemed it of the highest consequence that Root should be succeeded by you. . . . Thank heaven you are to be with me. . . ."

When the Tafts, as a friendly gesture of departure, gave a huge Venetian masked ball and carnival, considerable difficulty was encountered in deciding upon a suitable Venetian character for the Governor to represent, since his physique did not readily lend itself to disguise. He wrote to his brother Charles,

"It is a humiliating fact to me that every suggestion of a character for me by me has been summarily rejected by Nellie unless it involved the wearing of a gown of such voluminous proportions as to conceal my Apollo-like form completely. The proposal that I assume the character of an Igorrote chieftain because of the slight drain on capital and our costuming resources did not meet with favor. So it is settled that I must assume the robes and headgear of the husband of the Adriatic, the Doge of Venice. The question is whether the robe can be made historically accurate and at the same time so conceal my nether extremities as to make it unnecessary for me to dye my nether undergarments to a proper color, for the entire Orient cannot produce tights of a sufficient size. The Council of War, meaning Nellie, has not advised me on the subject, but tights or no tights we shall have a Doge of Venice that never was on land or sea."

165

Taft left the Philippine Islands, with a unique and an enviable record of achievement. Supplanting the military government with a civil administration, he had created, out of confusion and chaos, a well-organized, efficiently functioning government, a government well-endowed with progressive and liberal laws executed by competent and well-trained officials. He had, as President Roosevelt said in an address at the University of California, rendered inestimable service and

> "not only have peace and material well being come to those Islands to a degree never before known in their recorded history, and to a degree infinitely greater than had ever been dreamed possible by those who knew them best, but more than that, a greater measure of self-government has been given to them than is now given to any other Asiatic people under alien rule, than to any other Asiatic people under their own rulers, save Japan alone. . . ."

CHAPTER XVIII

INTERNATIONAL COMPLICATIONS

THE announcement by Roosevelt that he had selected Taft to succeed Elihu Root as Secretary of War had preceded Taft's departure from the Philippines. Stopping off at Nagasaki in Japan, on his way home, Taft found a reception committee of Japanese army officials eagerly awaiting his arrival. A special train was placed at his disposal, a luncheon arranged with the Emperor and the Empress, and, graciously enough, the Japanese paraded a large unit of their crack troops before Taft so that he might view the precision of their drill and movements.

The high military officers composing the official entertaining committee had assumed that Mr. Taft, in common with the Japanese War Minister, General Terauchi, was a soldier and had been educated in the technicalities of military skill. Eager to impress the newly-appointed American Cabinet official with their abundance of knowledge, certain of the Japanese officers recounted their experiences to him at length, while others, seeking information, questioned him. One of these, General Kodama, who had been Military Governor of Formosa, later Japanese Chief of Staff in the war with Russia, was greatly interested in Taft and in the problems with which he had had to deal as Governor General of the Philippines.

Believing that his administration in Formosa had paralleled Taft's trials in the Archipelago, Kodama grew confidential and said, "We had to kill a good many thousands of those people before they would be good. But then, of course, you understand, you know—you know."

Taft, hastening to explain to the Japanese General that all of his efforts to pacify the Filipinos had been friendly, and that he had never harmed a single native, was greeted with a slightly perplexed but knowing smile.[1]

When Taft assumed the duties of his new post, he found them multifarious, varied, exacting; and upon his already heavily laden shoulders, President Roosevelt placed the additional burden of supervising and directing the construction of the Panama Canal. An Isthmian Canal Commission had been appointed by President Roosevelt to supervise the actual work of excavation and construction. The task of familiarizing themselves with conditions and initiating engineering calculations was the first of this Commission's undertakings, and while they were thus engaged, Roosevelt shifted the responsibility of directing their exertions to his newly-appointed Secretary of War.

Immediately upon the signing of the Hay-Bunau-Varilla Convention, by which the United States was granted full and complete sovereignty in Panama over a strip of land ten miles in width, extending from sea to sea (in return for which the United States covenanted to guarantee the integrity of Panama and to pay the Republic ten million dollars and an annual rental for the Canal), the American people expected operations in the Isthmus to begin to hum.

[1] "Recollections of Full Years," by Helen Herron Taft. Dodd, Mead & Company, New York, 1914.

SECRETARY OF WAR

They were disappointed, of course, for the various members of the Commission, lacking decision, began a voluminous correspondence with Taft. Before long, his office became a clearing house for disheartening reports, ignorant inquiries by Congress, and the harassing taunts of the public. This very unsatisfactory situation was aggravated by discouraging rumors of friction between the American Minister, the Canal Commission, and the Government of Panama. Alarmed at what they considered an encroachment by the Americans upon their rights and interests, the people of Panama, by failing to coöperate, were impeding the progress of the work.

Believing that Taft could conciliate the opposing factions, and convince the people of Panama that America harbored no desire or intention to interfere with their Government, President Roosevelt instructed Taft to proceed to Panama. Accompanied by Mrs. Taft, the Minister from Panama to the United States, Senor Obaldia, Admiral John G. Walker, the chairman of the Isthmian Canal Commission, and Mr. Nelson W. Cromwell, counsel for the Government of Panama, Taft left Washington for New Orleans. The party proceeded from there to Pensacola and embarked on the cruiser *Columbia.*

Once Taft had settled himself in a comfortable chair in the wardroom of the *Columbia,* he must have ruminated on the events of the past few months, and on the colossal scope of the work now confronting him. The fact that President Roosevelt had entrusted him with the labor of supervising the building of the Panama Canal must have delighted him, yet he must have felt uncertain of his ability

169

to complete so gigantic an undertaking, where others had failed.

Taft disembarked at Colon, the Caribbean port of Panama, on the twenty-seventh of November, 1904, and began a series of secret conferences with President Amador.

Taft examined the Canal project and found it to be a "sorry sight," for

> "All along the line of operations the old French machinery lay buried in pathetic ruin in a tropic jungle which all but effaced the evidences of the French enterprise, and such conditions of general unhealthiness prevailed as made it seem almost too much to expect that any kind of clean-up program could be made effectual." [1]

He found that rails had to be laid for a railroad, so that when excavation was begun there would be adequate transportation facilities to carry the immense quantities of material needed in the interior. Docks had to be erected. Considerable effort had to be spent in draining the towns in the interior between Colon and Panama. Large tracts of swamp land had to be filled in, and streets had to be paved, for they were full of stagnant pools, breeding places for millions of tropical insects. As the natives depended upon fetid cistern water for drinking purposes, a modern waterworks had to be installed. A complete sewerage system had to be laid. Quarters, hospitals and canteens for the workers had to be erected. All this reconstruction work, which had to be completed before excavation could begin, must necessarily delay the building of the Canal.

[1] "Recollections of Full Years," by Helen Herron Taft. Dodd, Mead & Company, New York, 1914.

With all this in mind, Taft hastened to complete his negotiations with President Amador. The agreement, as finally drafted, stipulated that no trade for the Canal Zone or the Republic of Panama would be permitted to enter the ports established by the United States at either end of the Zone, except articles in transit and such supplies as were to be used for the construction of the Canal. The Government of Panama promised to reduce its high tariff and consular fees, to revise its postage rates, and to build and maintain certain roads and highways to run into the Canal Zone. Free trade between Panama and the Canal Zone was agreed upon, and Panama granted to the United States the right to make quarantine regulations for the cities of Colon and Panama.

While this agreement removed much of the friction between the Government of Panama and the United States officials, it failed to silence the reports fostered by petty jealousies, and the innumerable complaints about improper living quarters, inadequate material and insufficient labor, that flooded Taft's office. Taft was more patient than President Roosevelt, who, exasperated by the endless bickerings between the officials in charge of operations, and by the persistent public criticism of the enterprise, told his Secretary of War that he was disgusted with conditions in the Canal Zone, that changes would have to be made in the personnel of the Isthmian Canal Commission, and that he wished "to heaven I could get Root at a salary of fifty to a hundred thousand dollars which I would cheerfully give him to take complete charge and run this whole business."

The early months of 1905 found the American Government engaged in many international controversies. The President was endeavoring to terminate the sanguinary Russo-Japanese War. Diplomatic negotiations were being conducted in order to prevent a European war from growing out of the Moroccan dispute. Venezuela was still troubling our State Department. The Japanese residents of Hawaii, who outnumbered the whites, were showing an insolent temper and threatening trouble, and, above all, disquieting rumors of dissatisfaction came out of the Philippines. In the midst of all these difficulties, President Roosevelt departed from Washington for a vacation at Glenwood Springs, Colorado, saying, with an assurance inspired only by the greatest confidence, "Oh, things will be all right; I have left Taft sitting on the lid." So, in addition to the innumerable details connected with his administration of the War Department, to Taft was delegated the task of conducting the President's delicate negotiations with those foreign nations.

How well he handled them and how pleased the President was with his conduct is shown in an excerpt from one of Roosevelt's letters to Taft.

"You are handling everything just right. As for the Japanese demands, I have been expecting that they would be materially increased after the smashing overthrow of Kuropatkin at Mukden. My own view is that the Russians would do well to close with them even now; but the Czar knows neither how to make war or make peace. If he had an ounce of sense he would have acted upon my suggestion last January and have made peace then. There is nothing for us to do but sit still and wait events. . . . You are acting exactly right about Morocco. I wish to heaven our excellent friend the Kaiser was not so jumpy and did not have so many pipe dreams. . . . Fortunately you and I play the diplomatic game exactly alike. . . ." [1]

When the reports of discontent emanating from the Philippines increased, it was decided that Taft should revisit the Archipelago, accompanied by a Congressional party. When this trip was originally projected, it was looked upon with disfavor by a critical public as being a costly and useless journey. But Roosevelt was firm in his determination that Taft should go to the Philippines. He felt that Taft, on the spot, could ascertain the truth as to conditions, and that he might, also, stop off in Japan to better Japanese relations, which Roosevelt had jeopardized by apparently favoring Russia and interfering with the peace negotiations at Portsmouth.

Accompanied by a party of Congressmen, Taft left Washington on the thirtieth of June, 1905. Secretary of State John Hay died the day after Taft's departure. President Roosevelt thought of making Taft Hay's successor, but he hesitated about removing his Secretary of War from his labors in the Philippines and Panama. The President conferred with his friend Senator Henry Cabot Lodge, of Massachusetts, whose reply apparently convinced the President of the inadvisability of doing this, for on the day on which he received the Massachusetts Senator's letter, Roosevelt wrote Taft: "I shall probably ask Root to become

[1] "Theodore Roosevelt and His Time," by Joseph Bucklin Bishop. Chas. Scribner's Sons, New York, 1920.

173

Secretary of State, though I doubt if he accepts. I should greatly like to have him able to deal with the Venezuela and Dominican problems, as well as with this peace conference matter this summer, while you have to be in the Philippines."

Unselfishly, Taft urged the President to appoint Root Secretary of State, if Root desired to return to public life. Roosevelt then offered the post to Root, who accepted. Writing Taft of Root's acceptance, Roosevelt said, "He will be an added strength to all of us. My dear fellow, as for your own attitude in the matter, I could say nothing higher of you than that it was just exactly characteristic of you. I do not believe that you will ever quite understand what strength and comfort and help you are to me. . . ."

The newspapers acclaimed the public announcement of Root's appointment. Taft, who had been much in the public eye and constantly referred to as the probable Republican nominee for the Presidency in 1908, was dropped, and Root was now hailed as the most prominent contender for that honor. The antics of the newspapers both amused and disgusted Roosevelt, who, writing to Taft, expressed contempt for their comments.

"Up to the first of July," he wrote, "you were the one person in the popular eye. Then you started for the Philippines, and Root suddenly appeared on the stage, and the great American public, to use a simile from the nursery, dropped its woolly horse and turned with frantic delight to the new cloth doll. The more lunatic portion of the press insisted that I had made a bargain by which Root was to have the next Presidency. The fact that to make such a bargain would show both of us to be not only scoundrels but idiots was treated as an unimportant detail. By the time you come back they will probably drop Root like dross and take you up as a new returned hero from the Orient and they will then vividly portray Root's bitter— and entirely imaginary—chagrin at my having abandoned him for you."

In May of that year, before going to the Philippines, Taft, as temporary chairman of the Ohio Republican State Convention, delivered the keynote speech for the campaign. In his speech, he opposed Bryan's plan for government ownership of the railroads, but said that he did favor a law fixing railroad rates. This address attracted widespread attention and received much favorable comment. The *Boston Transcript* said,

"The Ohio Republicans know all about his (Taft's) record on the Philippine question. They are familiar with what he said about railroad organization and they are not deterred thereby in any purpose to do him honor. In this purpose, both Secretary Taft's personality and political antecedents aid and encourage. He is a big-brained, big-bodied men. He has a cordial manner. He is a man-mountain full of kindness, and at the same time as is apt to be the case with men large according to the standards of moral and mental measurements, he is not without plenty of force. He can be strenuous if need be, but he prefers to be suave. In this request he resembles, in no small degree, President McKinley, who entertained for him the warmest regard and personal affection.

"Indeed Secretary Taft was one of President McKinley's discoveries. From his appointment as Chairman of the Philippine Commission dates Mr. Taft's prominence before the people of the United States, and he has grown steadily year by year in their estimation. So rapid was his growth that in January, 1903,

175

there was a considerable comment and movement looking to his nomination as the Republican candidate in 1904. . . . If Ohio should in 1908 bring forward the name of William H. Taft it might have the force of combining, oddly enough, the support of two such elements, ordinarily diverse, as the Roosevelt Republicans and the Republicans who followed Marcus A. Hanna."

Later, after his return from the Philippines, Taft was requested by the Ohio Republican leaders to deliver an address at Akron on behalf of Myron Herrick, of Cleveland, the party candidate for Governor. The old Campbell "gang," so powerful in Taft's earlier days in Cincinnati, had become part of the Republican organization of George B. Cox, who had served in the Cincinnati City Council and on the Decennial Board of Equalization. At the time of the Blaine campaign, after receiving a sizeable campaign fund from the none-too-squeamish up-state leaders, Cox had turned in a substantial Republican majority from Hamilton County, in spite of adverse conditions.

This victory made Cox the successor of Campbell, acknowledged leader and boss of the Republican machine, and also marked the beginning of his ascendancy in state political circles. For some years after the Blaine campaign, Cox, from a bare room over the notorious "Mecca" saloon, worked to strengthen his organization. He maneuvered his corrupt satellites into important city offices, where they and he profited from ensuing graft. Finally his organization became so powerful that for years it really determined the policies of Ohio Republicanism.

The early months of 1905 had seen the reputable politi-

176

cal element of Cincinnati organized to combat Cox. They published a small newspaper called *The Citizen's Bulletin,* at first nothing more than a handbill, in which they assailed the Republican boss. The movement gained such momentum that it became necessary for the up-state Republican leaders to determine with which group they should align themselves. Taft did not straddle. He courageously attacked the Cox-Foraker machine, and in his Akron address said,

> "But power secured by the boss and his assistants under the machine has undoubtedly inured to their pecuniary benefit and it is seen in the large fortunes they now have. How their money was made has not been disclosed. . . . If I were able as I fear I shall not be because public duty calls me elsewhere, to cast my vote in Cincinnati, in the coming election, I should vote against the municipal ticket nominated by the Republican organization and for the state ticket."

CHAPTER XIX

THE MISSION TO CUBA

WHILE serving as Secretary of War, Taft was once again honored by being tendered a place on the United States Supreme Court. In a conference with the President, Taft asked Roosevelt for time to consider the advisability of accepting the appointment. Roosevelt told him to take as long as he liked, and after the interview the President issued the following statement,

> "As Mr. Justice Brown will not retire until June, when the Supreme Court will take a vacation until the second Monday in October, and no public inconvenience will arise from the vacancy continuing through the vacation, the President will take further time to decide the question of Mr. Justice Brown's successor. Several names, including that of Secretary Taft, have been under consideration, but no decision has been or is likely to be reached or announced in the near future."

Shortly after this conference the President wrote Taft,

> "I think I have been in error as to your feeling. You say that it is your decided preference to continue your present work. This I had not understood. On the contrary I gathered that what you really wanted to do was to go on the bench and that my urging was in the line of your inclinations, but in a matter in which you were in doubt as to your duty.
> "My dear Will, it is preëminently a matter in which no other man can take the responsibility of deciding for you what is

178

best for you to do. Nobody could decide for me whether I should go to the war or stay as Assistant Secretary of the Navy. Nobody could decide for me whether I should accept the Vice Presidency or try to continue as Governor. In each case it is the man himself who is to lead his life after having decided one way or the other. No one can lead that life for him, and neither he nor anyone else can afford to have anyone else make the decision for him, because the vital factor in the decision must be an equation of the man himself.

"So far as I am personally concerned, I could not put myself in your place, because I am not a lawyer, and would under no circumstances, even if I had been trained for a lawyer, have any leaning toward the bench; so in your case I should, as a matter of course, accept the three years of service in the War Department dealing with the Panama and the Philippine questions, and then abide in the event as to whether I became President or continued in public life in some less conspicuous position or went back to the practice of the law.

"But I appreciate, as every thoughtful man must, the importance of the part to be played by the Supreme Court in the next twenty-five years. I don't at all like the social conditions at the present. The dull, purblind folly of the very rich men, their greed and arrogance, and the way in which they have unduly prospered by the help of the ablest lawyers, and too, often through the weaknesses and short-sightedness of the judges, or by their unfortunate possession of meticulous minds; these facts and the corruption in business and politics have tended to produce a very unhealthy condition of excitement and irritation in the popular mind, which shows itself in part in the enormous increase in the socialistic propaganda.

"Nothing effective, because nothing at once honest and intelligent is being done to combat the great amount of evil which, mixed with a little good, a little truth, is contained in these outpourings. . . . Some of these socialists, some of them lurid sentimentalists; but they are all building up a revolutionary feeling, which will, most probably, take the form of a political campaign. Then we may have to do too late, or almost too late, what had to be done in the silver campaign, when in one summer we had to convince a good many people that what they had been laboriously taught several years ago was untrue.

"Under such circumstances, you would be the best possible leader, and with your leadership we could rest assured that only good methods would prevail. In such a contest you could do very much if you were on the bench; you could do very much if you were in political life outside. I think you could do most as President but you could do very much as an Associate Justice. Where you can fight best I cannot say for you know where your soul turns to better than I can.

"As I see the situation it is this; there are strong arguments against your taking this justiceship. In the first place my belief is that of all the men who have appeared so far you are the man who is most likely to receive the Republican nomination, and who is, I think, the best man to receive it. It is not a light thing to cast aside the chance of the Presidency, even though, of course, it is a chance, however a good one.

"It would be a very foolish thing for you to get it into your thoughts so that your sweet and fine nature would be warped and you would become bitter and sour as Henry Clay became; and, thank heaven, that is impossible. But it is well to remember that the shadow of the Presidency falls on no man twice, save in most exceptional circumstances.

"Now, my dear Will, there is the situation as I see it. It is a hard choice to make, and you yourself have to make it. You have two alternatives before you, each with uncertain possibilities, and you cannot feel sure that whichever you take you will not afterward feel that it would have been better if you had taken the other. But whichever you take I know that you will render great and durable service to the nation for many years to come, and I feel sure that you should decide in accordance with the promptings of your own liking, of your own belief as to where you can render the service which most appeals to you, as well as which you feel is most beneficial to the nation. No one can with wisdom advise you." [1]

From Murray Bay, where he had gone for a short five weeks' vacation, came Taft's response,

"I know that few, if any, even among my friends, will credit me with anything but a desire, unconscious perhaps, to run for the Presidency, and that I must face and bear this misconstruction of what I do. But I am confident you credit my reasons as I give them to you, and will believe me when I say that I would prefer to go on the Supreme Bench for life than to run for the Presidency, and that in twenty years of judicial service I could make myself more useful to the country than as President, even if my election should come about.

"Please do not misunderstand me to think that I am indispensable or that the world would not run on much the same if I were to disappear in the St. Lawrence River. But circumstances seem to me to have impressed something in the nature of a trust to me personally that I should not discharge by succeeding Justice Brown. In the nature of things the trust must end with this administration, and one or two years is short to do much. Yet the next session of Congress may result in much for the benefit of the Filipino, and it seems to me it is my duty to be in the fight."

The fact that the press was violently attacking the administration for alleged muddling in the Philippines and Panama, must have definitely influenced Taft to decline

[1] "Theodore Roosevelt and His Time," by Joseph Bucklin Bishop. Chas. Scribner's Sons, New York, 1920.

the Supreme Court appointment, for he told President Roosevelt that he would remain in the Cabinet.

Declaring himself "as pleased as Punch that Taft was to stay in the Cabinet," Roosevelt told his Secretary of War that

"One element in my enjoyment was, as it always is with you, my un-Christian delight in finding that you, whom I admire as much not only as any public man of the present but as any public man of the past, bar Lincoln and Washington—indeed, whom I suppose I admire more than any other public man bar these two—get yourself into just the same kind of hot water that I from time to time get in myself. The water is not so hot, and you never deserve to have gotten into it, as I am sorry to say I abundantly do; but it is a comfort to feel that the man I love and admire and respect encounters the difficulties I encounter and it makes me feel that perhaps in my gloomier moments I exaggerate my culpability and the blame with which I shall be visited, when I see that not only do you ludicrously exaggerate the weight of the attack that will be made upon you, but ascribe to yourself a culpability that is wholly non-existent."

By the Treaty of Paris, which terminated the Spanish-American War, the United States had undertaken certain obligations not only in respect to the Philippines, but also in regard to Cuba, but for some inexplicable reason we were more generous in our treatment of the Cubans than of the Filipinos. Possessing neither tradition, experience nor education in self-government, the Cubans were as ignorant of the meaning of civil and personal liberty as were the Filipinos. Again like the Filipinos, they understood "government" to mean a single omnipotent ruler, whose decrees were law. Yet in spite of their obvious inability to govern themselves, the United States relinquished its supervision over the Cubans after a short period of tutelage, freeing them and permitting them to conduct their own government. But as a condition precedent to our withdrawal from the island, Secretary of War Root had insisted upon and secured the adoption by Cuba of a constitution which the United States could approve.

In this constitution Root had caused to be incorporated a provision, later known as the Platt Amendment, Article Three of which reads,

> "That the government of Cuba consents that the United States may exercise the right to intervene for the preservation of Cuban independence, the maintenance of a government adequate for the protection of life, property and individual liberty, and for the discharge of the obligations with respect to Cuba imposed by the Treaty of Paris on the United States now to be assumed and undertaken by the Government of Cuba."

The first election in Cuba to be held without the quieting effort of the American armed forces took place in 1905. Two major political parties, alike in that both used their power as a means of profit and gain, differing only in the methods they employed, placed candidates for the Presidency in the field. There were other smaller political groups, but none had sufficient strength to be a real factor. Don Tomas Estrada Palma, a veteran of the ten years' war with Spain, sought to succeed himself as President, campaigning on the Moderate ticket. A distinguished Havana lawyer, Mendez Capote, had been made his running mate. To oppose Palma and Capote, the Liberal party nominated General Jose Miguel Gomez, a man of the people and a soldier. As the campaign progressed it became apparent that bribery, intimidation, and almost wholesale incarceration to prevent the members of the Liberal party from voting, had been resorted to by the party in power, the Moderates. These practices made the result inevitable. The Moderates were successful and Palma was overwhelmingly reëlected.

Their minds inflamed by the many injustices they had suffered at the hands of their opponents, the Liberals rebelled against the Moderates. At the outset it was believed that these disturbances were nothing more than sporadic lawless outbreaks, so common in tropical countries, that could be quelled by a show of force, but with the passing of the spring and summer the revolutionary movement assumed such proportions as to imperil the industrial prosperity and alarm the business interests of the island.

Palma called the reservists to the colors. For weeks and months Pino Guerra, the outstanding leader among the insurrectionists, had roved as he pleased throughout the length and breadth of the Province of Pinar del Rio. His army had grown by leaps and bounds, by scores and hundreds, and his time was largely devoted to arming, drilling, marching, and making soldiers out of raw civilians. The Federals constantly sought this boyish rebel chieftain, who fought in an ordinary business suit and leather riding leggings with a little whip dangling from his wrist, but they always found the insurgent troops so firmly entrenched in a strategic position that to fight would mean sure defeat. Out-maneuvered, they had no recourse but to retreat. August, 1906, found the Cuban revolution assuming ominous proportions and threatening the Moderate Government.

The attitude of the American people at this time, if viewed without prejudice and in the cool, calm light of reason, seems, at best, paradoxical. Almost fanatically eager to ensure Cuban independence, they placed the blame for the insurrection upon the American sugar and tobacco interests, who were operating large holdings in Cuba. Arguing that the "trusts" were importing their products from Cuba into the United States under a heavy duty, American public opinion accused these corporations of conniving with the insurgents to overthrow the Palma Government, annex Cuba to the United States, and thus remove the exorbitant duties that they were compelled to pay.

The situation was acute. With the passing of the days it became more and more threatening. Exerting himself to suppress the threatening disorders, President Palma strengthened the military and increased the numbers of the rural guard. But he reckoned without the strength of the rebel forces. For in a series of engagements between the rural guards and the insurrectionists, the rural guards were defeated time after time with very severe losses. Constantly retreating they soon found themselves on the outskirts of Havana with over twenty thousand insurrectionist troops, poorly armed but formidable, facing and enveloping them.

Taft had only just returned from his vacation at Murray Bay when Roosevelt, impressed with the gravity of the Cuban situation, called a special Cabinet meeting to consider it. On the fourteenth of September, 1906, the members of the Cabinet gathered at Sagamore Hill, Oyster Bay, to learn from the President that Palma had wired that he intended to resign.

Once again a diplomatic mission of the utmost delicacy fell to Taft's lot. Instructed by President Roosevelt to proceed to Havana and there endeavor to adjust and pacify the differences of the contending factions, Taft left Washington for Key West on the sixteenth of September, just two days after the Cabinet meeting. He was accompanied by a very small staff. Only Assistant Secretary of State Bacon, an aide, Captain Frank McCoy, who had served on General Wood's staff when Wood had been Military Governor of Cuba, Frank Cairns, a former Cuban secret service operative, and Major E. F. Ladd, were detailed to go with him.

When word reached Cuba that the United States intended to intervene, the contending factions prepared for battle with a grim despatch never before attained. And only a few hours before Taft landed on Cuban soil the Battle of Wajay was fought by the government and insurrectionist troops.

Taft's plans were indefinite. Such information as had emanated from Cuba was too vague and untrustworthy to make it possible for him to devise a plan of action. So he determined to accommodate himself to conditions as he found them.

When the cruiser *Des Moines,* carrying Taft and Bacon, docked at Havana, there were no members of the Liberal Party present to welcome the American Secretary of War and his staff, on behalf of the Cuban Government; only government officials and leaders of the Moderate Party.

Escorted to the palace, Taft found the Cuban president, Palma, surrounded by his Cabinet, awaiting him in the apartment of state, the famous Red Room. In a very few words Taft said that he would like to interview the Liberal leaders as well as the members of the Governmental Party, and asked where they could be found. The air of serenity, of happiness, and of confidence that had prevailed in the Red Room was immediately altered. The Moderates, who had gathered for this "love feast" between the American Commissioners and the Cuban Governmental officials, gazed at one another in stupefaction. And when Taft and Bacon took their departure from the apartment of state, bound for the palatial home of United States Minister Morgan at Marianao on the outskirts of Havana, they left behind them a very dazed group.

Deciding to hold hearings to discover the truth, Taft accepted the invitation of Minister Morgan who offered his palace to the Commissioners for their consultations. There in a salon, off a great patio filled with palms and gorgeous blossoming plants, Taft and Bacon received all sorts and types of men who had anything to offer in the way of information. Laborers, bankers, lawyers, merchants, politicians, men from every station of life, appeared before them.

Slowly, after days had been expended in conferences, the truth was sifted from the mass of evidence. The testimony was mephitic with its taint of corruption, and clearly showed that there had been fraud in the election. When

187

this was brought to the attention of the Moderates, they merely shrugged their shoulders and said, "But that, after all, was a mere matter of detail. We did it for the good of Cuba. And the other fellows, if they had the chance, would have done the same thing."

As a result of these disclosures, Taft was exceedingly doubtful about the wisdom of keeping Palma in the Presidency, and he wrote Roosevelt that Palma

"professes to be anxious to resign but claims that if he would resign he would have no money to support his family. The truth is that Palma is one of the very few men who are really honest and patriotic, in either of the parties, and of sufficient age to be President. His continuance in office would be valuable to the Island in that everybody accords him honesty and the property holders and the conservatives would be gratified by his continuance. The outrages were not committed by Palma, and I doubt if he was advised of the extent of the abuses, but it is necessary to make a mixed Cabinet to secure a compromise and I am not sure of the permanency of that arrangement. . . . What is needed here, as in the Philippines and elsewhere in the tropics, in dealing with people like this, is patience; but the trouble lies in the irresponsible character of the men in arms, who, although they represent a great majority of the people in their cause, are themselves, many of them, lawless persons of no particular standing in times of peace, and whose motive for continuing in arms is very strong because of the importance they enjoy under such conditions while peace means to them that which they most hate—work."

On the twenty-first of September the Executive Committee of the Moderate Party gathered, in response to a summons, and unanimously voted to accept any compromise that might be proposed by Taft. Palma and his Cabinet were then instructed that he would call at the palace on the evening of the twenty-third of September, to submit a plan of compromise. When he arrived he found the government officials, as usual, awaiting him in the Red Room. In a kindly tone which was at the same time firm, Taft proposed that President Palma remain in office, the Cabinet resign, new Congressional elections be held forthwith, and that the Cuban constitution be amended so as to extend autonomy to the cities of the Island.

Palma listened in silence. When Taft had finished, he said, his voice trembling with emotion:

"I cannot accept this solution of our difficulties, Sir. My honor, the honor of my country, the honor of my advisers, all are at stake. We owe it to our patriotism to stand firm."

"But, Mr. President," Taft replied, "there comes a time when patriotism demands a sacrifice. . . ."

"Mr. Secretary," Palma interrupted Taft heatedly, "I do not intend to take any lessons in patriotism from you."

And the aged man's head sank low on his breast, as emotion overpowered him. Taft remained standing before Palma in sympathetic silence.

Suddenly Secretary O'Faril y. Chapotin, of the Department of State and Justice, broke the silence by upbraiding the Americans, "Is it for this that you Americans have come here?" he cried out. "We could have settled this matter ourselves, and put down the revolution unaided. Yet you came here and deal with men in arms against the Government."

Taft turned on the little Cabinet officer. "Such acts as

yours," he began in a scathing tone, "are killing the Republic of Cuba." And for ten minutes he recited the facts of the election as he had elicited them from the witnesses who had appeared before him. He recounted specific instances of fraud, violence, and even assassination. The room became painfully still. He finished, and departed, leaving the Government officials in somber silence, still standing in the same positions in which they had greeted him, and withal much wiser men.

The following day Taft wrote President Palma requesting that he reconsider his resignation and remain in office as President. But Palma replied that he would go with the others, and, at the same time, he called an extraordinary session of Congress to meet in joint session to receive the resignation of himself and his official family.

Havana was seething with excitement. General Freyre Andrade, a small, relentless man of great force, called upon Taft and Bacon and informed them that the Moderate party would convene Congress, receive President Palma's resignation, appoint a committee to ask him not to resign. When he declined, they would return to Congress, report their failure, break the quorum and disappear. Andrade was emphatic in his belief that the only solution of the problem now was for the United States to intervene.

In a last effort to bring about an amicable adjustment, Taft asked the Moderates to confer with him. They did so, and immediately after the meeting, Taft said, in a public statement,

"The Government officials, instead of coöperating with us to save the Republic, have resorted to every kind of obstruction

190

with the object of continuing their control of the administration. President Palma and his advisers have rejected terms of peace which were honorable to them though in the form of a compromise with their opponents. We are still striving to arrange a settlement and we trust that the American people will give us credit for doing everything possible to accomplish a settlement without resorting to force.

"I cannot say that we are hopeful for I have never known a more disgusting situation. Investigation convinces us that the election was thoroughly rotten. We do not want to intervene but the conditions afield may necessitate it. Our reports show that the insurgent commanders have lost control of their forces which are now lawless bands. The situation seems to demand the use of force."

Scores of prominent Cuban, as well as American, citizens called upon Taft and warned him that General Rafael Montalvo y. Morales, Secretary of the Interior and Public Works, had ordered the rural guard to fire upon the Congressmen when they assembled for their joint session. As these reports increased in volume, Taft sent for the Secretary. Morales admitted that he had ordered fifteen hundred troops to the arsenal, which was located near the House of Representatives, to be on hand in the event of trouble. Taft warned him, and, as a matter of precaution, had two thousand American bluejackets and marines made ready for active duty ashore.

The days that followed were full of kaleidoscopic changes, of fervid oratory, and passionate protestations about patriotism, dignity and honor. However, when the time came for the session of Congress to begin all was comparatively quiet. Ricardo Dolz, the President of the Senate, sat in a chair high above the floor and presided over this joint meeting of the Cuban House of Representatives and Senate. On his right sat the fourteen Senators, and on his left the forty members of the House of Representatives. The ceremony attached to the convening of the session was meticulously followed. General Andrade, the Speaker of the House, ascended the Tribune and shook hands with Senor Dolz. Senator Alfredo Zayas, chief of the Liberals, ascended the Tribune from the opposite side, and did likewise, and then, smiling coldly, turned and faced the Moderate leader. They shook hands, and each returned to his chair. A little bell tinkled and the extraordinary session had begun.

After roll call, the clerk read the letters of resignation. Almost immediately Senator Betancourt Manduley, a man of full and generous proportions, arose and requested the right to offer a resolution. As he spoke his voice became a trifle husky. "We are assembled," he said, "not as members of this party or that, but as Cuban legislators, for our beloved country is in peril. I move that a Commission of Moderate, Liberals and Independents go to President Palma and beseech him to withdraw his resignation."

As Manduley proceeded, his voice broke and shook with emotion, while his arms were thrust outward in a gesture of appeal. When he had concluded, Zayas objected, but after considerable debate, a vote was taken. The motion prevailed, and the crowd of citizens, who had packed in on the floor and aisles, and in the back of the room—for there was no gallery—cheered wildly and applauded. Congress then adjourned until late that evening.

Once against the scene shifted to the Red Room of the palace, where Palma received the congressmen, who pled with him to withdraw his resignation. When Dolz, acting as spokesman for the delegates, had completed his plea, Palma said, "But here we have a question of the dignity of the government. We are deprived of authority by an armed element which has arisen against us. I must go." No one spoke. No one dared speak for fear of betraying emotion. And as the legislators filed out of the room, defeated, they appeared overwhelmed; many of them had tears standing in their eyes. Congress again gathered in extraordinary session, adjourned, and reassembled, only to lack a quorum and adjourn without naming a successor to President Palma.

Whereupon Taft assumed control of the Cuban Government. American Marines were landed to guard the Treasury, and to disarm the rebel and government forces. Taft issued a proclamation in which he said,

"The failure of Congress to act on the irrevocable resignation of the President of the Republic of Cuba or to elect a successor leaves the country without a Government at a time when great disorder prevails, and requires that, pursuant to the request of Mr. Palma, the necessary steps be taken in the name and authority of the President of the United States to restore order and protect life and property in the Island of Cuba and the islands and keys adjacent thereto, and for this purpose to establish therein a provisional government.

"The Provisional Government hereby established will be maintained only long enough to restore order, peace and public confidence, by the direction of and in the name of the President of the United States, and then to hold such elections

193

as may be necessary to determine in those persons upon whom the permanent Government of the Republic should be devolved.

"In so far as is consistent with the nature of the Provisional Government established under the authority of the United States, this will be a Cuban Government conforming with the constitution of Cuba. The Cuban flag will be hoisted as usual over the Government buildings of the Island, all the executive departments and the provisional and municipal governments, including that of the City of Havana, and all laws not in their nature inapplicable by reason of the temporary and emergent character of the Government will be in force."

Concerning his administration of Cuban affairs, Taft said, in a letter to President Roosevelt,

"Bacon and I have attempted, both in the proclamation and in this speech and in everything else, to conform as nearly as possible to Root's views as expounded by him in his trip to South America and to show the South Americans that we are here against our will and only for the purpose of aiding Cuba. . . .

"My theory in respect to our Government here, which I have attempted to carry out in every way, is that we are simply carrying on the Republic of Cuba under the Platt Amendment, as a Receiver carries on the business of a corporation, or a trustee the business of his ward; that this in its nature suspends the functions of the legislature and of the elected executive but that it leaves them in such a situation that their functions will at once revive when the receivership or trusteeship is at an end. . . . This is, of course, a novel situation, but the Platt Amendment was novel in that one independent government agreed with another independent government that the latter might intervene in the former and maintain the former in law and order. All this effort is apparently exceedingly gratifying to the Cuban people and softens much the humiliation that they have suffered from the intervention."

On the third of October, Roosevelt appointed Charles E. Magoon, a once obscure law clerk in the War Department, as Provisional Governor of Cuba, and, in wiring Taft to return home, said, "I doubt whether you have ever rendered our country a greater service than the one you are now rendering." Ten days later Taft, leaving behind him "those awful twenty days," as he afterward called his stay in Cuba, sailed from Havana on the battleship *Louisiana* to resume his interrupted War Department labors.

CHAPTER XX

THE PANAMA CANAL

THE beginnings of reconstruction and excavation work on the Panama Canal had demonstrated the inefficiency and consequent failure of a large Commission with divided responsibility. Because it failed to agree, Roosevelt had forced the resignation of the seven members composing the original Panama Canal Commission. The same members were appointed to the second Commission, but to assure unanimity and coöperation, three of the members were made an Executive Committee and four became an Advisory Committee. This plan also had failed. The final solution, that of conferring upon a single person absolute powers of direction and control, was decided upon in a conference between Taft and Roosevelt, during which they determined that the building of the canal should be withdrawn from private engineering companies and placed under the direction of the army engineers. In an address at a dinner of the Ohio Society of New York, Taft afterward explained how the job of completing the canal came to be entrusted to Colonel George Washington Goethals:

"President Roosevelt asked me if I could suggest an engineer officer best qualified to tackle the great problem there in the Isthmus. I told him I thought I could. I said the man was a Brooklyn Dutchman, and his name was Goethals."

The most harassing of all the vexing Canal questions was the labor problem. After having a thorough survey made of the United States' labor resources, in hope of finding a supply which he might employ in the Canal Zone, Taft found that there was nowhere in this country any overplus of labor which could be attracted to the Isthmus. He had considered the securing of negro labor from America, but learned that to remove the negroes from any section of the country would result in labor disturbance there, and that the American negroes were earning more wages than they would be in Panama. Hence he abandoned this plan.

But labor was needed, and needed badly. Taft turned then to the West Indies, where the wages received were less than those the American government would pay in the Canal Zone, and made attractive offers to Indian laborers, so that a large number of these West Indies blacks was imported into Panama. After a time, however, these negroes were found to be unsatisfactory. Inducements were then held out to Spaniards from the Northern Provinces of Spain, for they had labored effectively in Cuba, but only about five hundred of them responded. Almost as a last resort, invitations were issued for bids for the furnishing of Chinese labor, but American labor organizations objected to the introduction of any coolie labor in the Canal Zone, and the invitations had to be withdrawn.

While the preliminary work of construction was going on, a sharp controversy arose as to the type of canal to be built. Should it be a lock canal above sea level or one at sea level? In authorizing the President to build the Canal,

Congress had left this question open. In order to get expert opinion, President Roosevelt appointed a Board of Consulting Engineers, consisting of thirteen eminent Dutch, French, English, German and American engineers. The Board disagreed, eight of the members recommending a sea level canal, five favoring the lock type. When the reports reached Taft's desk, he studied them carefully. Concluding that a lock canal would not cost as much, that it could be completed in less time, and that the expense of maintenance would be appreciably less, Taft sided with the minority and forwarded the reports, with his views and recommendations, to the President. In the face of the adverse majority report, Roosevelt supported Taft and the minority recommendation, and the lock canal became the administration program. After several weeks of debate, Congress approved this plan. To remove friction between American officials and those of Panama, to smooth irate feelings, conciliate conflicting factions and generally to supervise the work on the Canal, Taft made several other trips to Panama during his four years as Secretary of War.

Taft's years in the Cabinet were not devoted solely to the administration of the duties of his office. President Roosevelt, in order that the administration should always appear to be, as he termed it, in the "fight up to the hilt," often employed his Secretary of War in speech-making and political tours on his behalf. The newspapers called Taft, Root and Roosevelt "The Three Musketeers" on account of their unceasing—and united—political activities, Taft being Porthos, Root Athos, and Roosevelt D'Artagnan.

TAFT AND ENGINEERS AT CULEBRA

Not merely pleased, but greatly tickled by these nicknames, the three statesmen used them in letters to one another.

Taft's numerous journeys, his Philippine tours, the trip around the world, impelled a New York newspaper editorial writer to comment thus:

"Merely to record the movements and missions of the Secretary of War requires a nimble mind. He journeys from Washington to Manila to reassure ten millions of natives restive under an experimental scheme of civil government and turns up in Panama to speed the digging of the Isthmian Canal. To give a fillip to a campaign for reform in some western state, or direct the southern Republicans in the way they should go, or enlighten the people down East as to the President's home policy, or illuminate the recesses of a problem in jurisdiction for the benefit of a Bar Association, is only a matter of grabbing a time table and throwing a change of clothing into a traveling bag. Such are mere relaxations and holiday jaunts for the Honorable William H. Taft.

"A Cuban revolution would be a poser to most statesmen, and to an ordinary Secretary of War a labour of Hercules; but to the business of bringing peace with honor to a distracted land, deposing one government and setting up another, meanwhile gratifying everybody and winning the esteem of the fiercest warrior, Mr. Taft devotes only one page of the calendar and takes ship for the States to resume his routine duties as if he had done nothing out of the common.

"But routine duties in Washington do not hold him long. An itinerary is made up for him and he plunges into the stress and turmoil of a political campaign. He is to make speeches in Ohio and Illinois, and Idaho claims him too. From Havana to Pocatello is something of a change and a far cry, but it is all in the day's work for William H. Taft. . . . All nice problems look alike to the Secretary of War who should be called the Secretary of Peace, so uniform is his success in smoothing the wrinkled front of conflict and making two laughs reach where one groan was heard before."

CHAPTER XXI

THE NOMINATION FOR PRESIDENCY

O<small>N</small> the fifth of September, 1906, Taft declared in a speech at Bath, Maine, that since the passage of the Dingley Bill there had, in his opinion, been "such changes in the business conditions of the country as to make it wise and just to revise certain of the schedules of the tariff." He recognized that this sentiment was growing in the Republican party and that, in the near future, its members would have to agree upon a reasonable revision. This speech, elucidating Taft's views upon the vital and pressing issue of the tariff, was popularly regarded as being the opening of his campaign for the Presidency. The field for the Republican nomination for the Presidency was an open one. President Roosevelt was, without doubt, the strongest man in his party, despite the fact that he was constantly issuing distempered forecasts of business conditions and making violent attacks upon prominent business men. Still, he dominated the party as no single person except, perhaps, Andrew Jackson, had ever dominated an American political party.

But Roosevelt had eliminated himself from being regarded as Presidential timber by the statement that he issued on election night, 1904, when he said, "The wise custom which limits the President to two terms regards the substance and not the form, and under no circumstances will I be a candidate for or accept another nomination." In repudiating the declarations of many of his supporters, who contended that he had served but one elective term, and was, therefore, eligible for another, Roosevelt had stated that he regarded his completion of the unfinished term of President McKinley as one term, and his election to the Presidency in 1904 as another.

As time went on it became apparent that no one man, except Taft, and possibly Root, had achieved sufficient national prominence to be included in that very select group created once every four years and known as Presidential possibilities. Fairbanks, of Indiana, Knox of Pennsylvania, Hughes of New York, and Cummins, of Iowa, were all considered but no one of them had become sufficiently distinguished outside of his own state to be anything more than a favorite son. It was evident, very early, therefore, that President Roosevelt would have much to do with the nomination of the Republican Presidential candidate for the 1908 campaign.

Although Roosevelt's tactics had embittered a large faction in his own party, so that they were showing a refractory disposition, he still controlled his political organization, which was stronger than any of the political machines of his opponents. Thus it was a certainty that his choice for the Presidency would be the choice of the Republican National Convention, and it was a foregone conclusion that Roosevelt would desire a man who would not relax the vigor of the combat against the vested interests, which he had begun and was carrying on.

His choice lay between his Secretary of State, Elihu Root,

and his Secretary of War, William Howard Taft, both of whom were open and unrestrained exponents of his policies. To prefer one and disregard the other—for both possessed every qualification for the Presidency and were eminently satisfactory as regards capabilities—was a difficult task for Roosevelt. Root, by reason of his connections with large corporations, would not make a good candidate. This the President knew, and this fact, coupled with Taft's popularity with the people of the country, caused him to favor the nomination of his Secretary of War.

Taft, however, must not have been particularly eager for the honor, for on different occasions he had told various friends, "I am not a politician and I dislike politics. I do want to go on the bench, and my ambition is to be Chief Justice of the United States. I would be of more service there to the United States than I could be as President."

But when he returned to the United States from his tour around the world, in late December, 1907, Taft found Roosevelt impatiently awaiting him. The severe depressions, caused by financial and business disturbances of that year, bordered upon a national calamity and resulted in the Panic of 1907. This had enabled the President's critics to charge that the financial chaos was directly attributable to the administration's meddling in business affairs. The President was eager that Taft, by answering these charges on behalf of the administration, should begin at once his campaign for the Presidency. In accepting, shortly after his return, an invitation to address the Merchant's Association at Boston, Taft had intended discussing conditions in the

203

Philippines, but Roosevelt prevailed upon him to "fire the opening gun of his campaign" by speaking on the financial situation.

This Taft did, and quite outspokenly riddled the claims of the "standpatters" by saying,

> "The economic and political history of the past four years is that of a great struggle between the national administration and certain powerful combinations in the financial world. . . . If the abuses of monopoly and discriminations cannot be restrained, if the concentration of power made possible by such abuses continues and increases, and it is manifest that under the system of individualism and private property the tyranny and oppression of an oligarchy of wealth cannot be avoided, then socialism will triumph, and the institution of private property will perish."

The preliminary campaign for the nomination was for the most part comparatively dull. Taft's cordiality, his unflinching sense of duty, his power to do long, tedious hours of hard work had already won for him many followers, and this Boston speech definitely increased their number. His brother Charles P. Taft installed campaign quarters in both Washington and Cincinnati, and the campaign got under way. Conditions made Ohio the pivotal state and it became strategically necessary for Taft to gain the support of his party in his own state before his nomination could be assured. And it was just here that many elements bespoke possible failure. The labor organizations and the negroes, who formed a substantial portion of the Republican votes of the state, were both opposing him. Senator Joseph Benson Foraker, who, with Senator Dick, had inherited the powerful Hanna machine, was also seeking to prevent the Ohio Republicans from instructing their delegation for Taft.

As part of his program of obstruction Foraker announced his own candidacy for the Presidency. But as Foraker's return to the Senate from Ohio was by no means certain, his motive in seeking the Presidential nomination may be attributed to an acute and remarkable political foresight, which made him willing to trade an endorsement of Taft for the Presidency by the Republican State Committee, for the Ohio Senatorship. In aligning his forces for the battle to control the Republican State Committee, Foraker solicited the support of George B. Cox, the notorious Republican leader of Cincinnati, and of a Central Ohio newspaperman, Warren G. Harding, who owned and published *The Marion Star,* an ardent and powerful Republican newspaper. Harding, who some nine years earlier had taken what he termed "his first whirl in politics" by running successfully for the Ohio Senate, was cautious. He was growing steadily in political strength in the state and had become a considerable factor in determining the policies of the Republican machine, but he was fully aware that a false step might prove his undoing and wipe away the power which it had taken him nine years to gain.

At the outset Harding endorsed Foraker. Later, however, changing his mind, he jumped to the Taft camp. It was this defection among his supporters that made Foraker more than eager for the compromise suggested by that genius for peace, Senator Murray Crane of Massachusetts. In hope of pacifying the turbulent elements in the Ohio political maelstrom, Crane approached Foraker with the suggestion that the Senator support the Secretary of War for the Presidency, and that, in return, Taft agree to promote Foraker's reëlection to the Senate.

The Senator was more than enthusiastic in his approval of this suggestion and Crane hurried on to Washington to report to the President the success of his mission. Roosevelt directed him to see Taft. During the ensuing interview Taft said,

> "You ask for a compact between Foraker and myself,—that if Foraker supports me I shall ask my friends to support Foraker. Personally I have no objection to Foraker. I have kindly feelings toward him. If it was individual support, I could do it. But my individual support isn't requested. Many of my friends in Ohio are opposed to Foraker's return to the Senate. They have determined to oppose him. If I make a pledge with you it is for them. I will be expected to control them. In other words to help myself, I must limit their freedom of action, induce them to do something which they do not wish to do, something against their convictions. In plain English, to secure harmony, I must sell out my friends. I refuse to do that. A man might pay too high a price for the Presidency."

This incident dissolved the opposition to the nomination of Taft in his own state, and it became certain that the Ohio Republicans would proceed to the Convention instructed to vote for the Secretary of War. But his nomination was by no means assured. Factions in other states still opposed him, and in their efforts to discredit him with the people of the country, seized upon and misconstrued his every act and speech.

To alienate the large Jewish vote, they charged that Taft had evinced his opposition to that race when he visited the Czar of Russia. To estrange the negroes they assailed his action, as Secretary of War, in disciplining a battalion of negro troops for their unpardonable offense in what had come to be known as The Brownsville Affair. To disaffect the military elements of the party, they pointed out that in a Memorial Day address at Grant's Tomb, Taft had slurred them when he mentioned the fact that General Grant had been given to strong drink.

Taft was much distressed over this latter charge. He explained that his opponents were deliberately distorting his words, and said,

> "In my Memorial Day address I attributed his resignation from the army in 1854 to his weakness for strong drink, because from Mr. Garland's *'Life of General Grant,'* and evidence that he cites, and other histories, I supposed it was undoubtedly true. I referred to the matter only because it seemed to me that it was one of the great victories of his life that he subsequently overcame the weakness."

The fact that Taft, while a Federal Judge, had issued injunctions against labor bodies had incarcerated certain of their members for the violation of these injunctions, had aroused the antagonism of labor and placed Taft in disfavor with their leaders. They early showed that they were opposed to his nomination, and in a letter to Taft, Mr. Llewellyn Lewis of Martins Ferry, Ohio, Secretary of the Ohio Federation of Labor, asked that the Secretary of War define specifically his views on the rights and limitations of labor.

Affirming the principles that he had so carefully thought out and pronounced while a judge on the State and Federal benches, Taft answered Lewis' letter by writing,

"Before taking up the specific questions and in order to understand my answers to those questions, I should shortly state my opinion with reference to the organizations of labor. . . . I believe it to be highly beneficial and entirely lawful for laborers to unite in their common interests. They have labor to sell, and if they stand together they are often able, all of them, to command better prices for their labor, more advantageous terms of employment than when dealing singly, for the necessities of the single employee may compel him to accept any terms offered him. The accumulation of funds for the support of those who propose to enter into the controversy with the employer by striking, is one of the legitimate objects of such an organization. Its members have the right to appoint officers, who shall advise them as to the course to be taken by them in their relations to their employers, and if the members choose to repose such authority in anyone, the officers may order the members, on pain of expulsion, to join the strike. Having left their employment, they have the right, by persuasion and other peaceable means, to induce those who would take their places to join the strike and their union. They may not do this by violence, threats of violence, or any other conduct equivalent to duress. It is only when the object is not betterment of the terms of their employment, or some other lawful purpose, or when the means they are using are unlawful that they can be properly restrained by law. . . ."

The Republican National Convention met in Chicago. In spite of many efforts to discredit him, Taft's strength had steadily grown until there was no longer any doubt of his nomination for the Presidency. He was chosen on the first ballot, the only untoward incident occurring, when the "die-hards" among Roosevelt's followers made one last effort to renominate the President. John Seibert, a man who was later identified as one of the elevator operators in the capitol building, arose in his chair above the speaker's platform and raised an umbrella, revolving it so that a likeness of Roosevelt was revealed, painted upon its upper surface. Immediately a chant of "four, four, four years more" filled the air, and, as though it had been perfectly planned, an American flag, with a large picture of Roosevelt, was flung free from the balcony.

Although the uproar became deafening, the delegates, as a whole, were unmoved. And after Chairman Lodge had restored order, by furiously pounding his gavel, the first ballot was taken and Taft made the party nominee. The only contest occurred in the choosing of a candidate for the Vice-Presidency. John Hays Hammond, Secretary Cortelyou, Senator Dolliver of Iowa, and Governor Murphy of New Jersey, were all mentioned as contenders for the honor, but Congressman James S. Sherman, of New York, was finally selected as Taft's running mate.

CHAPTER XXII

THE CAMPAIGN OF 1908

THE spring following his nomination, Taft went to New Haven for the Yale Commencement and, religiously following the prescribed customs of reunion classes, enjoyed a refreshing holiday from politics. He joined his classmates on the steps of old Center Church, where they had their picture taken, attended the meeting of the Yale Corporation and the graduating exercises of the law and medical schools. He rode with his class in a trolley car to the baseball field and marched through the mud to his seat, heading a procession of alumni. The other reunion classes then made a circuit of the field and halted in front of the stand where he sat, cheering him lustily, each class, as it passed, giving the yell,

> "Everyone takes his hat off to Taft,
> Hat off to Taft, hat off to Taft, hat off to Taft."

After the game he marched, again with his own and the other reunion classes, to the home of President Hadley, where the President regaled them with tales of Taft's undergraduate days. The next day he was off to the boat races at New London, where he saw the Yale crew lose to Harvard.

Meanwhile his nomination was being well received by the people and press of the country.

When Taft resigned as Secretary of War, to be succeeded by General Luke Wright of Tennessee, his former associate in the Philippines, many people pushed past the portly, jolly old negro messenger at the door of the War Office, to felicitate him upon his nomination and bid him at least a temporary good-bye. Among these visitors was Archie Butt, the President's Aide, who told of his call upon Taft in a letter to his mother, written that evening.

> "While I was in the office," he wrote, "he saw at least a dozen people on business and settled many questions. He is capable of a great amount of labor, but those of us who have served with him in the Philippines have seen this capacity for work almost overworked at times. I have seen him in the Philippines, lying flat on his back and suffering intense pain, transact business from his bed with a cheerfulness which many of those on top do not exercise in their comfortable offices. He thinks he is going to be elected, but does not feel at all certain. . . ." [1]

In order to get an opportunity to do the preliminary work of organizing the Republican forces for the campaign, Taft went to Virginia Hot Springs, after his retirement from the Cabinet. Here, instead of the helpful cooperation that he had expected to receive from the party leaders, he found that these men desired to make him the arbiter of their bickerings and petty quarrels. It exasperated him, but, knowing the political situation — that the Panic of 1907 had estranged many voters from the Republican ranks; that labor and the negroes were both opposing his

[1] "The Letters of Archie Butt," by Lawrence F. Abbott. Doubleday, Page & Company, New York, 1924.

election; that by reason of the extreme aggressiveness of Roosevelt's administration there were already two factions within the party — Taft felt that he should conciliate, instead of antagonizing, these conflicting elements. To have made them hostile would have resulted in a cleavage within the party ranks and made defeat inevitable. So he set about the arduous and uncertain task of harmonizing the discordant factions.

Upon learning of these quarrels, Roosevelt had told Taft, that he should take some forceful action to discipline the wranglers. But Taft, for these reasons, refused to do so. He did not care much about running for the Presidency, but, as he told Roosevelt, "I suppose the next four months will pass some way or other."

The President wrote sympathetically,

"Of course you are having a hard time; but, you old trump, surely you know how rare it is to find men who will give both disinterested and efficient service. There are a number of such disinterested men under me, whom I have appointed to office. You are the chief of them, and there are others, more or less like you."

On a hot August day in Cincinnati, Taft lucidly explained to the Notification Committee his interpretation of the Republican platform, in a speech of some twelve thousand words. That night he wrote Roosevelt,

"No matter what happens with regard to the election, the joy that we felt at our reception in Cincinnati was unalloyed. It was really a tremendous outpouring of citizens, without respect to party. The city was in gala attire, and there was not one discordant note to interfere with our pleasure. My speech was of such enormous length that I had to cut it in half in the delivery, and then it was very hot work getting through, both for the audience and for me, but the audience stood it well and seemed to receive it with great pleasure."

After his nomination to the Presidency and retirement from the Cabinet, Taft did not intend actively to campaign for the Presidency. He hoped that it would not be necessary to stump the country, and that it would be possible for him to remain in Cincinnati, where he could receive the many delegations that were expected to call upon him. This plan of action, however, did not conform to the intentions of his opponent, William Jennings Bryan.

Realizing that an active campaign was necessary and knowing that by attack he could force Taft to alter his original plan, the Commoner took the stump! With the slogan "Shall the people rule?", he began a vigorous campaign. Employing tariff revision and governmental ownership of the railroads as a premise upon which he based his argument and conclusion that the Republicans should be defeated and a Democrat elected, Bryan appealed to the people of the country. He charged that the Republican nominee was opposed to organized labor, and intolerantly said that the American people would never elect a Unitarian to the Presidency. At this point of the campaign the apparent indifference of the American public, as well as the attacks by Bryan, disturbed Taft. To arouse the people from their disinterested state and make them more enthusiastic, Taft countered by taking the stump. Characteristically, in his first addresses he revealed himself to Bryan.

Without fencing with words or agilely sidestepping the issues presented by the Commoner in many campaign speeches, Taft answered the charges, and defended his own judicial decisions and religious beliefs.

Bryan must soon have realized that he was wholly ignorant of the nature and character of his opponent. For Taft, by his sincerity, directness and fearlessness, in his campaign tour throughout the West and South, had adopted a course most disconcerting to the Democrat. In an address at Columbus, Taft defended his labor decisions, and at the same time, championed labor organizations, thus answering Bryan's charges that he was prejudiced against the laboring man.

He said,

"They say I am the 'father of injunctions in labor cases.' I have issued injunctions in labor cases, and I have done it because the rights of the plaintiff entitled him to an injunction, and when I am on the bench and enforcing the law, I enforce it and I do not make apologies for it. . . . When I am a judge in the bench in so far as I can decide cases according to the law and the facts, no matter whom it hurts. . . .

"Labor has the right to unite in organizations for the purpose of looking after the united interests of labor in its controversy with capital, because if it did not unite and was not permitted to unite, then it would be helpless. Laborers have the right not only to unite but to contribute funds, which in times when they wish to leave the employ of their employer, when they do not like his terms, may support their fellow-members. They have the right to appoint officers who shall control their action if they choose. They have the right to invite all other laborers to join with them in their controversy, and to withdraw if they

TAFT DURING HIS CAMPAIGN

choose from association with their employer; but they have not the right to injure the employer's property; they have not the right by what is called a 'secondary boycott' to invite a third person into the controversy who wishes to keep out, by threatening a boycott with him unless he assists in the fight. In this fight between employer and employee, they must fight it out between themselves, and they must not involve the rest of the community in it by a system of duress."

Despite the obvious justification of his conduct on the bench, Taft found that the labor leaders were still opposing him, and Democratic hopes of a Presidential victory in November were considerably brightened when Samuel Gompers, claiming that Taft was the representative of all the elements opposed to organized labor, came out for Bryan. The Democrats were jubilant. Their exultant feelings reached the point of ecstasy when, on the night of September the seventeenth, William Randolph Hearst, speaking at Columbus, on behalf of his newly-organized National Independence party, read a number of letters that had passed between John D. Archbold, a Vice President of the Standard Oil Company, and the Republican Senator, Joseph Benson Foraker.

In one of these letters Archbold had written,

"Responding to your favor of the twenty-fifth, it gives me pleasure to hand you herewith certificate of deposit for fifty thousand dollars, in accordance with our understanding. Your letter states the conditions correctly, and I trust that the transaction will be successfully consummated."

The letters were incriminating enough to reveal that Foraker, while a member of the United States Senate, had

215

been employed as counsel by the Standard Oil Company. To discredit Taft and shake public confidence in the Republican party, the Democrats seized upon his correspondence and endeavored to make political capital of it. Its effect might have been far-reaching had not the Republicans revealed the Murray Crane incident, showing that Taft had refused to bargain for Foraker's return to the Senate, and thus forestalled possible disastrous consequences.

In arranging the itinerary of his campaign tour, Taft had, contrary to the advice of his managers, included the South. He knew that he could not hope to break the Democratic hold on that section of the country, but he felt that he "had no right to ignore the Southern states any more than he had to ignore those states which seemed certain to give him the electoral vote." Taft resolved to visit many of the states which Bryan contemplated visiting or in which the Democratic nominees had already delivered campaign speeches. By this he hoped to stir up political interest. Hurrying through the West and South, he spoke to large crowds that gathered to greet him. His personality, his lucid and concisely arranged speeches, and his adherence to a definite set of policies, met with the approval of the audiences he addressed. Upon the completion of his tour, Taft, content with what he had done, viewed the apparent results with satisfaction.

Taft's campaign was singularly free from demagogic appeals. Not given to the practices of a charlatan, and with a dignity befitting one who was seeking the highest honor in the nation, he did not indulge in vulgar personalities, but restricted his addresses to cogent dissertations on legitimate political issues. Taft was not a great orator. He spoke well, but in the manner of a teacher. Swaying an audience was not his forte, but he could lead his listeners by sheer reasoning and logic. This was generally recognized, and President Roosevelt, when questioned, said "Taft has pitched this campaign on a higher plane than any campaign in the history of the country."

With the approach of election day the trend of public opinion in Taft's favor became more pronounced, and when Grover Cleveland's posthumous endorsement of Taft was announced and made public, there was no further doubt as to the final outcome of the campaign. The former Democratic President had written,

> "Personally and officially I have had the opportunity of knowing many things concerning Mr. Taft that were not a matter of general knowledge, and with a keen interest I have watched his large share in the conduct of our national affairs in very recent years. His excellence as a Federal Judge is something not to be underestimated or overemphasized. . . . His high ideals of honesty and of relative justice, his great capacity for severe labor, and his humorous wisdom in the face of the serious problems are attributes equally valuable and commendatory to a people seeking him to whom they may repose the trust of their collective interests while they turn their increased attention to their pressing individual demands."

Though practically all the political prognosticators had awarded the election to Taft, their auguries failed to foresee the overwhelming victory that he enjoyed. The complete results gave Taft three hundred and twenty-one elec-

217

toral votes and Bryan one hundred and sixty-one. The fact that Democratic Governors were elected in Ohio, Minnesota, North Dakota and Montana, while he, running far ahead of his party ticket, carried each of these states by a comfortable margin, was most gratifying.

CHAPTER XXIII

TAFT, ROOSEVELT, AND THE CABINET PROBLEM

TAFT much appreciated the assistance that President Roosevelt had rendered him in the election, and when the returns were in, his first letter was to the President. He wrote,

"I have just reached Hot Springs and have only now taken up my correspondence. The first letter that I wish to write is to you, because you have always been the chief agent in working out the present state of affairs and my selection and election are chiefly your work. You and my brother Charley made that possible which in all probability would not have occurred otherwise. I don't wish to be falsely modest in this, I know, as you have said to me when we have talked the matter over, that neither you nor he could probably have done the same thing with any other candidate, under the circumstances as they were, but that doesn't affect the fact as I have stated it, or my reason for feeling the deep gratitude which I do to you both for what has happened and the successful efforts which you have made, costing time and subjecting you to severe criticism, and, in some cases, the loss of personal friendships that you might have avoided.

"The great comfort that I have in being under such a heavy obligation to you is that I know that the easiest way for me to discharge it is to make a success of my administration and to justify you in your wish and effort to make me your successor.

"The election was not so much of a surprise to you as it was to me, judging from the remarkable forecast that you gave in a letter to Lodge. The tremendous popular majorities in New

York, New Jersey, Connecticut and Massachusetts were quite a surprise to me, and the large electoral vote was more, considerably, than I expected. The vote in New York City was the chief surprise. I attribute it to four causes; first, to the unanimity among business men, Republicans and Democrats, in their utter distrust of Bryan; second, the tremendous influence of the Catholic vote; third, the solid Jewish vote; and fourth, the breach in the ranks of labor made by Hearst's attack on Bryan, for I think that his influence through his papers is not to be measured by the votes cast for his candidates. . . .

"The phase of this election that seems most pronounced is the ability of the American people to scratch and defeat Governors by votes so widely different from those on the national ticket. . . . I am exceedingly anxious about the New York Senatorship. If you conclude that you don't want it in view of your absence and that you should prefer to wait until the Depew vacancy, I am exceedingly anxious that Root should secure it, if he will not remain in the Cabinet. He could be a tower of strength for me in the Senate. The personnel of the Senate is changing so rapidly that it has an important bearing on the entire administration.

"I am all right physically, but I am quite tired. The truth is I did not realize the strain I was going through at the time, and it is only now that the reaction has set in that I have a lassitude that needs open air exercise to overcome."

The people of the country failed to appreciate how sweeping had been Taft's victory over Bryan. They did not realize what an unqualified endorsement Taft had received when he carried Ohio, Minnesota, and Indiana, while Democratic Governors were elected in each of these states, or by the way in which he ran ahead of his own party ticket in the states of Michigan, Illinois, and New

York. Taft had won a great personal victory as well as a great victory for the Republican Party.

Almost immediately after the election Taft began the trying task of organizing his Cabinet. He wanted around him men with whom he could work to the best advantage, in his own way. To find them was not easy, for he was hampered by the exaggerated expectations of subordinates in the Republican ranks, who, believing him to be a sort of "crown prince," thought that he should carry on not only the policies but also the appointees, of his predecessor. Actuated by selfish motives and lacking sufficient political astuteness to realize the possible results of their actions, many of these men were pressing Roosevelt to intercede with Taft on their behalf. This Roosevelt refused to do, and, in fact, later stated in a letter that he had scrupulously avoided suggesting any appointees to any office.

Washington, however, was seething with the flotsam and jetsam, as well as the leaders, of the Republican party, all eagerly expecting rewards. In hopes of shaking off a considerable number of these job-hunters, Taft removed his headquarters to Augusta, Georgia, where, in the "Terrett Cottage," back of the Bon Air Hotel, he could receive visitors who called to urge the claims of their candidates for the Cabinet and where he could exercise daily by playing golf.

Taft's stay in Augusta was almost as trying as if he had remained in Washington, for the "job-hounds" who had made his life unbearable in the capital followed him to his new headquarters. They gathered, small groups of grave, important-appearing men, on the front porch of the hotel, while only a few yards away in his small cottage drawing-room, Taft was receiving his visitors and listening, without comment, to what they had to say concerning the capabilities of the man whose appointment they were soliciting. Almost without exception, these visitors would leave the President-elect with the conviction that Taft knew more concerning the qualifications of their candidates than they themselves possessed. Generally this was true, for Taft, with his customary forethought and thoroughness, had sent innumerable confidential inquiries to various friends and acquaintances in order to gain complete information concerning Cabinet possibilities. When, in early January, Henry Cabot Lodge came from Washington to Augusta to call upon him, Taft was busy, not only with Cabinet-making and appointments, but also in fulfilling engagements—eating possums and tasting innumerable cakes presented to him by visiting delegations as tokens of esteem.

Upon his return to Washington, Lodge, in reporting to the President, told Roosevelt that he had been in Augusta for two whole days before he had been able to see the President-elect alone. That the Massachusetts Senator was extremely selfish, self-centered, and without any great love for Taft, Roosevelt should have known. But his great fondness for Lodge made him short-sighted, and when the Senator told him that "not one of the present Cabinet would remain unless it be Meyer, and he would remain only through outside pressure. . . . That it was evidently the intention to get rid of every person who might keep President Taft in touch with the Roosevelt influence," [1] he became somewhat concerned, but not greatly worried, for he had the utmost confidence in Taft to do what he believed was best for his own administration.

Thus a campaign of detraction and vilification was begun. The President already knew that Taft did not intend asking Newberry, Cortelyou, and Bonaparte to serve in his cabinet, and concluded after his last conversation with Taft, shortly before the latter departed for Augusta, that neither Garfield or Straus were to be among Taft's constitutional advisers. Roosevelt must have felt that Lodge had misconstrued Taft's words, for he knew that George von L. Meyer was to be reappointed, and that there was also a possibility of Wilson's being asked to serve again. This must have been the case, for in writing Taft shortly after Lodge's visit and report, the President expressed himself as being "exceedingly pleased at the good news about Meyer," and asked whether Taft wanted him to notify those Cabinet members that they were not to remain during the coming administration.

Taft believed that he, not Roosevelt, should notify the members of Roosevelt's cabinet whom he did not expect to reappoint, although it is difficult, at this date, to perceive what prescriptive right they possessed to retain their positions. He had tried to free himself from the personal aspects of the situation, which were somewhat embarrassing in view of the fact that he had belonged to the same Cabinet himself. He wrote accordingly to Garfield, Straus,

---

[1] "The Letters of Archie Butt," by Lawrence F. Abbott. Doubleday, Page & Company, New York, 1924.

Cortelyou, Newberry and Bonaparte. At this time he was still uncertain about General Luke Wright, who had succeeded him as Secretary of War. Although he felt a strong comradeship for Wright, on account of their work together in the Philippines, he believed that a younger and more aggressive man should take over the Portfolio of War. Taft felt that the choice of a Cabinet was like "the making of a picture puzzle,"—he would have to fit the parts in to meet the necessities and complete a perfect whole. Acting as judicially as possible, he surveyed the field of possibilities and culled from numerous prospects the best possible talent.

Believing that the circumstances under which he was entering upon the duties of his administration were quite unlike those of the retiring President, Taft reasoned that the composition of his Cabinet should be somewhat different. So, in making his selections, he did so with a view to the changing state of the reforms which Roosevelt had initiated and which he must carry on. When he left for Panama, in early 1909, he had not definitely made up his mind, and it was not until after his return from the Isthmus that the new Cabinet really took form.

He had gone to the Canal Zone at the urgent request of Roosevelt. The Canal had been the most exacting and the most prolonged of all the responsibilities with which the retiring President had been burdened, and was evidently to be an equal ordeal for Taft. Realizing this, Roosevelt had urged Taft to visit the Canal Zone, once again, before assuming his duties as President. In this journey to Panama, Taft fully informed himself as to the progress that had

been made on the Canal, the obstacles that had been encountered and the immediate needs of the engineers. At
this time there were current rumors of a breach of the
friendly relations between Taft and Roosevelt. They were
all false. There was not the slightest disagreement between
the two men. In point of fact, Taft had submitted to Roosevelt the original draft of his proposed inaugural address,
and Roosevelt had expressed himself as being delighted
with it, saying, "I can not imagine a better inaugural, and
it marks just exactly what your administration will be."
Later, when Taft made some additions to the speech, he
referred these also to the President, who again had "no
suggestions to make."

In order to make as emphatic as possible the refutation
of any suggestion of a quarrel between the President and
his successor, President and Mrs. Roosevelt invited President-elect and Mrs. Taft to be their guests for dinner, and
to spend at the White House the night before the Taft
inaugural. The President-elect, welcoming the opportunity
of contradicting these false reports by staying at the White
House, accepted the Roosevelts' invitation.

The weather on the third of March was stormy, and
although forecasts predicted that it might clear for the
inaugural, the storm instead grew worse that night. And
when morning came, Washington was white with snow
and penetratingly cold. The trees gleamed like ghosts, their
limbs breaking and falling under the weight of the ice
which encased them, and snow still fell. Taft, rising early,
went downstairs to the great hall of the White House and
found the President awaiting him there.

"Well, Will," Roosevelt said, "The storm will soon be over. It isn't a regular storm. It's nature's echo of Senator Rayner's denunciation of me. As soon as I am out where I can do no further harm to the Constitution, it will cease."

"You're wrong," responded Taft. "It is my storm. I always said it would be a cold day when I got to be President of the United States." [1]

At twelve noon, Taft was sworn in as President of the United States. The inclement weather did not permit an outdoor inaugural, and the oath of office was administered in the Senate Chamber before a brilliant and colorful assembly.

Roosevelt left Washington immediately after the inaugural ceremony, and, a little over two weeks later, sailed from New York on his African trip. Taft sent the former President a boat letter in which he said:

"If I followed my impulse, I should still say 'My dear Mr. President.' I cannot overcome the habit. When I am addressed as 'Mr. President,' I turn to see whether you are not at my elbow. When I read in the newspapers of a conference between the Speaker and the President, or between Senator Aldrich and the President, I wonder what the subject of the conference was, and can hardly identify the report with the fact that I had had a talk with the two gentlemen. . . .

". . . Many questions have arisen since the inauguration with respect to which I should have liked to have consulted you, but I have foreborne to interrupt your well-earned quiet and to take up your time when it must have been so much occupied with preparations for your long trip. . . .

"I have no doubt that when you return you will find me

[1] "Recollections of Full Years," by Helon Herron Taft. Dodd, Mead & Company. New York, 1914.

very much under suspicion by our friends in the West. Indeed, I think I am already so, because I was not disposed to countenance an insurrection of thirty men against one hundred and eighty outside the caucus. I knew how this would be regarded, but I also knew that unless I sat steady in the boat, and did what I could to help Cannon and the great majority of the Republicans stand solid, I should make a capital error in the beginning of my administration in alienating the good will of these without whom I can do nothing to carry through the legislation to which the party and I are pledged. Cannon and Aldrich have promised to stand by the party platform and to follow my lead. They did so for you in the first Congress of your administration and this is the first Congress of mine. Of course, I have not the prestige which you had or the popular support in any such measure as you had, to enable you to put through the legislation which was so remarkable in your first Congress; but I am not attempting quite as much as you did then, and I am hopeful that what I do offer will be accepted and put through. . . .

"I want you to know that I do nothing in my work in the Executive office without considering what you would do under the same circumstances and without having in a sense a mental talk with you over the pros and cons of the situation. I have not the facility for educating the public as you had through talks with correspondents, and so I fear that a large part of the public will feel as though I had fallen away from your ideals; but you know me better and will understand that I am still working away on the same old plan and hope to realize in some measure the results that we both hold valuable and worth striving for."

Just before the boat sailed, on the twenty-third of March, 1909, Roosevelt wired Taft, "Am deeply touched by your gift, and even more by your letter. Greatly appreciate it. Everything will surely turn out all right, old man."

Taft told Jacob Schmidlapp of Cincinnati that, in forming his Cabinet he must "get the best men. I mean by that I must get the men with the best qualifications for the place." In making his appointments he followed this idea, exercising the greatest care and discrimination. Of Roosevelt's cabinet he retained George von L. Meyer of Massachusetts, Roosevelt's Postmaster General, and James Wilson of Iowa, who had been serving efficiently for twelve years, in the respective positions of Secretary of the Navy and Secretary of Agriculture. Philander C. Knox, a prominent Pittsburgh lawyer and United States Senator from Pennsylvania, who had served capably in the cabinets of McKinley and Roosevelt, succeeded Root as Secretary of State. For the Interior Portfolio, Taft selected Richard Ballinger, a distinguished Western lawyer and former mayor of Seattle. Two Democrats, Jacob N. Dickinson of Tennessee, a noted Southern railroad attorney, and Franklin MacVeagh of Illinois, were chosen for the War and Treasury Departments. Charles Nagel of Missouri became Secretary of Commerce and Labor, George W. Wickersham of New York was made Attorney General, and Frank H. Hitchcock of Massachusetts, Postmaster General.

Almost immediately a storm of denunciation broke over Taft's head. Charging him with a breach of faith in failing to reappoint Wright, Straus and Garfield, the malcontents assailed Taft, concentrating their displeasure on these appointments. In this they were aided by the press which, with screaming headlines, such as, *"Taft Has Surrounded*

228

Himself With Corporation Attorneys," and *"Taft Has Made Studied Effort To Repudiate Things Predecessor Stood For,"* began to lay the foundation for the distrust with which the administration was viewed.

Taft knew that in succeeding Roosevelt as President he was undertaking a difficult task. He was under no illusions as to the likelihood of his administration being a popular one, for the opponents of the President had determined to check what they considered, on Roosevelt's part, to be an over-reaching ambition, and there had ensued a series of savage assaults and drastic attacks. Consequently, it had become a day of "big words and small deeds." The Republican party was split, a sharp division having been created between the reactionaries and the insurgents within its ranks.

This legacy was bequeathed by Roosevelt to his successor, and Roosevelt himself thus testifies to it in his "Autobiography."

"On these great moral issues the Republican party was right, and the men who were opposed to it and who claimed to be radicals and their allies among the sentimentalists, were utterly and hopelessly wrong. This had, regrettably but perhaps inevitably, tended to throw the party into the hands not merely of the conservatives but of the reactionaries; of men who, sometimes for personal and improper reasons, but more often with entire sincerity and uprightness of purpose, distrusted everything that was progressive and dreaded radicalism. These men still from force of habit applauded what Lincoln had done in the way of radical dealing with the abuses of his day; but they did not apply the spirit in which Lincoln had worked to the abuses of their own day. Both Houses of Congress were controlled by these men. Their leaders in the Senate were Messrs. Aldrich and Hale. The Speaker of the House . . . Mr. Cannon, who, although widely different from Senator Aldrich in matters of detail, represented the same type of public sentiment. There were many points on which I agreed with Mr. Cannon and Mr. Aldrich, and some points on which I agreed with Mr. Hale. I made a resolute effort to get on with all three and with their followers, and I have no question that they made an equally resolute effort to get on with me. We succeeded in working together, although with increasing friction, for some years, I pushing forward and they hanging back. Gradually, however, I was forced to abandon the effort to persuade them to come my way, and then I achieved results only by appealing over the heads of the Senate and House leaders to the people, who were the master of both of us.

"I continued in this way to get results until almost the close of my administration; and, the Republican party became once more the progressive and, indeed, the fairly radical progressive party of the nation. When my successor was chosen, however, the leaders of the House and Senate, or most of them, felt that it was safe to come to a break with me, and the last or short session of Congress held between the election of my successor and his inauguration, four months later, saw a series of contests between the majorities in the two Houses of Congress and myself—quite as bitter as if they and I belonged to opposite political parties. However, I held my own. I was not able to push through the legislation I desired during those four months, but I was able to prevent them doing anything I did not desire, or undoing anything that I had already succeeded in getting done." [1]

This schism had been due entirely to Roosevelt's obstinacy. For although Roosevelt possessed great popularity,

[1] "Theodore Roosevelt, An Autobiography." Charles Scribner's Sons, New York, 1919.

it was a personal as distinguished from a political one. And by his many-sided nature, which astounded one moment and distressed the next, he had created these antagonisms within the Republican ranks and had also caused a bitterly hostile feeling toward the Executive and any program that he might advocate.

This feeling of antagonism on the part of Congress, toward the President, is reflected in the legislative measures enacted throughout Roosevelt's last administration, for his record as President, while not barren of achievement, is notable for the enactment of no great constructive legislation.

So it was with party disaster almost inevitable, that Taft assumed his duties as President of the United States.

CHAPTER XXIV

THE PAYNE-ALDRICH TARIFF ACT

Taft went to work immediately after his inauguration on that cold, sleety March day. The Republican platform of 1908 committed the party to a revision of the tariff, and Taft called a special session of Congress to convene on the fifteenth of March, 1909, to fulfill that pledge. During Roosevelt's administration a very decided effort had been made to force the President's hand on a revision of the tariff, but he had temporized. On the other hand, as far back as 1906, in his speech at Bath, Taft had declared himself in favor of revision. Again in 1908, he had made known his views when the Ohio Republican platform, which was drawn at his instance, declared in favor of revision and fixed the rule which should govern such proceedings.

Taft was only too well aware that he ran a risk of jeopardizing his entire legislative program by forcing the tariff issue, but he felt that the party should comply with its platform promises. What he hoped to secure was the enactment of a Bill to contain "within itself a provision for a permanent Tariff Commission, which could make its investigations and report each year the facts respecting products whose schedules should be increased or decreased."

Protectionist that he was, he proposed that the Bill should look to

232

"the reduction in the cost of production of articles behind the tariff wall by the operation of competition within the country, relying upon the greater ingenuity of American inventors, the greater enterprise of American business men, and the greater intelligence of American labor to effect this reduction in cost. . . . And that it was wise to reduce excessive rates in order to prevent the temptation of those engaged in making the articles thus protected, from attempting to monopolize the market and the manufacturer in this country from controlling the prices and taking advantage of the rates. . . ."

In the history of tariff legislation no committee of Congress ever devoted more labor to the preparation of a customs act. Since the tenth of November, a few days after Taft's election, the Republican members of the Ways and Means Committee had been in constant session, even on occasional evenings and Sundays, preparing this Bill.

After some hesitation, Taft had conferred with Cannon as Roosevelt had directed him to do. For the former President had told him that "it would of course be well if there was some first class men to put in his place as Speaker. But it is evident that four-fifths of the Republicans want Cannon, and I do not believe that it would be well to have him in a position of the sullen and hostile floor leader bound to bring your administration to grief, even though you were able to put someone else in as Speaker."

This interview with Cannon had been eminently satisfactory. The Speaker assured the President of his complete sympathy, and that he would help to carry out the party platform. Feeling that the temper of Congress was such that if the President intervened and sought to dictate con-

233

cerning the Tariff Bill he might bring disaster to his entire program of legislation, Cannon advised Taft not to interfere until the Bill had gone to conference. Representative Sereno Payne, Chairman of the Ways and Means Committee of the House of Representatives, and Senator Aldrich, Chairman of the Senate Committee on Finance, were of the same opinion. The three of them assured the President that they would confer with him whenever he desired it, and further agreed to make a Bill which would appeal, not only to the party, but to the country as well.

In deciding to follow the suggestions of Payne, Cannon and Aldrich, Taft felt that while he could not hope to have all of his proposals accepted, he would, nevertheless, by his willingness to coöperate with the legislative leaders, secure the enactment of a Tariff Act which would be substantially in compliance with the party platform and effect a reduction of the existing exorbitant duties. To Roosevelt's satellites, naturally distrustful of course, these conferences of Taft with Payne, Cannon and Aldrich appeared merely to confirm their suspicions that the President was consorting with the reactionaries, and departing from the policies of his predecessor. And when Congress convened for the short session, this group, without taking into consideration the circumstances under which Taft was working, joined the party insurgents in their campaign of criticism.

Organizing for this short session, the House of Representatives elected Joseph G. Cannon Speaker for the fourth consecutive time. The President, pointing out in his message to Congress the immediate necessity of a revision of the customs act, explained that the expenditures of the

234

Government exceeded the income and asked for a larger revenue although he said that he expected, at the same time, a revision downward. On the day following the reading of Taft's message, Representative Payne introduced the new Tariff Bill, which in general proposed to reduce the tariff duties. Exceptions were made, however, in the case of luxuries, on which the tax was increased.

Almost immediately came murmurs of dissatisfaction. The placing of hides on the free list alienated the West and Southwest, where it was said that this provision would surely destroy the cattle industry. The lumber interests insisted that the lumber tax remain the same, instead of being reduced as the Bill proposed. The oil and coal companies also complained because their products had been put on the free list. And the omnipresent influences that always play a part in the making of a Tariff Act were all on hand. For home political consumption, many Congressmen, although openly disapproving of certain features of the proposed Act and despite the detriment that it would cause to the nation as a whole, voted to increase the duties on many of the items. During the months that the Bill was in debate there was the usual trading and reciprocal voting.

It was not an easy task for Taft to sit back and watch the efforts of the trusts, who, in order to perpetuate their own existence, sought to increase the already exorbitant duties on their products. Nor did he remain silent. When the lumber interests tried to get the President to agree not to interfere with the lumber schedule, Taft told the senators who were its protagonists, that unless the reduction he demanded was affected he would veto the Tariff Act.

When the House Bill was sent to the Senate Taft was "convinced that the House committee, with Payne at its head, had gone to work conscientiously to carry out the plank of the platform. . . . The Payne Bill was a genuine effort in the right direction, and that while the step was not so great as I would have been glad to take, it contains much of what I approve." Although this committee had increased the tax on hosiery and gloves, and had made no reduction on wool because of the powerful wool lobby, they had, nevertheless, reduced the lumber tax, placed many articles on the free list, and reduced the duties on quite a large number of other items.

In the Senate the Bill was referred to the Finance Committee, where, under the guiding hand of Senator Nelson Aldrich, it was remolded. Immediately, the insurgent element of that body, whose battle-cry had become "the rights of the ultimate consumer," began their onslaught on the bill. Senator Dolliver of Iowa, charging that the wool and cotton schedules were higher than those of the Dingley Law, demanded that Taft veto the Bill. His colleague Cummins, after assuring Taft that he would applaud the President upon the floor of the Senate for his efforts, about-faced and accused Aldrich of "keeping promises to the ear and breaking them as to the hope." The other insurgents labeled the Act "a farce" and "an abomination."

While the Bill was in the Senate, Taft wrote his brother, Horace,

"It is a hot Sunday afternoon and with a kimono, and looking like a Chinese idol, I am walking my room dictating to you. I am doing it for the purpose not alone of informing you,

236

but of putting in permanent form, so to speak, my state of mind at the present moment as to the political situation. As you know, the Republican convention declared in favor of the tariff. I had declared my views in favor of this as long ago as 1906 in my speech at Bath, Maine, and had reiterated this expression of view when opportunity offered. At my instance the Ohio platform was drawn declaring in favor of a revision of the tariff and fixing the rule which should obtain in doing so, and the national Convention followed that plan. Now, the principles of the protective theory—if such a free trader as you will admit there are any principles in protection—look to the reduction in the cost of production of articles protected behind the tariff wall by the operation of competition within the country, relying upon the greater ingenuity of American inventors, the greater enterprise of American business-men and the greater intelligence of American labor to effect this reduction in cost, therefore, I said that as eleven years had elapsed since the Dingley Bill had passed, and great changes had taken place in the conditions affecting the cost of production, it was reasonable to infer that quite a large number of the schedules could be reduced; that the rates under them had become excessive; and that it was wise to reduce excessive rates in order to prevent the temptation of those engaged in making the articles thus protected, from attempting to monopolize the market and the manufacturer in this country from controlling the prices and taking advantage of the rates. That was my position and it is still. I said so in the canvass and I have not changed my views. . . .

". . . This carries me back to the time between my election and my inauguration when I made an investigation into the question whether Cannon could be beaten, and I found that he could not be beaten in a caucus vote. I therefore gave up any hope of doing so or any effort to do so. In fact, I received some most urgent telegrams and letters from Mr. Roosevelt

237

himself calling me to Washington, as I did in December, the first message from the White House was to see Cannon at once. I did see Cannon. I had a most satisfactory talk with him, in which he said that he was entirely in sympathy with my effort to carry out the pledges of the Chicago platform, and that he would assist me as loyally as possible. . . ."

After debate in the Senate, the Bill was ready for the Conference Committee. Here, for the first time, Cannon did not play square with the President. In naming the House members of that committee, he placed four high tariff men on it. This proved a boomerang against the higher tariff, however, because the members of the House, feeling that they had been tricked, supported those members of the committee who fought for lower duties.

Their feeling that they had been tricked also assisted Taft in his efforts to secure the enactment of his program, which included free hides, reduced tariff on boots and shoes, on iron ore, and quite considerably on cotton. The Bill was finally passed on the fifth of August, 1909, and Taft signed it that same afternoon. He felt that the result, on the whole, was a victory for him. He realized that the Payne-Aldrich Act was not perfect, but he felt that it was the best obtainable under the circumstances. It did, in effect, carry out the Republican platform pledges, for the rates were lower, and by its provisions a Tariff Board, "to secure information to assist the President in the discharge of his duties," had been created.

Vetoing the Bill, which would have been a spectacular gesture and in line with the demands of the Progressives, would have gained Taft, at best, only a temporary popularity. At the same time such a procedure would have been foolhardy for it would have increased the abuses of monopoly and jeopardized the President's position with the majority in his own party. The insurgents in Congress, reflecting the sentiment of the states west of the Mississippi River, beginning with Minnesota and running down to Kansas, denounced Taft for not breaking with the conservative element of his party and standing or falling on the low tariff issue.

Desirous of appealing to the people of the western states for support, Taft determined to make a speaking tour through those states, and within a month after he had signed the Payne-Aldrich Act, was on his way West. His first address was scheduled for Winona, Minnesota. This city was the residence of Representative Tawney, the sole member of the entire Minnesota delegation to vote for the Tariff Act. After praising Tawney to the large crowd which had gathered, Taft defended the Tariff Bill, by saying,

"Now, the promise of the Republican platform was not to revise everything downward, and in the speeches which have been taken as interpreting that platform which I made in the campaign, I did not promise that everything should go downward. What I promised was, that there should be many decreases, and that in some things increases would be found to be necessary; but that on the whole I conceived that the change of conditions would make the revision necessarily downward, and that, I contend, under the showing which I have made, has been the result of the Payne Bill.

"I did not agree nor did the Republican party agree, that we should reduce rates to such a point as to reduce prices by the introduction of foreign competition. This is what the free traders desire. . . . To repeat the statement with which I opened this speech, the proposition of the Republican party was to reduce rates so as to maintain a difference between the cost of production abroad and the cost of production here, insuring a reasonable profit to the manufacturer on all articles produced in this country. . . .

"On the whole, therefore, I am bound to say that I think the Payne-Tariff Bill is the best tariff bill that the Republican party ever passed; that in it the party has conceded the necessity for following the changed conditions and reducing tariff rates accordingly. This is a substantial achievement in the direction of lower tariffs and downward revision, and it ought to be accepted as such. . . .

"If the country desires free trade, and the country desires a revenue tariff and wishes the manufacturers all over the country to go out of business, and to have cheaper prices at the expense of the sacrifice of many of our manufacturing interests, then it ought to say so and put the Democratic party in power, if it thinks that party can be trusted to carry out any affirmative policy in favor of a revenue tariff."

Taft's use of the superlative instead of the comparative in describing the Payne-Aldrich Act and his praise of Tawney further alienated the West and widened the schism within the Republican ranks. Although unfortunate, perhaps, in his phraseology, he was nevertheless accurate in his statements. For the Payne-Aldrich Tariff Act was the best tariff act ever passed by the Republican Party up to that time.

The Act as finally passed contained six hundred and fifty-four decreases and two hundred and twenty increases; eleven hundred and fifty items on the dutiable list were left unchanged. It included a maximum and minimum tariff proviso, and provided for a Tariff Board. It gave free trade to the Philippines. Its provisions included a corporation tax of one per cent on the net income of corporations whose net earnings exceeded five thousand dollars.

Four years later during the campaign of 1912, Taft, justifying his signing of the Payne-Aldrich Act, explained in detail his reasons for so doing:

"The Payne-Aldrich Bill I approved, because, above all, it provided the machinery by which alone a just and intelligent revision of the tariff could be effected—a Tariff Board, which without political bias and free from political pressure, would ascertain those facts essential to any intelligent adjustment of the rates of duty; because it clothed the Executive with power, by means of maximum and minimum rates, to compel just treatment from foreign nations of American products and exports; because it imposed a tax on profits of corporations that at once gave to the government an insight into the operations of these important instrumentalities of business, which it had in no other way been able to obtain, and because it provided the machinery whereby increased revenues could be collected with facility in face of an emergency; because it granted to the Filipinos that measure of justice to which the nation stood pledged and which was essential to their prosperity; and, finally, because it effected a material reduction in the rates of duty — not so much of a reduction as I desired, but as much as I believe could be secured without the aid of that machinery, the Tariff Board, which it created."

CHAPTER XXV

BALLINGER AND PINCHOT

THE American Government had a two-fold purpose in disposing of its undeveloped western and territorial lands. By these sales, revenue was raised and arid tracts of land, which otherwise probably would have remained barren wastes, were developed. But many abuses, which grew into the proportions of a national scandal, had followed in the wake of many of these grants. Whereupon President Roosevelt, somewhat alarmed at the ease with which these evils had been propagated, inaugurated a policy of staying further grants, and in some instances of withdrawing from private hands certain of the lands already granted, although he had no legal authority for his actions. From these beginnings developed the conservation movement, the leading spirit of which was the Chief Forester in the Department of Agriculture, Gifford Pinchot, who led and fostered the movement with true missionary zeal. He was a man of apparently inexhaustible energy and boundless enthusiasm, who had been able to persuade Roosevelt that his mission was approved by the public.

Roosevelt, however, while coöperating with Pinchot in his efforts to deter speculators and great corporations from sequestering the public domain and to restore it to national ownership, had, at the same time, been encouraging private capital to develop the limitless possibilities Alaska afforded. Hoping to develop the natural resources of that territory, he had interested among others George W. Perkins, a representative of the Morgan interests, and shortly afterward the Alaska Syndicate, a Morgan company, came into being. This syndicate had acquired rich copper mines, upon beginning its operations, and, desiring further to extend its holdings, sought to buy the "Cunningham Coal Lands." These lands were named for Clarence Cunningham, who had gone to Alaska in February, 1903, at the instance of certain wealthy American investors, and under the general mining laws of that territory, located some thirty-three claims to rich coal land in the Bering River district. Later learning that, by reason of a special law, the validity of these locations might be contested, Cunningham had relocated the entire group of claims in the summer of 1904. H. K. Love, a special agent of the General Land Office of the department of the Interior, subsequently approved all these locations.

The General Land Office, at this time, urgently needed overhauling and rebuilding, if President Roosevelt were to carry his plan of conservation into effect. When Roosevelt appointed James Garfield Secretary of the Interior, the latter proposed that Richard Ballinger of Seattle, a former fellow-student of his at Williams College, be made Commissioner of that office. Garfield assured the President that Ballinger was especially well-qualified to undertake this job of reorganization. Thereupon Roosevelt offered the post to the Seattle lawyer, who first declined it, but after some persuasion yielded and agreed to accept.

In reorganizing the General Land Office, Ballinger

found conditions that bordered upon chaos. He learned that there were any number of claims which had been located, but that had not been "clear-listed," a condition precedent to the issuing of a patent of deed to the claimant. The Cunningham claims were among these locations, and after carefully scrutinizing the file in that matter and finding no reason why these claims should not be "clear-listed," Ballinger, without any personal knowledge of the claim and using Love's report as a basis, ordered the Chief of the Field Service, a Mr. Schwartz, to notify Louis Glavis, a young chief of the field division in charge of the territory of Alaska, of his decision. Within a few days after he had been informed of the Secretary's intentions, Glavis wired, "Coal entries mentioned in your letter should not be clear-listed." Ballinger then revoked the listing. Shortly afterward, on the fourth of March, 1908, he resigned to resume his law practice. Both President Roosevelt and Secretary Garfield praised Ballinger's efficiency and he was complimented generally upon the able manner in which he had reorganized the General Land Office. During the year that elapsed between Ballinger's resignation and Taft becoming President, nothing had been done on the Cunningham claims.

Taft decided not to retain James R. Garfield as Secretary of the Interior, and, on the twenty-second of January, 1909, wrote him,

"The most painful duty I have to perform is the selection of a Cabinet for my own administration. The circumstances under which I enter upon the duties of a new administration are quite different from those of a retiring administration, and they require that the complexion of the new Cabinet should be somewhat different from the old because of a difference in function that the new administration is to perform in carrying out the policies of the old, as I explained in my letter of acceptance. It means that I cannot retain in my Cabinet a good many who served Mr. Roosevelt in that capacity, although I have for them a warmth of affection and a great respect. . . . The truth is that in the selection of my Cabinet I have tried to act as judicially as possible and to free myself altogether from the personal aspect, which has embarrassed me not only with respect to you, but with respect to the members of the body of which we both formed a part."

Obviously, Garfield, who was politically ambitious, must have felt humiliated and greatly disappointed upon learning that he was not to be retained in the Cabinet. His later actions prove this, for, although he was without legal authority for any such act, he withdrew from entry, in February, 1909, hundreds of thousands of acres of land as waterpower sites. Very possibly this procedure was justifiable; but Garfield retired without mentioning these withdrawals to his successor, Ballinger, and that was unpardonable. It reeks of a malevolence which is emphasized by later events, for surely no motive, except ill-will, could have impelled Garfield to obtrude himself into the Pinchot-Ballinger controversy.

With his appointment by Taft as Secretary of the Interior, Ballinger returned to Washington. He found these wholesale withdrawals made by Garfield, and because Congress had passed a law that the public land should be open to entry, he considered it beyond the power of any administrative official to withdraw them by Executive order, and therefore cancelled the withdrawals made by his predecessor. Taft agreed with him. Ballinger also found that despite the urgent and repeated efforts of his superiors in the Department of the Interior to have him complete his Alaskan investigation, Glavis still procrastinated and had failed to make a field survey of the claims.

Ballinger immediately directed the field clerk to submit a complete report in these cases. After a month, during which Glavis continued to do nothing, Ballinger notified the Land Office Agent that his investigations would have to be completed within sixty days. At the end of that time, Glavis, without presenting a single reason for the delay, requested a further extension of sixty days, which was denied him. Appealing to the Forest Service of the Department of Agriculture, Glavis found the Chief Forester, Gifford Pinchot, not only ready but eager to help. Pinchot intervened and had final action on the Cunningham claims postponed until October.

In the meantime, on the sixth of August, 1909, Glavis met and talked with Pinchot in Spokane. A few days later the Chief Forester gave him a letter to President Taft, in which Pinchot stated that "by Mr. Ballinger's action in restoring water powers sites, which had been withdrawn by Secretary Garfield, valuable lands containing power sites had passed from the government." And in order to give greater credence to Glavis's story, Pinchot wrote that he had known Mr. Glavis for a number of years, although later events showed this statement to be inaccurate.

On August eighteenth, Glavis presented his complaint against Secretary Ballinger to President Taft at the summer White House in Beverly, Massachusetts. He told Taft that he had discovered, in the course of his official duties, certain facts that indicated a conspiracy to rob the United States of large tracts of valuable coal lands and other lands in the public domain. Directed to be more specific, Glavis charged Secretary Ballinger with maladministration of the public lands under his control. The President summoned Ballinger to answer Glavis' charges, and the Secretary delivered his statement to Taft on the sixth of September. A week later the President wrote Ballinger that he had examined the documentary evidence most carefully, and had concluded that the charges were unfounded. In this letter he directed the dismissal of Glavis from the Government service.

Because of the public interest in conservation, Congress was compelled to act. At Ballinger's request, a resolution to appoint a committee to inquire into Glavis' charges, and to investigate the Department of the Interior, was being debated in the Senate when Senator Dolliver took the floor. He read a letter which he had received from Gifford Pinchot, in which the Chief Forester referred to Louis Glavis as "the most vigorous defender of the people's interests." The letter continued by saying that he (Pinchot) had prepared, through his assistants in the Chief Forester's office of the Department of Agriculture, a systematic and organized publicity campaign to discredit the Secretary of the Interior, and that "having violated a rule of propriety as between the Departments, they deserved and had received a reprimand," but Pinchot went on to say that the motive of his subordinates was praiseworthy. In concluding, he de-

247

plored the dismissal of Glavis from the field service, and implied that President Taft had taken action under "a mistaken impression of the facts."

Nor did Pinchot stop with that, for his egoism and crusader spirit had apparently overcome his better judgment. Addressing the University Club in New York city in early January, 1910, he said,

> "The great conflict now being fought is to decide for whose benefit our natural resources are to be conserved; whether for the benefit of the many, or the use and profit of the few."

He claimed it to be an "honorable distinction" of the Forestry service that

> "it has been more constantly, more violently and more bitterly attacked than any government bureau. These attacks have increased in violence and bitterness just in proportion as the service has offered effective opposition to predatory wealth.
> "There is no other question before us that begins to be so important . . . as the great questions between the special interests and equal opportunity, between privileges of the few and rights of the many, between government by men for human welfare and government by money for profit, between the men who stand for Roosevelt's policies and the men who stand against them. That is the essence of the conservation problem today. . . ."

By forwarding this letter to Senator Dolliver to be read on the floor of the Senate, Pinchot had made his dismissal from the Forestry service inevitable. Soon afterward, Taft, writing to the Chief Forester to discharge him from the Government service, said,

"Your letter was in effect an improper appeal to Congress and the public to excuse in advance the guilt of your subordinates before I could act and against my decision in the Glavis case. . . . By your own conduct you have destroyed your usefulness as a helpful subordinate."

By a joint resolution of Congress, a joint committee of the two houses was appointed. Charges of delinquency in office were then preferred against Secretary Ballinger by Louis Glavis and Gifford Pinchot, in a formal written statement prepared and presented to the committee by Pinchot. It alleged that Ballinger had been untrue and unfaithful to the conservation policy inaugurated by President Roosevelt, and that he was an "enemy of the policy of conservation." Although Pinchot had formerly told Senator Lodge that the legislation in regard to conservation which Ballinger had recommended far exceeded his own recommendations, he asserted that the interests of the people were not safe in the Secretary's hands, and that Ballinger had deceived and betrayed the President.

When this committee began its sessions, Louis D. Brandeis of Boston, and Joseph B. Cotton of New York, appeared as counsel for Glavis. Gifford Pinchot retained George W. Pepper of Philadelphia. Ballinger was not represented by an attorney at the beginning of the proceedings, but after the proceedings had continued for a few days, Mr. John J. Vertrees appeared on his behalf. Glavis was the first witness, and when questioned as to the charges he wished to prefer against Ballinger, replied that he did not believe the Secretary guilty of corruption as was popularly supposed, but that he proposed to show a "sequence of events" which indicated impropriety on the part of Mr. Ballinger.

An hour's questioning, instead of eliciting the facts, resulted only in confusion, and finally a member of the committee suggested that counsel for Glavis outline what the critic of the Department of the Interior proposed to prove. This was done. Then, after a few preliminary questions, Senator Nelson asked,

"What, if anything, do you claim to have been amiss in the administration of the public lands?"

Glavis, who talked with a slight lisp and now appeared somewhat nervous, replied that he could not answer that question briefly.

"Go ahead and tell us in your own way," directed Nelson.

Glavis was questioned for days, but his evidence failed to substantiate any of the charges he made. He had a predilection "to avoid direct answers, to make insinuations, to reiterate, explain and amplify, generally leading the committee into collateral and irrelevant channels."

Gifford Pinchot followed Glavis to the stand. When questioning began as to the letter that Pinchot had sent Senator Dolliver, Senator Nelson adjourned the hearing until Secretary of Agriculture Wilson, who had signified his desire to be present when Pinchot testified, could be located. After Wilson had arrived, Pinchot, resuming, said, "We" (Wilson and himself) "discussed at some length the right of Senator Dolliver to get information from me. . . . I believed I had his consent."

His request for an opportunity to testify being granted,

Secretary Wilson refuted Pinchot's version of their conference by saying, "He never got my consent to send that
letter to the Senate. . . . Mr. Pinchot didn't tell me he was
going to send a letter of that kind dealing with the
President."

After hearing the evidence presented, the majority of the
Committee in their report found,

> "the charges against Mr. Ballinger appear to have had their
> origin in a strong feeling of animosity created by supposed
> differences in policy respecting the conservation of natural
> resources. The accusers evidently had this policy very deeply
> at heart and were evidently disposed to take a most unfavorable
> view of the character and motives of anyone whom they sup-
> posed to be opposed to their views. They thus came to regard
> Mr. Ballinger with suspicion and to regard the most natural
> and innocent acts occurring in the ordinary course of depart-
> ment administration as furnishing evidence of some sinister
> purpose. . . . The evidence has wholly failed to make out a
> case. Neither any fact nor all the facts put together exhibit Mr.
> Ballinger as being anything but a competent and honorable
> gentleman, honestly and faithfully performing the duties of
> his high office with an eye single to the public service."

Despite Ballinger's official vindication by the Congressional Committee, there was a widespread belief that Taft
had displayed unsound judgment in his dismissal of Pinchot. But what else could the President have done? Pinchot,
permitting his zeal to becloud his reason, had been unpar-
donably insubordinate. Even Theodore Roosevelt, partial as
he was to Pinchot, said, in a letter to Senator Lodge, that
Pinchot had acted improperly, which by implication justi-
fies Taft's action in dismissing the Chief Forester.

CHAPTER XXVI

POLITICAL STORMS

TAFT's interest in the creation of forward-looking legislation and his ability to foster it are indicated by the extensive program he outlined for his administration. When his first Congress, the sixty-first, met in December, 1909, several measures of utmost importance were presented by the President for its consideration—the Railroad Bill, providing for an increase of the powers of the Interstate Commerce Commission and facilitating the disposition of its orders in the courts; the Postal Savings Bill, and the Conservation Bill ratifying all withdrawals and giving greater power in express terms to the Executive, as well as a number of remedial bills concerning railway safety devices.

He also recommended a Federal Incorporation Bill, primarily to protect the rights of investors and to ensure the stability of securities placed upon the market by corporations created by virtue of the law; a bill limiting the use of injunctions; a bill requiring the publication of campaign expenditures, and a bill for the admission of the territories of New Mexico and Arizona as states of the Union.

When these recommendations were brought before Congress for action, the insurgent element demanded and secured certain alterations in the provisions of the Railroad Bill, making it more drastic upon the common carriers.

Although Taft did not wholly approve these changes, he agreed to them, not wishing to lose the whole law. When the Postal Savings Bill came up for debate, the Senate insurgents sought to have incorporated among its provisions an amendment prohibiting the government from removing the deposited money from the neighborhood in which the deposits were made, except in case of war or dire emergency. This amendment would have caused Taft to veto the Act, but fortunately it was defeated.

Commending Taft for the progressive legislative enactments that he had pushed through Congress, the *Springfield Republican* said, editorially, "The like is not to be found in the whole seven years of Roosevelt's administration. . . . Even the hysterical, screaming 'Back-from-Elba' army must now admit that as one who 'does things' the former President is being outclassed." And yet that session of Congress, which should immeasurably have benefited Taft's political status, became, in the public mind, an example of his inefficiency and lack of political acumen. This unjust estimate was due to political eruptions within the party ranks which obscured the real issues and clouded Taft's achievements. Chief among them was the revolt of the Representatives against Joseph G. Cannon.

Angered by his autocratic use of the office of Speaker of the House of Representatives, the insurgent Republicans and the Democrats formed a coalition to end Cannon's arbitrary and tyrannical rule. This was presaged by a series of defeats suffered by the regular Republicans at the hands of the insurgents, who in combining with the Democrats had found themselves in the majority. On the morning of the sixteenth of March, 1910, the revolt broke. A resolution had been offered proposing that the census of 1910 be taken. After the Speaker's ruling on this resolution, the House, upon being appealed to, reversed his decision, whereupon Cannon declined to rule again. Then, Norris of Nebraska, gaining the floor, introduced a resolution, which proposed a new Rules Committee and included a provision rendering the Speaker of the House ineligible for membership. As the power of the Speaker rested upon the fact that he appointed the House committees and was, ex officio, chairman of the Committee on Rules, which governed the introduction and debate of proposed legislation, the insurgents had determined to increase the membership of the Rules Committee to fifteen and at the same time decrease the Speaker's power by placing the appointment of the committee in the House itself.

Upon objection, the resolution was declared out of order, but Representative Norris was persistent. He pressed his resolution and appealed from the ruling. Throughout the remainder of that day and night and the day following, an unusually bitter debate took place. Hoping to gain sufficient strength to repel this curtailment of his powers, Cannon caused a short adjournment, during which time an effort was made to effect a compromise.

When the House re-convened on the morning of the nineteenth, it became known that all the attempts to reconcile the warring factions had failed. The galleries were filled with spectators when Cannon, with an elastic step and an air of deep concern, entered the chamber, debonair, as usual, with a red carnation in his coat. Instantly the regular Republicans were upon their feet, giving him a thunderous cheer of greeting. The insurgents remained silent, immobile.

When the House was called to order, Cannon took up a typewritten sheet of paper and read his ruling sustaining the point of order against the Norris amendment. A half dozen members leaped to their feet, shouting for the floor, but Representative Norris was recognized and once again took an appeal from the decision of the chair. For the second time, Cannon was rebuked by the House, when they overruled him by a vote.

Flinging the gauntlet to the insurgents, Cannon announced himself ready to entertain the motion to declare the chair of the Speaker vacant, so that the House might proceed with the election of a new Speaker. The insurgent leader, Representative Norris, stood silent. He did not wish to go that far. The Democratic leader, Champ Clark, was so obviously affected by Cannon's attitude that he wept unashamed. In the midst of the tumult on the floor of the House, Representative Burleson, a Texas Democrat, gained the floor and offered the motion, which was declared to be in order. Representative Underwood rushed to where Burleson stood and pled with him to withdraw his motion and allow one of the insurgents to offer it, but the Texan remained obdurate.

Calling Representative Payne to the chair, Cannon walked from the chamber. It was a dramatic moment—one in which the insurgents fully appreciated the power they could exercise by uniting with the minority party. But when the motion to declare the chair vacant was presented, they were reluctant to go so far in siding with the Democrats and therefore voted in the negative.

Another element which began at this time to shadow Taft's success with the public was the increase in rumors, at first without foundation, of a change in his relations with Theodore Roosevelt, rumors which insistently whispered that Roosevelt was disappointed in him. There had been no breach of their personal relations before Roosevelt's departure for Africa, for Taft, in late February, 1909, had written his predecessor telling him that both of them knew that many people had attempted, during the months since the election, to represent that they were at odds, but that these rumors were all false. Taft signed this letter "with love and affection, my dear Theodore." In answering, Roosevelt told Taft that his letter was so very nice, that while nice was not anything like a strong enough word to express his true feelings to use words as strong as he felt would look "sloppy," and said, "You put in the right way to address me at the end."

On a rainy day in middle June, 1910, Roosevelt returned to the United States from his African trip. After a riotous reception in New York, Roosevelt resumed his journey to his home at Oyster Bay, whence he wrote Taft, answering the President's long letter of greeting. There is no doubt that the personal relations of the two men were still extremely friendly and cordial at this time although the seeds of dissension had been sown by the detraction of Taft indulged in by Roosevelt's satellites.

The intolerant Gifford Pinchot evidently had been piqued by President Taft's action in removing him from the office of the Chief Forester, for, on the thirty-first of December, 1909, he had written Roosevelt a letter calculated to appeal to the former President's amenity of temper, vanity and ever-present desire for more power, which Pinchot, knowing Roosevelt intimately, understood very well. Yet, on the other hand, he was also cognizant of the very close personal relations that existed between the former President and his successor. Pinchot must have felt, however, that, if properly handled, Roosevelt was a tractable person. His apparent purpose therefore became to implant in Roosevelt's mind a belief that Taft had become disloyal and unfaithful to the policies for which Roosevelt had stood. In this way Roosevelt's resentment of the President's actions might be aroused and he might be inclined to give credence to Pinchot's claims.

In this letter Pinchot outlined at length what he considered to be his reasons for believing that the President had abandoned the policies which had been inaugurated by his predecessor. The former Chief Forester said that Taft had surrounded himself with a Cabinet of corporation attorneys and reactionaries, who, according to Mr. Pinchot, were necessarily in opposition to the Rooseveltian policies; that Taft had permitted attacks upon Roosevelt to continue without opposition during the last session of Congress; that after becoming President, Taft associated himself with all the leaders in Congress opposed to the Rooseveltian policies; that in appointing Richard Ballinger as Secretary of the Interior, the President had attacked Roosevelt's conservation program; that his handling of the Payne-Aldrich Tariff Bill had been disgraceful, and despite the many

257

shortcomings of that law Taft had signed and now defended it as the best tariff bill ever passed, and, finally, that Taft had publicly endorsed in his speeches both Senator Aldrich, the conservative Republican leader in the Senate, and Representative Tawney of Minnesota, whom Mr. Pinchot called Roosevelt's "bitterest enemy."

Pinchot followed this letter up by a journey to Europe, where he awaited Roosevelt's return from Africa. There they conferred, the former President receiving from the implacable conservationist his first detailed account of political conditions in the United States. Suffering from political distemper and believing that he had been unjustly treated by President Taft, Pinchot, no matter how admirable his intentions may have been, could hardly have been in a mood to take a calm, dispassionate and impersonal view of the actual facts. Of Pinchot's efforts, Taft knew. He was also well aware that all of Roosevelt's followers disapproved of him because of his failure to countenance and support the Republican insurgents in their revolt against the regulars of the party. Taft did not combat these men in their endeavors to propagate a popular distrust of his actions and discredit him politically, nor did he give much heed to their intriguing. He had every confidence that Roosevelt, by investigating the facts of each case, would detect their shortsightedness and narrow partisanship. Taft had looked forward eagerly to his predecessor's return to the United States. He had missed the former President's heartening words of encouragement and sympathetic understanding, and keenly anticipated an early resumption of their former friendly relations. So he had despatched not

PRESIDENT TAFT ON HIS FAVORITE MOUNT IN ROCK CREEK PARK

only an official welcoming committee to greet Roosevelt at New York, but also his aide, Captain Archie Butt, who carried the official letter of welcome and a personal letter from Taft inviting the Colonel and Mrs. Roosevelt to visit him and Mrs. Taft at the White House.

This invitation Roosevelt declined, telling Taft that while the invitation was greatly appreciated, he did not "think it well for an ex-President to go to the White House, or indeed to go to Washington, except when he can't help it." But when the President moved the White House for the summer to Beverly, Massachusetts, Roosevelt, accompanied by Senator Lodge, came to call upon his successor. Their greeting was most friendly, Roosevelt taking both of Taft's hands in his own and saying, "Mr. President, it is fine to see you looking so well."

"But why 'Mr. President'?" laughingly inquired Taft.

"Because," replied Mr. Roosevelt, "it used to be 'Mr. President' and 'Will,' and now it must be 'Mr. President' and 'Theodore.' " [1]

Roosevelt remained for two hours reminiscing with the President. He told of his trip and his experiences in foreign capitals, and regaled the President and Mrs. Taft with humorous anecdotes. Politics were not discussed. In his letter of welcome Taft had told his predecessor that, as he had predicted, he had "had a hard time." But he had assured Roosevelt that he had been "conscientiously trying to carry out your policies but my method of doing so has not worked smoothly." And he went on, "I did not follow up

[1] "Recollections of Full Years," by Helen Herron Taft. Dodd, Mead & Company, New York, 1914.

my letter delivered by Archie Butt to you on the steamer, with others, for the reason that I did not wish to invite your comment or judgment on matters at long range or to commit you in respect to issues that you ought perhaps only reach a decision upon after your return to the United States. . . . The Garfield-Pinchot-Ballinger controversy has given me a great deal of personal pain and suffering but I am not going to say a word to you on that subject. You will have to look into that wholly for yourself without influence by the parties if you will find the truth. . . ."

The contrast is marked between the intense campaign of detraction conducted by Pinchot and the others of his coterie and the self-effacement of Taft, his willingness to have Roosevelt judge his efforts by a personally conducted investigation without any influence. But in this course, as later events were to prove, the President was mistaken. He had judged the friendship and fairness of his predecessor by the standard of his own friendship and fairness, not only underestimating it, but also failing to appreciate the zeal with which the disgruntled Pinchot had acted. Early in August, Roosevelt set his face westward to fulfill a series of speaking engagements. That at this time he entertained no rancor, that he still held Taft in the highest esteem, and that their relations were most friendly, is borne out by indisputable evidence. But Roosevelt had still to hear the wild cheering and the applause of the western crowds in the many cities where he was to speak.

Before the Colorado legislature and at the John Brown battlefield in Kansas, he denounced the Supreme Court of the United States, and preached a doctrine which he called

"The New Nationalism," in which he advocated full publicity for the affairs of private corporations, and full responsibility for their directors and officials. The warmth of the welcome and the enthusiasm with which he was received in the West had its effect upon Roosevelt, and must have prompted him to heed, for the first time, the reports from Gifford Pinchot of the dissatisfaction of the people of the country with the Taft administration.

When the people went to the polls that November of 1910, they forgot many things. They were eager to reprimand Taft for what they considered his political blunders. Failing to understand properly all the facts about the Pinchot-Ballinger controversy, the Payne-Aldrich Tariff Act, and the insurgent insurrection against Cannon, they wrongly considered these incidents as examples of Taft's deficiencies as an executive. They not only neglected to remember that Taft as President had procured more progressive and forward-looking legislation in a single session of Congress than Roosevelt had been able to secure in his whole administration, but they also failed to recall that the Taft administration had turned, within a year, a national deficit of some fifty million dollars into a surplus of fourteen millions.

The struggles for supremacy within the party ranks certainly should not have deflected the attention of the people of the country from Taft's accomplishments, but they did just that, and the election changed the Republican majority of forty-seven in the House of Representatives to a Democratic majority of sixty-seven, while in the Senate the Republican majority was reduced from twenty-eight to ten. The Democrats also elected Governors in the usually Republican states of Ohio, New York, Connecticut, New Jersey and Massachusetts.

CHAPTER XXVII

RECIPROCITY

IN his message to Congress in December, 1910, Taft said that by his direction the Secretary of State had despatched two representatives of the United States, as Special Commissioners, to confer with the Government of Canada regarding the commercial relations of the two countries. He also said that these commissioners had been empowered to negotiate a "reciprocal trade agreement" with the Dominion.

Taft had long had such an idea in mind. The large volume of trade between the two countries, coupled with the similarity of conditions in labor, material, soil and resources, prompted Taft's belief that such a measure would find favor. Having sounded a Canadian Cabinet Minister, Fielding, on the subject, the President found him favorably disposed and of the opinion that the citizens of Canada would look upon such an agreement as advantageous. Subsequently, when the two men met, further negotiations took place, which resulted in the despatching of the two American representatives to meet the Canadian emissaries at Ottawa.

Conferences began there in November, 1910, and adjourned to be reopened later in Washington. They were continued in the American capital until the seventh of January, 1911, when a Reciprocity Trade Agreement was signed by the representatives of the two governments. Before submitting the Reciprocity Agreement to the legislators Taft had forwarded the text of the agreement to Roosevelt for comment, as he had his message to Congress. After considering the proposed convention, the former President wrote Taft that,

> "it seems to me that what you propose to do with Canada is admirable from every standpoint. I firmly believe in free trade with Canada for both economic and political reasons. As you say, labor cost is substantially the same in the two countries so that you are amply justified by the platform. Whether Canada will accept such reciprocity, I do not know, but it is greatly to your credit to make the effort. It may damage the Republican party for awhile, but it will surely benefit the party in the end. . . ."

Committing himself to the agreement, Taft by a special message on the twenty-sixth of January, 1911, submitted it to Congress. The agreement provided for free trade on some Canadian products and reduced duties on others; in return, Canada was to make similar concessions on American goods. To say the least, the situation was a unique one. A President belonging to the protectionist party, was seeking, in the form of reciprocity, free trade and reduced tariff duties, and in order to procure the enactment of his proposal, it had become necessary for him to rely upon his political opponents, the Democrats. Taft was taking indeed a courageous step.

Taft fully expected the Republican insurgents not only to support the Reciprocity Bill, but to claim that he was only trailing after them and coming belatedly to their views. Instead, to his great surprise, they repudiated the agreement, because as they alleged, it discriminated against the West and Northwest and favored the East. Debate on the measure in the American House of Representatives caused the ghost of annexation to haunt the Canadian electorate. Speaker Champ Clark, in an address to the House, unwisely went so far as to say that "I am for this Bill, because I hope to see the day when the American flag will float over every square foot of the British North American possessions clear to the North Pole. They are people of our blood. They speak our language. Their institutions are much like ours. They are trained in the difficult art of self-government."

In accordance with Taft's plans, Samuel W. McCall of Massachusetts cleverly manipulated the Reciprocity Bill and procured its passage by the House of Representatives. The Senate, however, was obdurate; the Bill met a stone wall of opposition, and Congress adjourned without having taken any final action on the measure. Taft immediately called a special session of the new Congress, in which the Democrats had the majority. Convening on the fourth of April, 1911, the House promptly passed the Bill. It was sent to the Senate and this time, with the aid of the Democrats, was passed by a vote of fifty-three to twenty-seven.

Taft was elated by his success. And he had a right to be, for the Bill had been well conceived and admirably handled. James Bryce, the British Ambassador to the United States, congratulated Taft by saying,

"May I congratulate you heartily on the victory just won in the Senate by your patient, luminous advocacy of your plan? It is only most privately and confidentially I can venture to do this, lest I be accused in Canada and England of being an accomplice in the work of Delilah, sweeping up, perhaps, the locks that fall from the head of the shorn Fielding. . . ."

In Canada, Sir Wilfred Laurier enthusiastically committed his party to the agreement. Submitting the matter to Parliament, he soon found that the opposition, under the able direction of Mr. Borden, was obstructing the passage of the bill. Unable to get the agreement to a vote, Laurier dissolved Parliament and ordered a general election. The campaign that followed this dissolution of Parliament was exceedingly bitter.

At Montreal, such prominent Canadians as Z. A. Lash, K. C., of Toronto, Clifford Sifton, a former Cabinet member, and the humorist and college professor, Stephen Leacock, addressed large assemblages. Lash labeled the Reciprocity Agreement "preposterous," while Leacock said,

"Shall two old gentlemen in a hurry sneak down to fat entertainments in Washington and come back to us, fellow-citizens, with a paper in their hands and say 'La Chose est faite'? (The thing is done.) Is this the way our democracy is to be conducted? . . . I do not wish to speak any evil of the American Republic. The Americans are a great people, but fifty years ago we settled the question as to what our lot was to be with respect to them. We have decided once and for all that the British flag was good enough for us."

Similar meetings were held in every Province in the Dominion.

266

In middle September, 1911, the newly elected Canadian Parliament convened and again took the matter of Reciprocity under consideration. By the creation of a so-called "national policy," stimulated by the belief that reciprocity would make the Dominion economically dependent upon the United States, Borden had been triumphant in the elections and his party had been returned to Parliament with a large majority. On the twenty-first of September, 1911, it was announced that Canada had finally rejected Reciprocity.

Taft's administration as President was a singularly productive one. This statement is borne out by John Spencer Bassett, who wrote,

"The struggle for party supremacy under Taft ought not to divert our attention from the many reform measures which he helped to carry through Congress. Never has the attention of the people been more vigorously directed to matters connected with the development of good government on a democratic basis." [1]

The excellence of his judicial appointments, also, has been universally recognized. During his four years as President, he appointed six justices, more than any other President except Washington had done, to our highest judicial tribunal. Considering the United States Supreme Court as the "chief bulwark of the institutions of civil liberty created by the constitution," Taft viewed these appointments as the most sacred duty with which he was charged. He chose Horace H. Lurton, of the Sixth Federal Circuit Court of

[1] "Short History of the United States," by John Spencer Bassett. The Macmillan Company, New York.

Appeals, to succeed Justice Peckham, and Charles Evans Hughes of New York, to take Justice Brewer's place. He elevated Willis Van Devanter, a native of the state of Indiana but a resident of Wyoming, whom Roosevelt had appointed to the Federal Circuit Court, to the Supreme Court succeeding Justice Moody. Taft made Edward D. White of Louisiana, a Roman Catholic and former Confederate soldier, who had served the court as an Associate Justice for sixteen years, the Chief Justice. He also appointed Joseph Lamar of the Georgia Supreme Court, and in 1913, shortly before his retirement, selected Mahlon Pitney of New Jersey to take Justice Harlan's place.

Taft also took a step forward in an effort to ensure world peace. In a speech before the National Geographic Society, he had said that he hoped the United States would be able to complete a treaty with some prominent European nation, whereby the two countries would agree to arbitrate every controversy that might arise between their respective governments. After Taft had completed his address and resumed his seat, the French Ambassador, seated nearby, leaned toward him and said, "We will make such a treaty with you."

Instantly Taft replied, "I'm your man."

A few days later, Sir Edward Grey, publicly deploring the stupendous increase in naval expenditures, declared that England would be willing to enter into such a treaty with the United States, and subsequently Mr. Balfour, the leader of the opposition, in agreeing with Grey, stated that his party also would support such a treaty.

As a result of these two avowals, negotiations were instituted by Secretary of State Knox with Ambassador Bryce and Ambassador Jusserand, which resulted, on the eleventh of May, in the texts of the treaties being made public. They were almost identical and both provided,

"first, that all questions determinable by the principles of law and equity shall be submitted to arbitration under the rules and terms of the Hague Convention; second, for the creation, as the occasion might demand, of a Joint High Commission to be composed of three Americans and three others, to be named by the country with whom there is a controversy; thirdly, that when a question could not be settled by the ordinary methods of diplomacy it should be referred to this Commission, upon the application of either party to the controversy, such reference to take place at the end of one year, and that the Commission, after due deliberation and a thorough investigation, should make a report with such recommendations as should seem proper; and finally, that when there should be a disagreement as to whether a given difference were determinable by the principles of law and equity, that disagreement should be referred to the Commission, and a decision by it, when concurred in by not fewer than five of the six members, should be binding."

Taft's efforts to conclude these treaties were negatived by the Senate, where two amendments to their text were proposed. These amendments would have destroyed the effectiveness of the treaties and it became doubtful whether either France or England would accept them in their modified form, so Taft, discontinuing his efforts to force concurrence by the Senate, abandoned the treaties.

Speaking at a later date, Taft said,

"It was not that those treaties would have abolished war; nobody said they would; but it was that they were a step in the right direction toward the practical ideal under which war might have been impossible. Other nations might have followed our lead with one another, and we would have an interlacing of treaties. The Senate has put so many amendments to the Treaty that it is doubtful whether the adoption of the same would be a step forward."

CHAPTER XXVIII

THE BREAK WITH ROOSEVELT

In relating the Taft-Roosevelt break which resulted in the memorable campaign of 1912, it becomes necessary first of all to consider especially the motive power in the campaign—Theodore Roosevelt, that unique person, a complex mixture of inconsistencies, the force of whose personality was to divide a great political party. He was a striking figure, a crusader, made so by his apparently tireless vitality, his superabundance of energy and utter fearlessness—a person who might in many ways be considered an ideal American, a hero to be emulated. But perspicacity should not be blinded by the emotions he aroused, for an impartial study of his acts and statements before and during the campaign of 1912 reveals Roosevelt in the rôle of an unusually gifted politician, but nevertheless a politician of the common sort. Yet he was above all the stuff of which popular heroes are made—dynamic, magnetic, acting always with a dash, having a gift for the pungent and quotable phrase.

Taft on the other hand never mastered the technique of popularity in so far as it depended upon manner. Any conscious effort to do so would have been repugnant to a man of his absolutely just nature. When Taft stepped to the edge of a platform to address a crowd, he stood passive and kindly; there went out from him none of that eager paternal warmth and cordiality which seems to take each man by the hand. His appeal was to their minds, on behalf of reason, not charm, which he possessed to such abundance in private acquaintance. Roosevelt was "Teddy" to vociferous thousands; Taft's staunchest admirers cannot quite be imagined calling him "Billy."

In policy, conduct and manner, in little things, and in large, when Taft and Roosevelt worked together they perfectly complemented one another; each threw the other's best qualities into bold relief. When they were at variance, each suffered from comparison with the other—one reason why the break was politically fatal to both.

Shortly after his return from his western tour, in September, 1910, Roosevelt told George von L. Meyer, Secretary of the Navy, that he intended to work for Taft's renomination and election. Then came the New York State Republican convention, in which Roosevelt sought the Temporary Chairmanship. The Vice President of the United States, James S. Sherman, was put up in opposition to him and Roosevelt accused Taft of being responsible, although he had every reason to know that the President was not, for Taft in a telegram had advised the leaders against a contest of any kind and had urged them to confer with Roosevelt before doing anything. When the convention assembled Roosevelt dominated it. He was made Temporary Chairman and, as one of his biographers has written, "he carried all points." This convention endorsed the Taft administration and platform and praised the Payne-Aldrich Tariff Act.

The first indication that Pinchot's intrigues were bearing

fruit came shortly after the New York State convention, when Gilson Gardiner, a newspaper man, called upon the former President. After this conference, Gardiner sought out the Senate leader of the insurgent movement, Senator Robert M. La Follette of Wisconsin. Representing himself as a confidant of Roosevelt, Gardiner informed La Follette that the former President had instructed him to tell the Senator that he had altered his opinion of Taft; that he now believed the Progressive Republicans should place a candidate in the field to compete with the President, and that Roosevelt wished to urge La Follette to present himself that candidate for the Republican nomination.

Continuing, Gardiner stated that Roosevelt was not yet in a position where he could openly endorse La Follette, but that he had promised to employ the columns of the *Outlook,* of which he was an associate editor, to commend the attitude of the Wisconsin Senator upon public questions. Gardiner ventured his own opinion that should La Follette declare himself a candidate, with the support of Roosevelt, his nomination would be assured.

Blinded by political aspirations and failing to discern Roosevelt's real purpose in putting him forward as a candidate, La Follette, an able and fearless man, although of the most imperious and demagogic nature politically, determined to seek the nomination. Had La Follette been astute, he might have known that he was to be nothing more than a cat's-paw to test out the Progressive strength.

Acting on Gardiner's suggestion, La Follette appointed Walter L. Houser, former Secretary of State of Wisconsin, his campaign manager. Houser, desirous of securing an endorsement for La Follette, called a meeting of the Progressives to be held in Chicago in mid-October, 1911. Only a short time before this meeting, President Taft had filled a series of speaking engagements in the Middle West, including Gilson Gardiner in his entourage, in the rôle of a newspaper correspondent. And in reporting the situation to Roosevelt upon the completion of this trip, Gardiner stated that there were three hundred and fifty potential Progressive delegates in the West.

Roosevelt then conferred with his former Secretary of the Interior, James Garfield of Ohio, who planned to attend the Progressive convention in Chicago. What was discussed has never been disclosed, but when the Progressives convened and proceeded to endorse La Follette's candidacy, Garfield protested. But finding that he stood alone and that the other delegates were determined upon such a course, he withdrew his opposition. The *Outlook,* commenting editorially upon the endorsement of La Follette, said this was to be considered a "recommendation rather than a committal of the movement to any one man."

On the eleventh of December, 1907, in answer to an inquiry, and referring to the third term statement he had made on election night, 1904, Roosevelt had said, "I have not changed and shall not change that decision thus announced." But after the New York state convention, as insurgents in increasing numbers called upon the former President, his determined tone became gradually modified. He first stated that "I am not and shall not be a candidate. I shall never seek the nomination, nor would I accept it if it came to me as a result of any intrigue."

Later, he said, "that under no circumstances would he accept another nomination." And still later, "If the utterly unexpected happens and I am nominated, I may very probably be defeated, in which case I shall be not only assailed, but derided." But again, he said, "If at this particular crisis, with the particular problems ahead of us at this particular time, the people feel that I am the man in sight to do the job, then I should regard myself as shirking a plain duty if I refused to do it."

Taft had long possessed misgivings as to Roosevelt's sincerity and outward manifestations of sympathy with his policies. He wondered if Roosevelt were not dissembling, and in truth seeking for an excuse, or a number of excuses, for an open break with the President. The rumors of the former President's disappointment with his successor were increasing in volume all the time. Still Taft could not understand, much less explain, Roosevelt's attitude. Their relations had been such that the President was not conscious of having offended his predecessor and Roosevelt had, in both public and private statements, endorsed practically all of Taft's policies.

Reports, apparently authentic, came to the President that Roosevelt had resented the letter which Taft had written him on the day following his election in 1908, in which Taft had said, "You and my brother Charley made that possible which in all probability would not have occurred otherwise." That Roosevelt should regard this letter as an occasion for feeling bitter toward Taft, because he had dared to include his brother in the same class with Roosevelt, surprised the President, as indeed it might. It seemed

275

petty that a letter written in the fulness of gratitude, as this letter was, should hurt his vanity because Taft had included his own brother as entitled to gratitude.

Taft could hardly believe that a man of Roosevelt's capacities would stoop to such a trifling excuse for breaking with him. To the President the idea of an open break with his predecessor was repellent. He was sincerely fond of Roosevelt and moreover felt deeply indebted to him. So Taft made up his mind to "sit tight" and remain silent. This attitude has since been misconstrued and misinterpreted, but only by persons who are ill-informed and not in possession of the facts.

Taft placed the active management of his campaign in the hands of Congressman William B. McKinley of Illinois, who set about aligning the party forces.

Taft felt that the candidacy of La Follette, whose views were at variance with the opinions entertained by the great conservative element of the country, would not develop sufficient strength to defeat him for the nomination, but he regarded the possible candidacy of Roosevelt with some apprehension. To him it meant a political combat with a man who not only possessed an expert knowledge of politics, but also one who had never known defeat and who would stop at nothing to achieve victory. He knew that he would be in for a hard fight, but he had determined to stay in anyhow, for two reasons,

"one is, that I believe I represent a safer and saner view of our government and its constitution than does Theodore Roosevelt, and whether beaten or not I mean to continue to labor in the vineyard for those principles and to aid the party or body of men that wish to uphold them and wish to stamp out the pernicious theory that the method of reforming the defects in a representative government is to impose more numerous and more burdensome political duties upon the people when their inability properly to discharge their present duties is the cause of every ground of complaint.

"Second, I am not conscious of having done anything which disentitles me to stand as a candidate for a second term or requires a departure from the time-honored and very safe tradition against a third term. I am, of course, conscious of having made errors, but there are few Presidents who do not, and, on the whole, I believe I can show as good a balance on the credit side as most administrations."

Taft well knew that Roosevelt's great popularity with the rank and file of the Republican party might seriously jeopardize his own chances of renomination, if the former President entered the race.

"The only cloud is Roosevelt," said Taft in a personal letter. "His is a most difficult part for him to play as he has marked it out for himself. He seems to be rousing the enmity of La Follette and his followers by not keeping his name out of the primaries, although I believe he would do me more damage."

With the approach of 1912 the equivocal rôle played by Roosevelt became more puzzling. Roosevelt's spokesmen were constantly reiterating and reassuring the baffled La Follette leaders that the former President had promised "that the wires would not be crossed," and that Roosevelt had no intention of becoming a candidate. Despite these assurances, the situation became more distracting to the La Follette forces when, at a meeting of the Progressives held at the Pinchot residence in Washington, Medill McCormick, Gifford Pinchot and Gilson Gardiner informed the Wisconsin Senator that there must not be a break with Roosevelt and that should one come, they would go over to the former President.

The political situation in many states was also indicative of the fact that Roosevelt had been duping La Follette, and that it was his intention in the near future to supersede the Wisconsin Senator as the Progressive candidate for the Presidency. That the former President feared defeat and lessened prestige, if he announced prematurely his intention of becoming a candidate for the nomination, is the only explanation that can be offered for his silence, and his indecision inspired much flippant newspaper doggerel, such as:

> "On Sagamore's house there was silence as deep
> As falls from the stars when the sea is asleep
> Or blows from the pole o'er a desolate land
> Where rival explorers are frozen or canned.

> "On Sagamore's lawn stood reporters with tabs
> And hosts of Progressives drove up in their cabs
> With Pinchot and Garfield—and riding between
> Frank Munsey, proud bearing a marked magazine.

> "And now and anon galloped out of the west
> Some envoy indignantly smiting his chest
> Crying 'Why art thou silent, O voice of our spiel,
> While the Guggs and the Morgans are hogging the deal?

> "The Ballingers plot and the Gallingers scheme
> The Coxes and Knoxes combine like a team
> The Lorimer's loom and the Pen-roses bloom
> While Taft blesses all with his usual beam."

278

It was early in 1912 apparently that Roosevelt first decided that he could beat Taft for the nomination. He had won the support of an ardent La Follette follower, Hiram Johnson, by dangling before him the hope of becoming the party's Vice Presidential nominee, after which Johnson abandoned La Follette to advocate the nomination of Roosevelt. Plans were formulated by which Roosevelt was to be "sprung" for the nomination. His adherents expected him to take like wildfire, and that the people and the press of the country would acclaim the announcement of his candidacy with wild enthusiasm. Late in January, paving the way for this announcement, Gifford Pinchot presented to La Follette the alternative of either withdrawing in favor of Roosevelt, with reservations as to differences of opinion, and continuing to stump for the Progressives, or withdrawing without committing himself to the support of any candidate, and continuing to stump. La Follette characteristically declined to accept either proposition.

Encountering a noticeable lack of enthusiasm over Roosevelt's candidacy, and fearing that the announcement had already been too long delayed, Pinchot and his fellow-Progressives decided to play their trump cards. To stimulate the boom for Roosevelt, eight governors declared themselves in favor of his candidacy—Stubbs of Kansas, Hadley of Missouri, Glasscock of West Virginia, Osborne of Michigan, Aldrich of Nevada, Johnson of California, Bass of New Hampshire, and Vessey of South Dakota. These men drafted a letter to Roosevelt requesting that he accept the call should the Republican party resolve upon him as the logical nominee.

On February eighteenth, Pinchot followed this letter with the publication of a statement announcing that he had withdrawn his support from La Follette and would thereafter advocate Roosevelt's nomination. In this statement he said, "Senator La Follette's candidacy was undertaken for two clear and specific purposes, first, to hold the Progressives together as an effective fighting force, and second, to prevent the renomination of a reactionary Republican President." [1]

After months of vacillation, on the twenty-sixth of February, 1912, Roosevelt made the long expected announcement that his "hat was in the ring." And in an interview with the newspaper correspondents, he said, "I want it understood that I have not changed my mind. My position has simply been misunderstood. I said I would not accept a nomination for a third term under any circumstances. Meaning, of course, a third consecutive term." He must have realized the inconsistency of this stand, for H. H. Kohlsaat testifies that Roosevelt told him that he "would cut that hand off right there," putting his finger on his wrist, "if I could have recalled that 1904 statement." [2]

The campaign got under way. Taft's organization, under McKinley's direction, was rapidly being perfected, and the President began to view his renomination as something more than a possibility. As he tersely expressed it, "Nothing but death can keep me out of the fight now."

Taft realized the necessity of having an able and wholly

---

[1] "The Autobiography of Robert M. LaFollette," Robert M. La Follette Company. Madison, 1913.
[2] "From McKinley to Harding," by Henry H. Kohlsaat. Chas. Scribner's Sons. New York, 1923.

independent judiciary, who would serve as a check upon the capricious judgments of the people. Roosevelt, by his "New Nationalism" theories, proposed to abolish this check and made it a campaign issue. The former President had joined that group of political emotionalists who had so lost their sense of proportion as to consider that the country had succumbed to a tyranny of wealth, full of evil and corruption. He proposed to have the affairs of the Government depend upon the momentary passions of the people, who were of course indifferently informed as to the merits of a particular question. With no definite object in view, Roosevelt proposed to reconstruct our society according to some fanciful, unformulated plan.

Taft's innate conservatism made him apprehensive of what might occur and he took issue with the former President by denouncing the proposed changes and being quite outspoken in his defense of the present system. He did not abuse Roosevelt in his addresses. He had selected what he considered to be the most vulnerable point of Roosevelt's political program and, without indulging in vulgar personalities, made a legitimate campaign issue out of the former President's "New Nationalism" theories. But Roosevelt began a campaign which for vituperation, vehemence and bitterness is unparalleled in American political history.

Roosevelt evidently forgot, by a convenient lapse of memory, what he had said in praise of Taft at the time of the 1908 campaign:

> "The true friend of reform, the true foe of abuses, is the man who steadily perseveres in righting wrongs, in warring against abuses, but whose character and training are such that he never

281

promises what he cannot perform, that he always a little more than makes good what he does promise, that while steadily advancing, he never permits himself to be led into foolish excesses, which would damage the very cause he champions. In Mr. Taft we have a man who combines all of these qualities to a degree which no other man in our public life since the Civil War has surpassed."

For now he assured the people of the country that Taft was a hypocrite, a man of flabby intellect, and the promoter and beneficiary of fraud. Through his managers, Roosevelt charged the President of the United States with prostituting his office by employing Federal patronage in order to control the election of Southern delegates to the Republican National Convention.

The former President declared the Supreme Court's decrees in the Standard Oil and Tobacco cases to be worthless and ineffective, although the decrees were drawn exactly as Roosevelt's own Attorney-General, in the bill filed against the companies, by direction of the former President, had asked that it be drawn. He accused Taft of being in league with Lorimer, although he had even then in his possession a letter from the President which read, "I have read as much of the evidence as I could get at and am convinced that there was a mass and mess of corruption, upon which his (Lorimer's) election was founded that ought to be stamped with the disapproval of the Senate. I want this movement to oust him to succeed."

With such expressions as, "The Republican Party would have died of dry-rot if we had not made this fight," "It is a bad trait to bite the hand that feeds you," and "This is not a dress parade, but a fight to the finish," Roosevelt campaigned. He called Taft a "man with brains of about three guinea-pig power." His campaign had become an undignified, abusive, hurly-burly, brawling affair that caused the *New York Evening Post* to state editorially "the whole spectacle which he presents to-day is pathetic in the extreme, and for the sake of his own fame, and in order that his brilliant career may not go out like a lamp with a bad smell, his true friends ought from this moment make every effort to induce him to withdraw."

Taft disliked pitting himself against the embittered attacks of Roosevelt, for, as he told his brother, Charles P. Taft,

"The fight has not been a pleasant one because of the antics of my opponent, who has misrepresented and distorted everything I have said in order to charge me with a distrust of the American people. . . . I have not answered Roosevelt and his charges. I have ignored him and let the newspapers attend to him and they are doing it. He is now engaged in attacking the newspapers. They can be trusted to answer for themselves, both Democratic and Republican. . . ."

Finally, Roosevelt's campaign became so abusive and violent that Taft broke his prolonged silence and scathingly replied to the many charges made by the former President. In Springfield, Massachusetts, the President said,

"Although Roosevelt posed as the apostle of the square deal, he has garbled and misrepresented my language and has indulged in loose and vague indictment, thereby clouding the real and critical issues and misleading a great many good and patriotic people. . . .

"I dislike to involve myself in a personal controversy with a man to whom I am so greatly indebted and the debt of gratitude I have never denied, and therefore kept peace for two months of misrepresentation, because I wanted to go through the campaign without being compelled to speak. But my dear friends, when you are backed up against a wall and a man is hitting you in the eye, and punishing you in every way both above and below the belt, by George, if you have any manhood in you, you have got to fight."

To Roosevelt's accusation that all the bosses were in favor of Taft and against himself, the President replied,

"The truth with respect to me is the same as it is with respect to Mr. Roosevelt. When I am running for the Presidency, I gratefully accept such support as comes to me. Mr. Roosevelt has done so in the past; he is doing so now."

In answer to the imputations made by Roosevelt that he had been "receiving stolen goods and profiting by the use of dirty instruments to secure delegates," Taft challenged his opponent to specify a particular instance of such fraud. He stated that no such charge ever brought to his attention had been sustained by a scintilla of evidence. Roosevelt ignored this challenge.

Taxed with having employed patronage in his efforts to procure the nomination, Taft exclaimed,

"I do not deny that under the present system of appointments Federal officeholders will be interested in politics and take part therein and will support those to whose appointment they attribute their preferment. Under present conditions, however, and under the policy which has been pursued in this administration, there are in office today at least seventy percent of

284

those who were in office by the appointment of Theodore Roosevelt. In view of his candidacy it is natural that a great number of these officeholders should favor him rather than me, and such is the fact, and Mr. Roosevelt cannot be ignorant of it. In spite of the great activity of a number of such individuals against me, not a single man of them has been removed."

CHAPTER XXIX

1912—THE CAMPAIGN AND ELECTION

EARLY June found the Republican hosts gathering in Chicago for their National Convention. In accordance with the established procedure of referring the contests for seats to the National Committee, and because of the great number of contests, the National Committee held its first meeting ten days before the convening of the delegates on the seventh of June, 1912. The Committee went into executive session at the appointed time and immediately adopted a body of regulations to govern their proceedings. In order to expedite the hearings and to have a report in readiness for presentation to the convention when it gathered, a rule was passed, providing that a roll call could be required only upon the demand of twenty or more members. Throughout the remainder of the week the sessions of the National Committee continued. Contrary to all forecasts, the meetings were surprisingly peaceful and, except for an occasional outburst from Francis J. Heney of California, the expected explosions did not take place. In all the cases decided during the first day, except one involving the contests from the States of Alabama and Arkansas, there was a unanimous vote for the Taft delegates, the Roosevelt members of the Committee voting with the Taft members and freely admitting that the "evidence on which was based the

286

Colonel's contest to the Alabama districts was too flimsy to merit consideration."

The second day's sessions repeated those of the preceding day. Forty-eight delegates were awarded to Taft, bringing the number of contests decided in his favor to seventy-two. All of these were settled by a viva voce vote, most of the contests being so weak that the Roosevelt adherents did not demand a roll call. At one juncture, Ormsby MacHarg, Roosevelt lieutenant appearing before the Committee on behalf of the former President, threw up his hands and declared his willingness to "bunch" ten contests in order to save time. Former Senator Dick, of Ohio, representing President Taft, rejected MacHarg's proposal and urged that the Committee determine each individual case upon its merits. When the Florida contests were heard, C. H. Alston, a negro contestant for Roosevelt, appeared and based his claim to a seat in the convention upon the fact that he had been denied admittance to the room where the regular Florida Republican convention was being held.

Alston said, "We walked in, and then in a couple of minutes we were walked out again."

And he went on to say that when he and other negroes who were supporting Roosevelt, made a second effort to gain admittance to the hall "one of the men wheeled on me and I wheeled on him, and they wheeled me out."

The National Committeemen were in paroxysms of laughter.

While he was standing on the street endeavoring to devise some way of entering the convention hall, Alston said a delegate "came out and gave me a ticket of admittance.

I sneaked back in again and hid way back in the hall, but they found me and put me out again. So I kept my ticket and brought it here and filed it with the Secretary."

Another negro from Florida appeared to claim a seat. As he presented a rather threadbare appearance, Senator Dick asked him who had supplied him with the necessary funds to come to Chicago.

"The Lawd be praised," replied the negro, "The folks done raise de' jackpot in the church."

A roar of laughter went up, drowning the vote, which was against the Roosevelt delegate. Senator Borah of Idaho, and Cecil Lyon of Texas, both ardent Roosevelt supporters, left the Committee room "freely expressing their disgust that they should be compelled to waste their time in such farcical proceedings."

In order to camouflage the unwarranted contests that had been filed, a smoke screen, in the guise of an alleged steam roller, was thrown out by Roosevelt's managers. The Roosevelt shock-troops on the National Committee were reinforced by Francis J. Heney, the "graft-hunting attorney of San Francisco," and Governor Herbert Hadley of Missouri, who sat in the hearings on the respective proxies of Thomas Thorson of South Dakota, and Sidney Bieber of the District of Columbia.

The voting on the contests continued with interruptions from Heney who occasionally shouted "robbery," "fraud," and "steal." The Taft delegates were seated as on the preceding days, not only receiving the votes of the Taft members of the Committee but also those of the Roosevelt adherents. After the Indiana contests, Roosevelt telephoned

288

from Oyster Bay to his manager, Senator Dixon, and up-
braided Senator Borah and Frank Kellogg of Minnesota
for their stand on the contests. The former President also
gave an interview to the newspaper reporters, in which he
called the members of the National Committee thieves and
robbers.

Unable to remain in Oyster Bay and away from the
battle front any longer, Roosevelt left New York for Chicago on Friday, June the fourteenth. He journeyed across
the country clamorously. At every possible railway station
where a large enough crowd had gathered, he delivered
a speech, including the inevitable charge that "it was just
a plain case of steal."

Meanwhile the crowds were gathering in Chicago. There
were innumerable impromptu parades with blaring horns,
throbbing drums. Hawked on the streets were flags, buttons, noise-making devices, bunting, and sheet music,
written especially for the convention. One Roosevelt symbol took the form of a cardboard arrangement of the former
president's face, under a Rough Rider's hat, revealing and
then concealing the famous toothsome grin.

Wearing a new felt hat with four dents, and a flaming
necktie, Roosevelt alighted from his Pullman amid these
crowds in the late afternoon of the fifteenth of June. The
day was hot and sticky, but that did not deter the former
President from energetically shaking hands with everybody in reach. Roosevelt was quickly ushered to a waiting
automobile, and the procession, which had been elaborately
advertised, started through the crowded streets for his headquarters at the Congress Hotel. Arriving there he gave out

289

a newspaper interview in which he shouted his defiance at the National Committee and "everyone else who dares to thwart the will of the people." He continued by saying that he had summoned his leaders to tell them, as he expressed it, "what they must do to prevent the control of the convention by the thieves, robbers and highbinders, who would steal the people's liberties." While he was holding secret sessions with his managers, a German band took its stand outside the hotel to serenade him. As *Harper's Weekly* recorded it in a diary of the convention, Roosevelt shoved his way through a window and appeared upon the hotel balcony to answer the plaudits of the crowd assembled below in the street. The diary reads:

"THEODORE—My friends (applause)
    Chicago is a bad place to steal in.
    (great laughter)
BAND— Everybody's doin' it, doin' it. (cheers)
THEODORE—The receiver of stolen goods is no better than the thief. This is a contest between the people and the politicians and the people will win. (applause) It is a naked fight against theft, thieves—thieves!
BAND— What the Hell do we care?
Theodore retires and the crowd exits."

The following day, Sunday the sixteenth, found the Massachusetts delegation arriving for the convention. Among the Taft delegates was a Mr. Keyes, who bore, in stature and general appearance, a marked resemblance to Roosevelt. In order to increase the likeness he put on large eye-glasses, a light suit, a sombrero and a turned-down soft collar. Through the day he amused himself and others by facetiously dashing in and out of the crowded lobbies, with a swarm of friends trailing behind him and shouting, "Out of the way, please." Whereupon the crowds, of course halted, spied Keyes, surrounded him and cheered frantically for "Teddy." Acting the part, Keyes grinned expansively, displaying a wide array of very white teeth, snatched his hat from his head, waved his arms in spectacular fashion and, biting off his words, shouted, "I will not be robbed. The people shall not be robbed. I thank you, my friends," or, again, "My friends, the people are fighting for a square deal and, by Godfrey, we're going to have it."

Cheers —— ——, while Keyes's friends, hovering in the background, shouted as they moved on, "Got 'em again."

When the delegates gathered at the Coliseum at noon on Tuesday the eighteenth of June, there was not the usual friendly conversation and exchange of badinage. It was an ill-tempered, sullen gathering. The band played, but even the music seemed apathetic. Just before the convention was called to order, Chairman Rosewater announced that a flashlight picture was to be taken and requested that everybody look pleasant.

An Indiana delegate prophetically shouted, "It's the last time the convention will look pleasant."

There were no echoing cheers as the strains of The Star Spangled Banner died away, and Victor Rosewater, the diminutive Chairman of the National Committee, called the convention to order.

The temporary roll made up by the National Committee

was presented, showing that Taft had been victorious in two hundred and thirty-five of the contests for seats and that Roosevelt had been awarded nineteen. The Roosevelt floor leader, Governor Hadley of Missouri, dashed forward and immediately moved an amendment to this temporary roll, by substituting the names of seventy-two delegates. Hadley, with a penetrating voice and compelling, vigorous gestures, said in support of his motion,

> "If it is in the power of twenty-seven men to say who shall constitute a National Convention, then we shall have ceased to have a representative government. The only government we have in this country is through political parties and if we allow a handful of men on a National Committee to say who shall sit in the convention of these parties we enable these men, if their party is successful at the polls, to direct the destinies of the government."

Senator Watson of Indiana, the Taft floor leader, made a point of order upon Hadley's motion, Rosewater sustained it and allotted a period for discussion. Former Governor Fort of New Jersey took the floor to support Hadley's motion, but his efforts to speak ended in dismal failure, for every time he opened his mouth, William Barnes, the New York boss and Taft supporter, threw back his head and laughed uproariously. The cue was taken by the Taft delegates, who made the Coliseum resound with laughter. Fort endeavored to continue, only to have Barnes, after an interval free from interruption, give the signal at which the Taft forces again fairly shrieked with laughter. Fort's speech was utterly ruined, but he refused to be discouraged or to leave the platform until several of the Roosevelt leaders told him to sit down.

Resenting the treatment accorded Fort, the Roosevelt men determined to resort to the same tactics when Congressman Sereno Payne, of New York, assumed the floor to speak on behalf of Watson's point of order. He had just begun when a Roosevelt delegate yelled, "What about that Tariff Bill of yours?" Pandemonium reigned. Payne stood on the platform watching the disturbance with a placid and impervious smile on his lips. It was impossible for him to go on. After awhile, he started again with, "The question is, shall we organize in the usual way through the National Committee. . . ."

A great shout answered him.

"No!" yelled the Roosevelt followers.

But Payne finally finished his speech and Rosewater made a final ruling, declaring Hadley's motion out of order. Hadley appealed to the convention to over-rule Rosewater, only to have the chair sustained.

When nominations for Temporary Chairman were called for, Elihu Root, about whom Theodore Roosevelt had once said, "I would walk on my hands and knees from Oyster Bay to Washington to make him President," and of whom Roosevelt was now saying, "He stands as the representative of the men and policies of reaction; he is put forward by the bosses and the representatives of special privilege," was nominated by the Taft forces for Temporary Chairman of the convention.

To oppose Root, the Roosevelt managers had planned what they believed to be a masterpiece of strategy. A La

293

Follette follower, Henry L. Cochems of Wisconsin, who four years before had placed La Follette in nomination for the Presidency, took the floor and proposed the name of Governor F. E. McGovern for Temporary Chairman. This nomination was made although the Wisconsin delegation, in a caucus prior to the convention, had decided not to offer McGovern's name, by a vote of fifteen to eleven. After Cochem's speech, La Follette's manager, Walter L. Houser, was recognized by the chair, and, as the late Wisconsin Senator described it, "In a speech thrilling with passion, laid the La Follette cards upon the convention table. 'This nomination is without Senator La Follette's consent,' Houser shouted; 'we make no deals with Roosevelt.' " [1] And to counter this stroke, the La Follette forces placed Judge W. S. Lauder, of North Dakota, in nomination.

The convention hall was in a bedlam, when Job E. Hedges of New York, took the floor to second Root's nomination. He began,

"As everybody cannot talk at the same time and as, unlike some gentlemen who have stood upon this platform, I do not pretend to be endowed with the sacred gift of prophecy, so as to be able to tell what will happen after something has been done first, I second the nomination of the man whom Theodore Roosevelt tells me is the ablest man in public life. (Applause and cheers for Roosevelt.) You need not hesitate to cheer Roosevelt in my presence. I cheered him seven years and I am just taking a day off, that is all. (Laughter.) I leave Elihu Root with you. He was good enough for Roosevelt and he is good enough for me. (Applause.)"

[1] "The Autobiography of Robert M. LaFollette," Robert M. La Follette Company. Madison, 1913.

Another Root supporter, Senator Bradley of Kentucky, rose to second again the nomination of the former Secretary of State. He had hardly begun when Francis Heney of California, interrupted him with, "Did you vote for Lorimer?"

Bradley's face became livid. He walked the entire length of the platform, until he stood directly in front of Heney. Pointing his finger accusingly at the Californian, he shouted, "Yes, I voted for Lorimer, and when I did I voted for a man ten thousand times better than you." The uproar that followed was just dying down, when Bradley, who had remained standing in front of Heney, now bent almost double and contemptuously snarled at the Roosevelt follower, "And the time shall never come when the great state of Kentucky will fall so low as to take moral advice from Francis J. Heney."

Again pandemonium reigned. Men stood in their chairs, shaking their fists and shouting epithets of the vilest sort at one another. Hissing and booing became the order of the day, and it was five minutes before Senator Bradley could resume. When he did, he once again addressed himself to Heney, by saying, "If a man could get under the cuticle he would find a meaner man than Lorimer." Catcalls, whistles, shouts and sirens! Chairman Rosewater's cries of "Order!" were drowned out and unheeded, as the police, in order to restore quiet, were obliged, after vain efforts to use gentler methods, to hurl some of the delegates bodily into their seats.

For the second time the Roosevelt forces tried their strength and were out-voted by the Taft delegates. Upon roll call Elihu Root was elected and when he thanked the convention for the confidence reposed in him, he was greeted with cheers and laughter. The Committee on Credentials then reported and the permanent organization was perfected, but not before Delegate Heney had shouted, "If President Taft now accepts the vote of these two men" (referring to the two Taft delegates who had been seated in the California contest) "in this convention, he will be guilty of high treason."

When the delegates assembled on Saturday, June twenty-second, Henry Allen of Kansas read to the convention a statement, which Roosevelt had prepared, to the effect that

"Under the direction and with the encouragement of Mr. Taft the majority of the National Committee, by the so-called 'steam-roller' methods, and with scandalous disregard of every principle of elementary honesty and decency, stole eighty or ninety delegates, putting on the temporary roll call, a sufficient number of fraudulent delegates to defeat the legally expressed will of the people, and to substitute a dishonest for an honest majority.

"The convention has now declined to purge the roll of the fraudulent delegates placed thereon by the defunct National Committee, and the majority which thus endorsed fraud was made a majority only because it included the fraudulent delegates themselves, who all sat as judge's on one another's cases. . . . This action makes the convention in no proper sense any longer a Republican convention representing the real Republican party. Therefore, I hope the men elected as Roosevelt delegates will now decline to vote on any matter before the convention. I do not release any delegate from his honorable obligation to vote for me, if he votes at all, but under the actual conditions I hope he will not vote at all. . . ."

296

After Allen had finished, a delegate called out, "If a man does not know when he is dead, his friends ought to know."

Bedlam again broke loose, but as the fight had gone out of the convention, the volume of noise was not so great as on the first days. When the roll call for nominations for President began, out of the gallery came shrill "toot-toots" from hundreds of toy whistles. Shouts of "Slip her in high," "What about the speed limit," "Sand the tracks, Watson, you're slipping," "More gasoline, more gas," and "All Aboard," resounded through the Coliseum.

After Warren G. Harding, of Ohio, had placed Taft's name in nomination, the roll was called. Taft, receiving five hundred and sixty-one votes, was again made the standard bearer of the party, and Vice President James S. Sherman, of New York, was once again made his running mate.

The week of the convention Taft spent quietly in Washington. He golfed, went to a baseball game, and quietly celebrated with his family the twenty-sixth anniversary of his marriage.

On the Sunday immediately preceding the Republican convention, Roosevelt characterized as utter nonsense the current rumors that he intended to bolt the convention, in the event that he was not nominated. Yet this was just what happened. Immediately after the regular Republican convention adjourned, the Roosevelt followers assembled in Orchestra Hall, where they organized a new party which came to be known as the Progressive or "Bull Moose" party. Theodore Roosevelt was made this party's standard bearer, while Hiram Johnson, of California, was made the Vice-Presidential nominee.

The campaign thus became a three-cornered fight, with Taft opposed by Roosevelt and the Democratic nominee, Woodrow Wilson. Taft conducted a quiet but resolute campaign. He did not enter into the bitter debates between Wilson, who designated Roosevelt as the tool of the steel trust, and Roosevelt, whose vehemence in expression reached new heights . . . or depths.

Early in the campaign Roosevelt had made overtures for the support and coöperation of La Follette, but the Wisconsin Senator rejected these advances, believing himself to be the victim of Roosevelt's perfidy. La Follette said,

> "In the history of American politics there has never been a primary campaign for the Presidential nomination an approach to the extravagant expenditures made in Roosevelt's campaign. . . . Stimulated by an overmastering desire to win they denounce loyalty to conviction and principle as stubborn and selfishness. In the convention they put forth no platform, no issues, and they made no fight against the reactionary platform adopted. They substituted vulgar personalities and coarse epithets of the prize ring for the serious consideration of great economic problems, and for the time being brought ridicule and contempt upon a great cause." [1]

Political prognosticators held out little hope for Taft's reëlection. Taft himself doubted that he would be successful in winning a second term. In July, 1912, he wrote Mrs. Buckner Wallingford, of Cincinnati,

[1] "The Autobiography of Robert M. La Follette," Robert M. La Follette Company, Madison, 1913.

Photograph, Underwood and Underwood, N. Y.

PRESIDENT TAFT IN FEBRUARY, 1913

"It is hard for one to understand, who has views like yours and mine, how the Bull Moose Party could find any considerable support and I don't think it could be unless there were a great many people without that saving sense of humor that has really at times been the only means of rescuing the country from a dangerous or foolish situation. At present, the lines are not formed, and chaos prevails, and it is very difficult to prophesy what is going to happen. . . .

"He (Roosevelt) is really the greatest menace to our institutions that we have had in a long time—indeed I don't remember one in our history so dangerous and so powerful because of his hold upon the less intelligent votes and the discontented. I don't mean by anything I may say to give up hope that in the end, in November, the people of this country will have so clarified their sense perception that they may give a Republican victory.

"If they do not, the Democratic administration which will follow will be under a man whose characteristics are such as to make it certain that he will try his own party and the country and call for vigorous opposition during his term and at its end.

"The Republican party needs the discipline of defeat, and the great object that I have in carrying on this campaign is saving the parts of the party which can be saved and making a solid disciplined force which will be ready to take advantage of the errors of our old-time enemy the Democrats. . . . The great trouble that we are facing in this campaign is a division of parties into groups, such as they have in France and Germany, and now in England. This destroys the possibility of intelligent and systematic progress in government, because everything which is done then becomes a compromise between experiments, which always means little progress and the whole energy of those engaged in politics is taken up not in the adoption of useful measures but in advertising their support of measures which they claim to be useful which are really useful only for the purpose of fooling the voters by promises. . . ."

Many conservative Republicans, fearful of Roosevelt's election, had abandoned Taft and were supporting Wilson. Aware of this, Taft urged these men to maintain their regular party alignment, and in a letter said,

"The great danger to Republican success this year is in the disposition on the part of the conservative business men and the voters generally to take it for granted that I will be defeated and to choose Mr. Wilson as the lesser of two evils, rather than run the risk of seeing Mr. Roosevelt elected.

"That belief has seriously hampered the starting of the campaign auspiciously, has added greatly to the troubles the committee has had to bear in respect to the tangled electoral tickets and has made it difficult to get subscriptions toward defraying the expenses of this campaign.

"You say and I agree with you, that a great host of voters are determined to prevent Mr. Roosevelt's success by any means in their power and that it is uppermost in the minds of a great many that they can do this most effectively by voting the Democratic ticket. That is the trouble. They go no farther than this year. If by their flocking to Mr. Wilson to insure the defeat of Mr. Roosevelt they lessen the gap between Roosevelt and me, he will be the logical candidate against Wilson or any other Democrat in 1916. A Democratic administration at this time is sure to bring on unsettled conditions and business disturbances and under the circumstances Roosevelt would very probably be elected in 1916. . . ."

The only untoward incident of the campaign was the shooting and wounding of Roosevelt by a fanatic at Milwaukee in October. In the election, Taft was the victim of too much Roosevelt, and carried but two states, Utah and Vermont, which gave him an electoral vote of eight. By defeating him, the American people renounced politically a man whose term of office had been a remarkable record of unselfish, laborious service and constructive achievement.

CHAPTER XXX

YALE—AND THE LEAGUE FOR PEACE

His defeat at the polls did not embitter Taft. He had never cared for politics and, even when he accepted the Presidency, had doubted whether it offered him the greatest scope of usefulness, for he knew that his gifts were more judicial than executive. He felt that his administration had been a forward-looking, progressive one, and hoped that the future would ultimately vindicate his judgment as expressed during the four years he served as President. In a letter to a friend, written shortly after the election, Taft said,

"The people of the United States did not owe me another election. I hope I am properly grateful for the one term of the Presidency which they gave me, and the fact that they withheld the second is no occasion for my resentment or feeling a sense of injustice.

"Under ordinary conditions, I think, perhaps, I might have been re-elected, but the conditions were not ordinary. One of my opponents was an extraordinary genius in politics, utterly unrestrained in the methods which he used, and wielding a power given to few men to wield. He was able to divide the party by his personality and his misrepresentations and that meant my defeat. . . . I have enjoyed the highest honors which can be given a man in this country and I have the great satisfaction of having been useful to my fellow-men in some substantial degree in the Presidential office and otherwise. No higher satisfaction than that can come to anyone.

302

"I do not carry in my heart the slightest resentment against the people or any bitterness of spirit with respect to their view of my administration. I think a good many of them have been misled by misrepresentations. . . . As I look out of my study window I see . . . the Washington monument which looks down upon me with benignity and encouragement. . . . This is the only country we have and we have to make the best of it; and such popular manifestations as we had the other day are not to be taken as an evidence of governmental incapacity. . . . There was nothing done which cannot be recalled and which will not be recalled promptly when the time comes, and in the end we shall see that popular government is the most enduring and most just and the most effective."

Shortly after the national election, on Monday, the eighteenth of November, 1912, Taft journeyed to New Haven to attend a meeting of the Yale Corporation. There he met President Arthur Hadley, of the University, who offered him the place on the Yale law faculty left vacant by the death of Professor E. J. Phelps. Outlining the scope of the professor's duties, which as a member of the Yale faculty Taft would ordinarily be required to fulfill, Hadley said that Taft would not be bound by them, but that he could make the position what he desired, and that he would be obligated only to lecture to the seniors of the academic department on Constitutional Law.

There had been much public speculation as to what Taft would do when he retired to private life. A rumor that he would resume the active practice of the law had been emphatically denied by the President, when he said in answer to an inquiry, "Six of the nine Supreme Court Justices bear my commission, and forty-five per cent of the

Federal judiciary have been appointed by me. That is the reason why I could not practice law as an advocate."

Taft, although he took Hadley's offer under advisement, was mightily inclined to accept at once. He believed that retirement to the academic shades of Yale would "approve itself to the general sense of propriety of the country," and in a measure would emulate Cleveland's retirement to Princeton. He thought it would be a very dignified way of escaping from the maelstrom of politics.

He did not, however, want to decide without consulting the members of his official family, the Cabinet. Without exception, they enthusiastically approved of his accepting the Yale professorship. So, after a few weeks, Taft told Hadley of his willingness to go to Yale, and his appointment as Kent Professor of Law followed.

When the public announcement of Taft's acceptance of the Yale professorship was made, the people of the country were too engrossed with the prospects of the coming administration and its effect upon the country to comment much upon the retiring President's modest and unassuming act. Taft himself, immersed in completing the unfinished business before him and preparing for his removal from the White House, was not devoting much time to contemplation of what the future held in store for him.

The fall of his retirement from the Presidency, on the fourth of September, 1913, Taft was nominated and unanimously elected President of the American Bar Association at its annual meeting in Montreal. In his acceptance address he made a strong plea for higher, broader and more comprehensive standards for admission to the bar, and denounced those members of the profession who practiced law solely with a merely mercenary point of view without taking into consideration the social and community aspects which should also command their attention. During the next eight years Taft occupied the professional chair at Yale, interspersing his activities there by traveling throughout the country, addressing bar associations, law schools and civic bodies.

The dramatic suddenness with which the great nations of Europe became locked in a life and death struggle made the people of the United States apprehensive of our own security and increased the demand for a more adequate army and navy. Taft, although an exponent of adequate protection, was an ardent advocate of the peaceful settlement of international disputes.

This was evidenced during his years as President, for while he was championing the arbitration treaties, he was perforce utilizing the army to protect the Texas border against the irregular incursions of Mexican armed forces. But in the main Taft was a proponent of peace. His arbitration treaties have since served as a model. He was the first head of any government unqualifiedly to endorse such treaties without the saving loop-hole of "national honor and vital interests."

Taft presided at the meetings at the Century Club in New York, begun in October, 1914, for the purpose of establishing the League to Enforce Peace, which eventually under his guidance prepared a platform containing four articles providing that the powers agreeing to it should combine against any of their number which committed hostile acts against another. And when it was formally organized in Philadelphia, June 17, 1915, Taft was made president, and conducted throughout the country a vigorous campaign for its principles, a campaign which had an almost incalculable part in acquainting the public with the League. Much later and after considerable hesitation, during which time a study of its political expediency was made, Woodrow Wilson followed Taft, but mistakenly went a step further by advocating the creation of a League of Nations.

The League to Enforce Peace gained popular favor in the United States, and many prominent British statesmen, also, found time to lend it their support.

The venerable James Bryce wrote to Taft,

"In the first months of the present war, many in England appalled not only by the horrors which Europe has witnessed, but by the thought that mankind may in the future be exposed to a recurrence of such calamities, began to consider the possibility, and the means of passing a scheme for reducing the risk of wars hereafter. More than one scheme has been prepared, but we have not embarked on the advocacy of any, because the mind of the British nation is so entirely occupied with the war and the measures required for prosecuting it that full attention could not at present be secured for deliberating on steps to be taken after the war.

"Meanwhile you in America have simultaneously been devoting yourselves to the same aim and we rejoice to know that the League to Enforce Peace over which you preside has already done such splendid work. . . . We, your fellow members here, congratulate you heartily on the results already attained, and confidently hope that the British people will, when the war comes to an end, most gladly join with you in the effort to

306

create a League for the preservation of an enduring peace such as you contemplate. . . ."

Bryce told Taft that Lord Grey sympathized with the objects of the League, though at the time he could not commit himself to the details of its program. He also said that Smuts of South Africa, Asquith, and many others prominent in the official, public and religious life of the Empire were all advocating such a League.

On the second of February, 1917, Taft, in an address before the National Chamber of Commerce in Washington, outlined the scope and functions of the League to Enforce Peace:

"The purpose of the League to Enforce Peace is to organize the world's strength into an international police to enforce a procedure with respect to issues likely to lead to war, which will prevent all wars but those which nothing can prevent. The procedure to be enforced is the submission of questions of a legal nature, the decision of which must be guided by rules of law, to an international court for its judgment, and the submission of all other questions to an impartial commission to hear and decide, its decision to take the form of a recommendation of compromise. The judgment of the legal questions by the court will be legally and in honor binding on the parties. That is implied in the submission to the court. The recommendation of compromise, however, is not in law or in honor binding, unless the party accepts it. The League does not propose to enforce either. Sometime, if the League comes into successful operation it may be thought well to enforce judgments just as domestic judgments are enforced. . . .

"If every issue between nations is forced to arbitration or recommendations, it will compel deliberation by those who think of war."

When the activities of the German submarines compelled America to join the Allies, Taft for the time being abandoned his peace-time activities and devoted himself wholeheartedly to the prosecution of war, becoming a member of the National War Labor Conference Board.

It was in May of the following year (1918) that the public reconciliation of Taft and Roosevelt took place, at the Blackstone Hotel in Chicago. Roosevelt, on his way to Des Moines in his campaign to further American participation in the World War, had stopped off at the hotel for dinner. He had taken a seat at a small table near a window when Taft arrived, on his way east from St. Louis, where he had been working on War Labor Board business. And Taft, the most undramatic of men, for once did the dramatic kind of thing all the world loves to see. He had taken the elevator to his room and was nearly there when he learned of Roosevelt's presence in the dining-room. Forgetting that at the funeral of Professor George W. Woodberry in New Haven Roosevelt had publicly refused his proffered hand, he immediately descended, entered the dining-room and started for the small table where Roosevelt sat. The other diners, of course, were already agog over the presence of Roosevelt, but when they saw Taft threading his way among the tables toward the former president, the cheering became deafening. The meeting is best described by John Leary in his book "Talks with T.R.," [1] who relates it as Roosevelt told it to him that night.

[1] "Talks with T. R.," by John Leary. Houghton Mifflin Company. Boston, 1920.

"Roosevelt said, 'I thought I heard someone call Theodore,' and I looked up just as Taft reached the table with his hand stuck out. There was so much noise being made by the people in the room I am not quite sure what he said. I think it was 'Theodore, I am glad to see you.' I grabbed his hand and told him how glad I was to see him. By Godfrey, I never was so surprised in my life. . . . But, wasn't it a gracious thing for him to do. . . . Jack, I don't mind telling you how delighted I am. I never felt happier over anything in my life. . . . It was splendid of Taft. . . . I've seen old Taft and we're in perfect harmony on everything."

Subsequently when Roosevelt was taken ill, Taft wrote him, and even later, when Roosevelt delivered his Maine Republican convention speech, he submitted the manuscript to Taft for his opinion. Once reconciled they remained friends until Roosevelt's death. And on the biting cold day that Roosevelt was buried in the little hillside cemetery at Oyster Bay, Taft, with his hands trembling and tears standing in his eyes, stood beside the snow-covered bier.

309

CHAPTER XXXI

CHIEF JUSTICE TAFT

EDWARD D. WHITE, Associate Justice and Chief Justice of the United States since 1894, had long been in poor health, and for some time had been considering retirement from the bench, but he died before resigning and on June thirtieth, 1921, President Harding appointed William Howard Taft his successor. When the news reached him, Taft was overjoyed. Asked by an interviewer whether he was pleased with President Harding's selection of a Chief Justice, he laughed and replied, "Well, you can judge for yourself about that. It has been the ambition of my life to be Chief Justice, but now that it has been gratified, I tremble to think whether I can worthily fill the position and be useful to the country."

Taft's appointment was everywhere viewed with satisfaction. The public realized that Taft entered upon his duties with a fine background of judicial training followed by long experience in dealing with great problems of state, which none of his predecessors on the bench had possessed. Typical laudatory newspaper editorials are these: from the *New York World,* "no man ever went on the Supreme Bench better equipped in learning and training and temperament"; from the *New York Times,* "On the score of fitness by training, temperament, and public service no better choice could have been made."

TAFT SHORTLY BEFORE HIS APPOINTMENT TO THE SUPREME COURT

Old political animosities, probably engendered in the campaign of 1912, undoubtedly caused La Follette, Borah and Johnson of California to oppose Taft's confirmation by the Senate, but their efforts were unavailing. Taft was confirmed, and on the thirteenth of October, 1921, took the oath of the Chief Justice administered to him by Justice McKenna.

Taft began his duties immediately. He was the administrative officer of the court, and attested all mandates and orders. Otherwise, except for the fact that he presided in open court, he possessed no more authority than his associates on the bench. From Monday to Friday, and from twelve to four-thirty, daily, the Supreme Court sat during its term from October to June, with Taft as Chief Justice, hearing arguments on the cases on its calendar. During the few precious hours of leisure, before twelve and after four-thirty, when the Supreme Court had adjourned for the day, Taft and the other Justices examined petitions and briefs on current applications for certiorari, and miscellaneous motions affecting cases already docketed. On Friday of each week, Taft forwarded to the Associate Justices a list of cases to be discussed during the conference held weekly at noon on Saturday. At these sessions, Taft presented each case by a brief statement of the facts and the questions of law. Then, as the case had not as yet been assigned to a particular judge, each Justice, in order of his seniority, discussed the case and gave his views. After each member of the court had been heard, a vote was taken, the Justice youngest in point of service, always voting first. That evening, Taft forwarded to each member of the court a memorandum advising him of the assignment of the cases for opinions.

Taft found soon after assuming his duties as Chief Justice that the Federal Courts were inadequately prepared to handle the enormous increase in litigation pending before them. For years the disposition of business in these courts, particularly courts of first instance, had been prompt and satisfactory. But with the war came increased legislation by Congress which called into action hitherto dormant federal powers. The number of statutes multiplied because, for one thing, traffic in intoxicating liquors was forbidden, and, apparently as a result of the war, crime was on the increase. The arranging and districting of the Federal Courts was of long standing, and had been outgrown even before these changed conditions gave a special impetus to federal business, and thus resulted a troublesome congestion of court dockets and delays.

Believing that the Federal Courts should be more expeditious and therefore more useful, Taft advocated an increase in the number of district judges and a simplification of procedure in the trial courts as a remedy for those conditions. And in the summer of 1922, he visited England to witness and study at first hand the English method of administering justice, stating his purpose, in a letter to George Harvey, American Ambassador to the Court of St. James:

". . . chiefly . . . of learning the procedure in the English courts of first instance, which I understand has now been reduced to the simplest form and brings about the greatest dispatch. We need such a system in the Federal District Courts."

Taft arrived in England on June the eighteenth, 1922. An interesting question of the status of a former President of the United States had arisen with his visit, and the King decided that Taft should be accorded the same honor that was paid a former chief of state of a European power and therefore should be entitled to special consideration. As a result of this ruling, Taft, wearing his judicial robes, and Mrs. Taft, attired in full court dress, were received privately by the King and Queen a half hour in advance of the regular reception.

Taft visited the Law Courts in London and was invited to a seat on the bench. The Attorney General, Sir Ernest Pollock, K.C., then arose and stated "that they could not observe that the head of the judiciary of the United States was present without wishing to offer him a welcome." Taft replied to Pollock's address, and the business of the court proceeded.

He was entertained at dinner by the Pilgrim Society at the Hotel Victoria, and after the Earl of Balfour had introduced him to the distinguished assemblage, which included several members of the Cabinet, Taft caused a ripple of merriment when he said "that he had retired from the Presidency of the United States with the full and unmistakable consent of the American people." He continued with a passage, which some consider the best epitome of Anglo-American history ever spoken or written:

"As a citizen with no official mandate, I beg the Britons whom I am addressing not to be misled by temporary ebullitions of one faction or another, but to count on the fundamental public opinion of the United States, in respect to our foreign relations which always prevail in a real exigency and which regards the maintenance of friendship with Great Britain as a most necessary security for the peace of the world."

Taft's stay was spent in a continuous round of activities. He was

"given honorary degrees by Oxford, Cambridge and Aberdeen, was the guest of the Honorable Society of Gray's Inn at a dinner in Gray's Inn Hall, and, later, of the Bench and Bar of England at a dinner in the Hall of the Honorable Society of the Middle Temple."

Taft labored unremittingly, during his years on the Supreme Court, for, as he told a correspondent, "The office of Chief Justice has more hard work connected with it than the Presidency, or, at any rate, more of a sustained intellectual effort. I like it better. There is not the nervous drain in it that the President has to stand."

As Chief Justice, Taft prepared and wrote so many judicial opinions that a separate volume would be necessary if one were adequately to record and analyze these decisions. Even then there would be differences of opinion as to the comparative significance of the more important cases. Therefore I shall limit myself to only two,—that of Myers vs. The United States, and the Coronado Case. By omitting or failing to mention any of Taft's other judicial decisions, it is not intended to underestimate Taft's career on the Supreme Court, importance of his judicial work or the significance of his other decisions. But these two are particularly interesting, and the Myers case is of special moment, for it is an able, lengthy and remarkably thorough dissertation, by a former President of the United States, sitting as an official in a separate division of the Government, the judiciary, and interpreting the powers of the Executive which he had once exercised. As Taft was the only man in the history of our nation who has served the United States as both Chief Justice and President, this decision must be the only case of its kind in the law books.

Taft, speaking for the majority of the court in the Myers case, declared that the President has the exclusive power to remove without the consent of the Senate executive officers of the United States, whom he has appointed by and with the consent of the Senate. A statute passed some fifty years before had provided "Postmasters of the first, second and third classes shall be appointed and may be removed by the President with the advice and consent of the Senate, and shall hold their offices for four years unless sooner removed or suspended according to law. . . ." The plaintiff Myers had been appointed postmaster of Portland, Oregon, in 1917. In 1920 he was removed, and subsequently brought action for his salary, in the Court of Claims. After the routine procedure, the case was appealed to the United States Supreme Court, where Taft wrote the majority opinion.

In this opinion, Taft gave a full discussion of the history of the executive power of removal. He discussed and summarized the debates appertaining thereto that took place in the first Congress. He attached considerable significance to these views for the reason that "this Congress numbered among its members many who had sat in the Constitutional Convention."

The opinion reads,

"This court has repeatedly laid down the principle that a contemporaneous legislative exposition of the Constitution when the founders of our Government and framers of our Constitution were actively participating in public affairs acquiesced in for a long term of years fixes the construction to be given its provisions.

"We are now asked to set aside this construction thus buttressed and adopt an adverse view, because the Congress of the United States did so during a heated political difference of opinion, between the then President and the majority leaders of Congress over the reconstruction measures adopted as a means of restoring to their proper status the States which attempted to withdraw from the Union at the time of the Civil War. The extremes to which the majorities in both Houses carried legislative measures in that matter are now recognized by all who calmly review the history of that episode in our Government leading to articles of impeachment against President Johnson and his acquittal.

"Without animadverting on the character of the measures taken, we are certainly justified in saying that they should not be given the weight to that reached by the first Congress of the United States during a political calm and acquiesced in by the whole Government for three-quarters of a century, especially when the new construction has never been acquiesced in by either the executive or the judicial departments. . . ."

Part of the opinion is devoted to discussion of the views of such famous contemporary lawyers as Story, Hamilton and Kent on the point involved, indicating that they accepted the theory "as settled law despite any doubts that they may have entertained as to the soundness of its policy."

And in summarizing the position of the majority of the court, Taft wrote,

"Our conclusion on the merits sustained by the arguments before stated is that Article Two grants to the President the executive power of the Government, i.e. the general administrative control of those executing the laws, including the power of appointment and removal of executive officers, a conclusion confirmed by his obligation to take care that the laws be faithfully executed; that Article Two excludes the exercise of legislative power by Congress to provide for appointments and removals except only as granted therein to Congress in the matter of inferior offices; that Congress is only given power to provide for appointments and removals of inferior officers after it has vested, and on condition that it does vest, their appointment in other authority than the President with the Senate's consent; that the provisions of the second section of Article Two, which blend action by the legislative branch, or by part of it, in the work of the executive are limitations to be strictly construed and not to be extended by implication; that the President's power of removal is further established as an incident to his specifically enumerated function of appointment by and with the advice of the Senate, but that such incident does not by implication extend to removals the Senate's power of checking appointments; and finally that to hold otherwise would make it impossible for the President in case of political or other difference with the Senate or Congress to take care that the laws be faithfully executed. . . .

"When on the merits we find our conclusion strongly favoring the view which prevailed in the first Congress, we have no hesitation in holding that conclusion to be correct; and it therefore follows that the Tenure of Office Act of 1867, in so far as it attempted to prevent the President from removing executive officers who had been appointed by him and with the advice and consent of the Senate, was invalid and that subsequent legislation of the same effect was equally so. For the reasons given, we must therefore hold that the provision of the law of 1876 by which the unrestricted power of removal of first class postmasters is denied to the President is in violation of the Constitution and invalid. . . ."

The Coronado Case, which also was viewed with wide interest and considered of importance, had its inception in a fight for the open shop and it involved the question of the extent to which labor unions could be held liable under the Sherman Act. The case arose in the Prairie Creek Valley of hilly Sebastian County, Arkansas, near the Oklahoma border line, where a group of nine corporations, inter-related in organization and physical location, were engaged as a unit in mining and shipping coal. One of the nine, the Bache-Denman Company, which owned the controlling interest in the other eight companies, was managed by a man named Franklin Bache. Bache had contracted with the United Mine Workers of America, through its Local District Unit No. 21, to engage union labor exclusively in his mining operations, which contract was due to expire on July 1, 1914. In March of 1914 Bache determined to close the mines, reorganize, and later to re-open them on an open shop basis. Bache wrote his Eastern principals:

"To do this means a bitter fight, but in my opinion it can be accomplished by proper organization."

He justified his action in this letter by stating that the change of policy would result in a substantial reduction in the cost of production. In endeavoring to avoid a charge of

318

breech of faith, Bache manipulated the holdings of his various corporations in such a manner that one of the companies, not under any obligations to the unions, agreed to run the mines. However, anticipating trouble, he made extensive preparation to forestall any damage that might be occasioned to the mining properties by reason of the change. A number of guards, including three Burns Detective operatives, were hired. A large stock of rifles and ammunition was purchased. Bache then proceeded to surround his mining plant with cable strung on posts, and notices warning trespassers not to trespass upon the property. When Bache discharged the miners, in anticipation of his re-opening, P. R. Stewart, the president of District No. 21, ordered out the remaining men at work. Bache planned to open the mines on a non-union basis on April 6, 1914. On Sunday, the 5th, a meeting of the union miners was held at one of the nearby towns and a decision was reached that a demonstration would be held to prevent the opening of the mines with non-union labor, and on the 6th a crowd gathered near the mines, and after many speeches appointed a committee, which included a constable of one of the neighboring villages, to call upon the superintendent and present their demands that the union men be re-engaged. The committee, accompanied by a large crowd of miners, proceeded to the mine, where one of the committee informed the superintendent that the company should abandon their attempt to run the mines on a non-union basis, "if they didn't want a repetition of Colorado."

Meanwhile two guards were assaulted by the crowd and so seriously injured that they had to be taken to a Fort

Smith Hospital. To prevent further trouble, the mines were closed, and on a coal tipple the miners raised an American flag, placing alongside of it a banner bearing the inscription, "This is a union man's country." Bache obtained a permanent injunction against the miners and then began the importation of non-union miners from without the state to operate the mines. In May a convention of the district was held at Fort Smith, and the president of one of the local unions of Oklahoma told an observer that the "miners of Oklahoma were going to come down to Prairie Creek and clean those scabs out." The president of the district, Stewart, announced in public that he would furnish guns to those people who would take them, saying, "We are not going to let them dig coal, the scabs."

In the trial it was proved that over forty rifles were secretly bought and paid for by a check signed by the officials of the district union. During the month of June, 1914, the miners proceeded with their plans to attack the mine. There was testimony tending to prove that on the night of July 16, 1914, the families of those miners who lived in Prairie Creek were warned to leave the vicinity. On the following morning the attack was begun by a volley of shots fired in the premises of the Coronado Company by the union miners. They then ignited the coal wash house and the coal tipple of one of the mines and destroyed the remainder of the plant by dynamite. A few of the non-union miners who were unable to escape and flee to the hills were captured and two of them, in the presence of the constable from a nearby town, were deliberately murdered. Six weeks after the destruction of the property, in September, 1914,

A. S. Dowd, as receiver of the Coronado Coal Company, brought an action for damages in the Federal Courts against the United Mine Workers of America, twenty-seven local unions of that body, and several individual members of that union. The complaint was demurred to by the defendants and the demurrer was sustained by the Court upon the specific ground "that the complaint fails to disclose that this court has any jurisdiction of the cause of action set forth for the reason that the acts of the defendants complained of, were not an interference with interstate commerce or a violation of the Federal statute upon which the complaint is predicated." This ruling on the demurrer was carried to the Circuit Court of Appeals, which Court reversed the District Court's decision and remanded the case to the lower Court, with instructions to overrule the demurrer and allow the defendants to answer. The case was later tried and resulted in a huge verdict for the plaintiff, which, under statutory authorization, was trebled in amount, to which was added interest and counsel fees.

The case was finally brought to the United States Supreme Court, and Chief Justice Taft wrote the opinion. Taft reviewed the organization of the International Union and its power to call strikes, and pointed out how admirably this machinery was devised so as to permit the members to act as a unit under direction of their national officers. He said:

"The membership of the union has reached 450,000. The dues received from them for the National and District Organizations make a very large annual total, and the obligations assumed in traveling expenses, holding of conventions and the general

321

overhead costs, but most of all in strikes, are so heavy that an extensive financial business is carried on. Money is borrowed; notes are given to banks, and in every way the union acts as a business entity, distinct from its members. No organized corporation has greater unity of action and in none is more power centered in the governing executive bodies."

He then cited a number of cases which supported the old doctrine that an unincorporated association can be sued only in the names of its members. Taft continued:

"But the growth and necessities of these great labor organizations have brought affirmative legal recognition of their existence and usefulness and provisions for their protection which their members have found necessary. Their right to maintain strikes when they do not violate law or the rights of others, has been declared. The embezzlement of funds of their officers has been especially taxed as a crime. The so-called union label, which is a quasi trademark to indicate the origin of manufactured products in union labor, has been protected against pirating and deceptive use by the statutes of most of the states, and in many states authority to enjoy its use has been conferred on unions. They have been given distinct and separate representation, and the right to appear to represent union interests in statutory arbitrations and before official labor boards."

Taft, after quoting a number of important Federal statutes in which the legality of labor unions was recognized, said:

"In this state of federal legislation, we think that such organizations are suable in the Federal Courts for their acts, and that funds accumulated to be expended in conducting strikes are subject to execution in suits for torts committed by such unions in strikes. . . . Our conclusion as to the suability of the

322

defendants is confirmed in the case at bar by the words of Sections 7 and 8 of the Anti-Trust Law. The persons who may be sued under Section 7 include 'corporations and associations existing under or authorized by the laws of either the United States or the laws of any of the territories, the laws of any state, the laws of any foreign country.' This language is very broad, and the words given very natural signification certainly include labor unions like these. They are, as has been abundantly shown, associations existing under the laws of the United States, of the territories thereof, and of the states of the Union. Congress was passing drastic legislation to remedy a threatening danger to the public welfare and did not intend that any persons or combinations of persons should escape in application. Their thought was especially directed against business associations and combinations that were unincorporated to do the things forbidden by the Act, but they used language broad enough to include all associations which might violate its provisions organized by the statutes of the United States or the States or the territories or foreign countries as lawfully existing, and this, of course, includes labor unions as the legislation referred to shows. . . . For these reasons we conclude that the International Union, District No. 21, and the twenty-seven Local Unions, were properly made parties defendant here and properly served by process on their proper officers."

The Coronado Coal case held that an International Union may be sued and held liable for the damage caused by unlawful injuries to private rights, in a strike authorized by it.

Whatever prestige Taft may have lost during the campaign of 1912, he regained during his nine years of distinguished work on the Supreme Court bench. Pleasant, politically uneventful years they were, of arduous work, the kind he liked best, relieved by hours of golf, which he played with more assiduity than skill. He loved the game, it was his favorite pastime, but he never became expert. Taft had the temperament, the fine type of mind, which the years enrich, and advancing age made him even more mellow, more human and humorous. He delighted in the company of his grandchildren when they romped and played all through the house at Murray Bay, climbing up and over the Chief Justice, welcomed with the famous chuckle which, as someone has said, became "a national possesssion."

He was so indefatigable, so incurably cheerful and uncomplaining, that even the people who knew Taft well were likely to lose sight of the fact that he had not been really well for years—probably not since his serious operation in the Philippines. When his elder brother Charles P. Taft, to whom he had always been devoted, died at the advanced age of eighty-six, Taft (against the advice of his physicians) insisted upon going to Cincinnati for the funeral. The exhausting trip overtaxed his strength, just as his medical advisers feared it would, but upon his return, in spite of his weariness, he drove directly from the railway station in Washington to the Supreme Court where he immediately resumed his judicial duties by attending a conference.

It proved too much for his over-tired physique. He was shortly afterward compelled to go to the Garfield Hospital in Washington for a rest. From there he was taken to Asheville, North Carolina, in hope that a change to a warmer climate might benefit him. His weakened consti-

THE CHIEF JUSTICE DURING HIS ILLNESS

tution failed to respond, however, and on February third, 1930, his son Robert Taft, preceding him to Washington, tendered his resignation to President Hoover. The President, in accepting Taft's resignation wrote to him:

"I was deeply pained at receiving your letter of resignation today. For some time I have been aware of the shock you received to your health and have been fearful lest this event should occur. In accepting your resignation I would like to add my personal appreciation of the long and distinguished service of a great American to his country."

Taft was brought to his home in Washington, where he had toiled for so many years in the service of the American people, since that gray February day in 1890 when he alighted at the deserted Pennsylvania Station. The trip so fatigued him that he had to be assisted to a wheel-chair and lifted from the vestibule of his car to the platform. While he was lying at his home, sick unto death, his associates on the Supreme Court sent him this heart-warming tribute:

"We call you Chief Justice still for we cannot quickly give up the title by which we have known you for all these later years and which you have made so dear to us. We cannot let you leave us without trying to tell you how dear you have made it. You came to us from achievements in other fields and with the prestige of the illustrious place that you lately held, and you showed in a new form your voluminous capacity for work and for getting work done, your humor that smoothed the rough places, your golden heart that has brought you love from every side, and, most of all, from your brethren whose tasks you have made happy and light. We grieve at your illness, but your spirit has given life an impulse that will abide whether you are with us or away."

For days Taft lay unconscious and nearly lifeless, rallying a little from time to time, only to sink again, and his physicians held out no hope of his recovery to an anxious and sorrowing nation. It was on March the eighth, late in the afternoon, that he finally drifted into the sleep from which he never awoke.

CHAPTER XXXII

IN RETROSPECT

WE are so close to Taft, he was so lately active among us, that it is difficult to appraise him with accuracy and judge him historically. Viewing his public life in retrospect, it is impressive to note how zealous and conscientious he was in the faithful discharge of his duties as Solicitor General, Federal Judge, Governor General of the Philippines, Secretary of War, President of the United States and Chief Justice. Taft's life was devoted almost solely to the public interests. He did not strive for the high offices which he so ably filled, nor did he particularly desire them. Taft left the Federal court bench with genuine reluctance to conduct an experiment in government at Manila, because the good of the state demanded it. After three and one-half years of arduous, exacting and merciless labor in the Archipelago, he returned to the United States to assume even greater responsibilities as a member of Theodore Roosevelt's Cabinet. Twice he declined appointment to the Supreme Court, which he greatly desired to accept, because to have done so meant leaving an important, if less congenial, task half-done; it would not have been fair to those with whom he was laboring; it would not have been, in Plato's phrase, "expedient for the state."

The four years that Taft served as a member of Roosevelt's Cabinet present a glorious record of achievement. Uncomplaining, he bore the brunt of inaugurating the construction of the Panama Canal. He effected a pacific settlement of the Cuban difficulty when the first independent government in that Island broke down. And these tasks he performed in addition to the ordinary functions of his office and his political duties.

Apparently Taft did not greatly desire to be President of the United States. Unlike Theodore Roosevelt, he made no effort to achieve the Presidency. He could not, of course, decline when it was proffered him, although he realized that it would bring him distress as well as satisfaction. He entered upon his duties determined to do his best. As he told Roosevelt, "The great comfort I have, in being under such a heavy obligation to you, is that I know that the easiest way for me to discharge it is to make a success of my administration and to justify you in your wish and effort to make me your successor."

In fulfilling the functions of his office, Taft was never partisan enough to please his Republican colleagues. As Joe Cannon said, "The trouble with Taft is that if he were Pope he would think it necessary to appoint a few Protestant Cardinals." And Taft himself said,

"Political considerations have never weighed heavily with me. I have tried to do in each case what seemed to me the wisest thing, regardless of its effect upon my own future. Indeed, in more than one case I have been perfectly conscious bad blood would be stirred by some act of mine or some refusal to act. The circumstance that the same persons who hail me, after one application of equal justice, as a far-seeing,

328

conservative patriot, denounce me after the next as an unreasoning radical, does not greatly disturb my equanimity. I set that down as all in a day's work."

Some of Taft's opponents charge him with having committed many blunders during his Presidential term, so many that he failed as President. If to recommend and procure an unparalleled amount of beneficent legislation with a hostile Congress and his own party split into factions; if to change a deficit of government finances into a surplus, is to fail, then Taft failed!

One cannot follow Taft's career for even a brief interval without being impressed with his conservatism, and his devotion to justice and the truth. These traits explain, in part, all of Taft's successes and, in full, his apparent blunders and failures. And to these traits Albert W. Gilchrist, Governor of Florida, paid tribute in this letter:

"I just wish to say that I feel very kindly toward you, and that I wish you and yours much happiness even to the end of the trail. Should you or any close friend of yours come to the little town, Punta Gorda, in which I live it will be a source of gratification to show you any attention possible. Of course I am a Democrat. Yet, I want to say that in my opinion you have performed the duties of your high office in a high-toned and in a conscientious manner, . . . in a manner worthy of the Chief Executive of the greatest nation on earth."

Taft emerged undisturbed, unresentful and without any malice from the campaign of 1912, a campaign made undignified and vulgar by the unrestrained behavior of his erstwhile friend, Theodore Roosevelt. For in expressing his

BIBLIOGRAPHY

In addition to the following partial list of authorities consulted, the author has made use of the files of newspapers in New York, Cincinnati, Brooklyn, Washington, and Chicago, and of many magazines.

The following newspapers:

New York Times
New York Tribune
New York World
New York Evening Post

Cincinnati Commercial
Brooklyn Eagle
Washington Star
Chicago Tribune

The following magazines:

Outlook
Review of Reviews
Harper's Weekly
Harvard Advocate
Independent
McClure's
The Saturday Evening Post
Forum
World's Work
Literary Digest
National Geographic
Century
Journal of Political Economy

American
New Republic
Nation
Atlantic
Current Literature
Everybody's
Collier's
Green Bag
North American
The World Today
Outing
Journal of American History

Abbott, L. F. *Impressions of Theodore Roosevelt.* Garden City, N. Y., Doubleday, Page, 1919.

Barry, D. S. *Forty years in Washington.* Boston, Little, Brown, 1924.

Bassett, J. S. *Expansion and reform.* 1889-1926. N. Y., Longmans, Green, 1926.

Beard, C. A. *The rise of American civilization.* N. Y., Macmillan, 1927.

Bennett, J. W. *Roosevelt and the republic.* N. Y., Broadway Pub. Co., 1908.

Bishop, J. B. *Theodore Roosevelt and his time.* N. Y., Scribner, 1920.

Bryan, W. J.*The memoirs of William Jennings Bryan.* Philadelphia, The John C. Winston Co., 1925.

Busbey, L. W. *Uncle Joe Cannon.* N. Y., Holt, 1927.

Butt, A. W. *Letters of Archie Butt,* Edited by L. F. Abbott, Garden City, N. Y., Doubleday, Page, 1924.

BIBLIOGRAPHY

Charnwood, G. R. B. *Theodore Roosevelt*. Boston, Atlantic Pr., 1923.
Cist, Charles. *Sketches and statistics of Cincinnati in 1851*. Cincinnati, W. H. Moore, 1851.
Clark, Champ. *My quarter century of American politics*. N. Y., Harper, 1920.
Cortesi, Salvatore. *My thirty years of friendships,* N. Y., Harper, 1927.

Davis, O. K. *Released for publication*. Boston, Houghton, Mifflin, 1925.
Davis, O. K. *William Howard Taft,* Philadelphia, P. W. Ziegler Co., 1908.
Dewey, George. *Autobiography of George Dewey, Admiral of the navy*. N. Y., Scribner, 1913.
Duncan-Clark, S. J. *The progressive movement; its principles and its programme*. Boston, Small, Maynard, 1913.
Dunn, A. W. *From Harrison to Harding*. N. Y., Putnam, 1922.
Dunn, R. L. *William Howard Taft, American.*

Egan, M. F. *Recollections of a happy life*. N. Y., Doran, 1924.
Elliott, C. B. *The Philippines to the end of the Commission Government*. Indianapolis, Bobbs-Merrill, 1917.
Elliott, C. B. *The Philippines to the end of the military régime*. Indianapolis, Bobbs-Merrill, 1917.

Fish, C. R. *American diplomacy. N. Y.,* Holt, 1923.
Foraker, J. B. *Notes of a busy life*. Cincinnati, Stewart & Kidd, 1916.
Foreman, John. *The Philippine Islands*. N. Y., Scribner, 1893.

Gompers, Samuel. *Seventy years of life and labor*. N. Y., Dutton, 1925.
Griffin, S. B. *People and politics observed by a Massachusetts editor*. Boston, Little, Brown, 1923.
Groat, G. G. *An introduction to the study of organized labor in America*. N. Y., Macmillan, 1926.

Hart, A. B. *American history as told by Contemporaries*. N. Y., Macmillan, 1897-1929. 5 vols.
House Documents. Nos. 1592-1595, 60th Congress, 2nd sess.
Howe, Henry. *Historical collections of Ohio*. Columbus, Howe & Sons, 1889, 2 vols.
Howe, M. A. De W. *George vonLengerke Meyer,* N. Y., Dodd, Mead, 1920.
Howland, H. J. *Theodore Roosevelt and his times*. New Haven, Yale Univ. Press, 1921.

Joblin, Maurice and Co. *Cincinnati, past and present*. Cincinnati, Edne St. Ptg. Co., 1872.
Johnson, W. F. *Four centuries of the Panama canal*. N. Y., Holt, 1906.

334

Joint Committee to investigate the Interior Department and Forestry Service. *Report in Senate Documents,* 61 Cong., 3 Sess. No. 719 (1911).

Kohlsaat, H. H. *From McKinley to Harding.* N. Y., Scribner, 1923.

La Follette, R. M. *La Follette's autobiography.* Madison, Wis., Robert M. La Follette Co., 1913.
Lane, F. K. *Letters of Franklin K. Lane,* Boston, Houghton, Mifflin, 1922.
Leary, J. J. *Talks with T. R., from the diaries of John J. Leary, Jr.* Boston, Houghton, Mifflin, 1920.
LeRoy, J. A. *The Americans in the Philippines.* Boston, Houghton, Mifflin, 1914. 2 vols.
Literary Club, Cincinnati. *The Literary Club of Cincinnati, 1849-1903.* Cincinnati, Ebbert and Richardson, 1903.

McRae, M. A. *Forty years in newspaperdom.* N. Y., Brentano, 1924.
Miller, Francis W. *Cincinnati's beginnings.* Cincinnati, P. G. Thomson, 1880.
Moses, Edith. *Unofficial letters of an official's wife.* N. Y., Appleton, 1908.

Olcott, C. S. *The life of William McKinley.*
Orth, S. P. *The boss and the machine.* New Haven, Yale Univ. Pr., 1919.

Paxson, F. L. *Recent history of the United States, 1865-1927.* Boston, Houghton, Mifflin, 1928.
Peck, H. T. *Twenty years of the republic, 1885-1905.* N. Y., Dodd, Mead, 1906.

Randall, E. O. and Ryan, D. J. *History of Ohio.* N. Y., Century Hist. Co., 1912. 5 vols.
Reed, G. I. *Bench and bar of Ohio.* Chicago, Century, Pub. and Eng. Co., 1897. vol. 2.
Rhodes, J. F. *The McKinley and Roosevelt administrations.* 1897-1909. N. Y., Macmillan, 1922.
Roosevelt, Theodore. *Letters from Theodore Roosevelt to Anna Roosevelt Cowles, 1870-1918.* N. Y., Scribner, 1924.
Roosevelt, Theodore. *The new nationalism.* N. Y., Outlook Co., 1910.
Roosevelt, Theodore. *Selections from the correspondence of Theodore Roosevelt and Henry Cabot Lodge, 1884-1918.* N. Y., Scribner, 1925. 2 vols.
Roosevelt, Theodore. *Theodore Roosevelt; an autobiography.* N. Y., Macmillan, 1913.

Schlesinger, A. M. *Political and social history of the United States, 1829-1925.* N. Y., Macmillan, 1925.

Schurman, J. G. *Philippine affairs; a retrospect and outlook.* N. Y., Scribner, 1902.

Senate Documents, 57th Congress, 1st Session, No. 331, parts 1-3.

Stanwood, Edward. *History of the presidency.* Boston, Houghton, Mifflin, 1916. 2 vols.

Stoddard, H. L. *As I knew them; presidents and politics from Grant to Coolidge.* N. Y., Harper, 1927.

Straus, O. S. *Under four administrations, from Cleveland to Taft.* Boston, Houghton, Mifflin, 1922.

Taft, Helen Herron. *Recollections of full years.* N. Y., Dodd, Mead, 1914.

Taft, W. H. *Presidential addresses and state papers.* N. Y., Doubleday, 1910.

Taussig, F. W. *Tariff history of the United States.* N. Y., Putnam, 1923.

Thayer, W. R. *The life and letters of John Hay.* Boston, Houghton, Mifflin, 1915. 2 vols.

Thayer, W. R. *Theodore Roosevelt,* Boston, Houghton, Mifflin, 1919.

Thompson, C. W. *Presidents I have known and two near presidents.* Indianapolis, Bobbs-Merrill, 1929.

Tumulty, J. P. *Woodrow Wilson as I knew him.* Garden City, N. Y., Garden City Pub. Co. 1925.

United States Supreme Court Reports of cases, 1921-

Walker, A. H. *Historical sketches of the administration of President Taft.* 4 vols. N. P., 1912.

Walker, A. H. *History of the Sherman law of the United States of America.* N. Y., Equity pr., 1910.

Watterson, Henry. *The editorials of Henry Watterson; compiled with an introduction and notes,* by Arthur Krock, N. Y., Doran, 1923.

White, W. A. *Masks in a pageant.* N. Y., Macmillan, 1928.

Williams, D. R. *The odyssey of the Philippine commission.* Chicago, McClurg, 1913.

Wilson, H. L. *Diplomatic episodes in Mexico, Belgium and Chile.* Garden City, N. Y., Doubleday, Page & Co. 1927.

Wilson, Woodrow. *Division and reunion, 1829-1889.* N. Y., Longmans, Green, 1893.

Worcester, D. C. *The Philippines, past and present.* N. Y., Macmillan, 1914.

INDEX

Addyston Pipe Case, 49-52, 78
Agoncilla, F., 59
Aguinaldo, Emilio, 57, 58, 61, 63, 64, 98, 123
Alaska, offer by Russia to sell, 29; treaty for purchase of completed, 30; boundaries defined by House Bill, 30, 242-244
Aldrich, Senator Nelson, 227, 230, 234, 236
Ali, Datto, 128
Allen, Henry, 296, 297
Alston, C. H., 287
Amador, President, of Panama, 171
American Bar Association, address of Taft before, 46; Taft president of, 304
American Federation of Labor, 19
American Railway Union, 37, 38, 45
Anderson, General, in Philippines, 63
Anderson, Lieutenant George, City Superintendent of Manila Schools, 122
Andrade, General Freyre, 190, 192
Anti-Imperialist, 65, 66; Taft an, 84
Archbold, John D., 215
Arellano, Judge, 133, 155
Arthur, P. M., 35, 36
Arthur, President Chester A., 8, 9
Asquith, Herbert H., 307
Attorney-General, 24, 25, 49
Augusti, Governor-General, 62

Bache, Franklin, 318, 319
Bacolor, 119, 120
Bacon, Robert, Assistant Secretary of State, 186, 187, 190, 194
Balangiga, Massacre of, 138
Balfour, Arthur, 268
Ballinger, Richard, Secretary of the Interior, 228, 246, 247, 249, 251, 257
Bandholtz, Captain, 115
Barnes, William, 292
Bassett, John Spencer, quoted, 267
Bayard, Thomas F., Secretary of State, 31
Bering Sea Controversy, 29-31
Berner Murder Case, The, 9, 10
Biacnabato, Treaty of, 58, 97
Bieber, Sidney, 288
Blaine, James G., succeeds Bayard as Secretary of State, 31

Bonaparte, Charles J., Attorney-General, 223
Borah, Senator William E., 288, 289, 311
Borden, of Canada, 266, 267
Boston, Taft's speech in, before Merchant's Association, 203, 204
Boston Transcript, The, 175, 176
Boston Watchman, The, 143
Bradley, Senator, of Kentucky, 295, 296
Brandeis, Louis D., Justice of the Supreme Court, 249
Bray, Howard, 61
Brewer, David J., Justice of the Supreme Court, 268
Bricklayers' Union, boycotts Moore's, 20
Brotherhood of Locomotive Engineers, 35, 36
Brown, Henry B., Justice of the Supreme Court, 78, 178, 181
Brownsville Affair, The, 207
Bryan, William Jennings, interviews Taft on train, 85, 96; endorsed by labor, 215; campaign of, 216; loses election, 218
Bryce, James, 265, 269, 306, 307
Burleson, Rep. Albert S., 255
Butt, Archie, 211, 259
Butterworth, Ben, 8, 24

Calderon, Don Felipe, 110, 142
Cairns, Frank, 186
Campbell, Tom, 9-12, 176
Campbell disbarment proceedings, 9-17
Canadian Reciprocity, agreement, 263
Canada, 263-266; Parliament of, 267; rejects reciprocity, 267
Canal Zone, 171, 197; Taft goes to, 224
Cannon, Joe, 227, 230, 233, 234, 253-255, 261; quoted, 328
Capote, Mendez, 184, 185
Carlisle, Calderon, 32
Catholic Church, 94; Filipinos members of, 105, 142, 143, 149; vote of Catholics, 220
Cebu, 101, 115, 124, 125, 129
Century Club, Taft presides at meeting at, 305
Chaffee, General, 133-136, 161
Chapman, Orlow W., 24

337

INDEX

INDEX

ganize Federal party, 114; receive limited self-government, 116; limitations of, 117; greet Commission on tour, 118, 119; placed on Civil Commission, 131; overjoyed at Taft's return, 151, 155, 156; protest against Taft's departure, 157, 158, 163, 168, 181, 182
First Philippine Commission, 68-71, 83
First Philippine Congress meets at Malolos, 107
Foraker, Joseph B., 9, 13-15, 25, 204, 205, 215, 216
Fort, former Governor of New Jersey, 292, 293
France, 67, 148, 269
Friar lands, 91, 105, 106, 107, 141, 146-148; dispute terminated, 149, 151
Frye, Senator William P., 67
Funston, General Frederick, 123, 139

Gardiner, Gilson, 273, 274, 278
Garfield, James R., 223, 230; as Secretary of the Interior, 243-245; attends Progressive Convention, 274
General Land Office, Ballinger in charge of, 243; reorganized, 244, 246
General Manager's Association, 36, 37
Gilchrist, Albert W., compliments Taft, 329
Glavis, Louis, 244-250
Goethals, General George Washington, 196
Gomez, Dr., Philippine labor agitator, 158
Gomez, Jose Miguel, 184
Gompers, Samuel, 19, 215
Gotti, Cardinal, 145
Grant's Tomb, Taft's address at, 207
Gray, Senator George, 67
Gray, Horace, Justice of the Supreme Court, 28
Great Britain, 29, 30; complains of seizure of English vessels, 31; proposes arbitration, 32; friendly in Spanish War, 60
Grey, Sir Edward, endorses Taft's arbitration plan, 268; approves League to Enforce Peace, 307
Guerra, Pino, 184
Guidi, Monseigneur, 148

Hadley, Arthur T., 210, 303, 304
Hadley, Governor Herbert S., 279, 288, 292, 293
Hale, Senator Eugene, 230
Hammond, John Hays, 209
Hanna, Marcus A., 176, 205

Harlan, John J., Justice of the Supreme Court, 93-95, 268
Harmon, Judson, 13, 14, 17
Harding, President Warren G., shifts to support Taft, 205; places Taft in nomination, 297; appoints Taft Chief Justice, 310
Harper's Weekly, diary of convention, 290
Harrison, President Benjamin, 31, 33
Harvard Advocate, The, 6
Harvey, George, 312
Hat trimmings cases, 28, 29
Havana, 60, 185-187, 194, 195, 199
Hawaii, 86, 90, 172
Hay, John, 75, 173
Hay-Bunau-Varilla Convention, signed, 168
Hayes, Rutherford B., 5
Hearst, William Randolph, 215
Hedges, Job E., 294
Heney, Francis J., 286, 288, 295, 296
Herrick, Myron T., 176
Herron, Harriett Collins, 15
Herron, John Williamson, 14, 15
Hitchcock, Frank, Postmaster-General, 228
Hoadley, Governor, of Ohio, 13
Hollister, Judge, with Taft at Yale, 6
Holmes, John R., 11
Hoover, President Herbert C., letter to Taft accepting resignation, 324
Houser, Walter L., 273, 294
Hughes, Charles E., 202, 268

Ide, Henry C., member of Second Philippine Commission, 82, 83, 91, 131
Igorrotes, 132
Imperialists, 65
Ireland, Archbishop, 147
Isthmian Canal Commission, 168-171

Jackson, Judge Howell, 78
Japan, 133, 166, 167
Johnson, Edgar, 13
Johnson, Hiram, 279, 298, 311
Jolo, 124-128, 160
Juan, Juan de, 100, 101
Jusserand, J. J., French Ambassador, 269

Kellogg, Frank B., 289
Kitteredge, E. W., 11, 17
Knights of Labor, 18, 19
Knox, Philander C., 202, 228, 269
Kodama, General, 167, 168
Kohlsaat, H. H., quoted, 280

339